I0070153

LABOUR LANDMINES

99 Ways to Succeed at the CCMA

Copyright © KR Publishing and Ivan Israelstam

All reasonable steps have been taken to ensure that the contents of this book do not, directly or indirectly, infringe any existing copyright of any third person and, further, that all quotations or extracts taken from any other publication or work have been appropriately acknowledged and referenced. The publisher, editors and printers take no responsibility for any copyright infringement committed by an author of this work.

Copyright subsists in this work. No part of this work may be reproduced in any form or by any means without the written consent of the publisher or the author.

While the publisher, editors and printers have taken all reasonable steps to ensure the accuracy of the contents of this work, they take no responsibility for any loss or damage suffered by any person as a result of that person relying on the information contained in this work.

First published in 2019.

ISBN: 978-1-86922-791-3 (Printed)
ISBN: 978-1-86922-792-0 (ePDF)

Published by KR Publishing
P O Box 3954
Randburg
2125
Republic of South Africa

Tel: (011) 706-6009
Fax: (011) 706-1127
E-mail: orders@knowres.co.za
Website: www.kr.co.za

Printed and bound: HartWood Digital Printing, 243 Alexandra Avenue, Halfway House, Midrand
Typesetting, layout and design: Cia Joubert, cia@knowres.co.za
Cover design: Marlene de'Lorme: marlene@knowres.co.za
Editing and proofreading: Valda Strauss: valda@global.co.za
Project management: Cia Joubert, cia@knowres.co.za
Index created with TExtract / www.Texyz.com

LABOUR LANDMINES

99 Ways to Succeed at the CCMA

by

Ivan Israelstam

kr
publishing

2019

"Fairness is not an attitude. It's a professional skill that must be developed and exercised."

– Brit Hume

TABLE OF CONTENTS

ABOUT THE AUTHOR   v
INTRODUCTION   vi

Chapter 1: SOUTH AFRICA'S LABOUR DISPENSATION – HOW IT
    AFFECTS THE STAKEHOLDERS   1

    EMPLOYEES – AN EXPENSE OR AN INVESTMENT?   1
    EMPLOYEES CANNOT HIDE BEHIND THE CORPORATE VEIL   3
    LABOUR BROKERS UNDER SEIGE   5
    USING LABOUR BROKERS AND TEMP AGENCIES NOT ALWAYS KOSHER   7
    BEWARE THE USE OF FIXED-TERM CONTRACTS   9
    NEDLAC PROCESS BESET BY CONFLICTING AGENDAS   11
    NEW LABOUR LAWS WEAKEN EMPLOYERS AND STRENGTHEN JOB LOSSES   13
    FOCUS OF SOUTH AFRICA'S LABOUR LAW DISPENSATION NEEDS TO BE
        BROADENED   15
    FOREIGN EMPLOYERS CAN'T ESCAPE SOUTH AFRICAN LABOUR LAWS   16

Chapter 2: UNDERSTANDING SOUTH AFRICA'S LABOUR DISPUTE SYSTEM   19

    THE LABOUR DISPUTE SYSTEM – HOW IT WORKS   19
    CON-ARB AT CCMA HAS PROS AND CONS   21
    CCMA GUIDELINES ON MISCONDUCT CRUCIAL   23
    THE AWARDS OF ARBITRATORS MUST BE RATIONAL   25
    EASIER TO TAKE ERRANT ARBITRATORS TO TASK   27
    WHAT POWERS DO THE LABOUR COURTS HAVE?   29
    INTERDICTS, DISCIPLINARY HEARINGS AND REPRESENTATION   31

Chapter 3: EMPLOYEES HAVE MORE RIGHTS THAN RESPONSIBILITIES   35

    WHEN DOES A JOB APPLICANT BECOME AN EMPLOYEE?   35
    TRAINEES COULD BE SEEN TO BE EMPLOYEES   37
    FORCED CHANGES TO EMPLOYMENT CONDITIONS NOT ON   39
    JAILED EMPLOYEES STILL HAVE RIGHTS   41
    TERMINATING FIXED-TERM CONTRACTS A HEADACHE   43
    AUTOMATIC TERMINATION CLAUSES DANGEROUS   45
    LABOUR LAWS PROTECT NEW MOTHERS   47
    EMPLOYMENT OF SEX OFFENDERS REGULATED   48
    ILLEGAL WORKERS ARE PROTECTED   50

SANGOMAS NOT YET REGISTERED TO PROVIDE MEDICAL CERTIFICATES   52

REFUSED PROMOTION CAUSES COMMOTION   54

UNPLEASANT CCMA SURPRISES FOR EMPLOYERS   56

DON'T MISS THE ARBITRATION HEARING!   58

DIRTY HANDS WILL BE CANED AT CCMA   60

Chapter 4: EMPLOYMENT EQUITY LAWS – ANTI-DISCRIMINATION AND AFFIRMATIVE ACTION   **63**

EMPLOYMENT EQUITY OBLIGATIONS MUST BE MET   63

CHINESE EMPLOYEES QUALIFY FOR AFFIRMATIVE ACTION   65

EQUAL PAY FOR WORK OF EQUAL VALUE NOW COMPULSORY   67

EMPLOYERS HAVE CLOSE SHAVE WITH RELIGIOUS DISCRIMINATION   69

SEXUAL RELATIONSHIPS HARASS EMPLOYERS   71

FALSE ACCUSATIONS OF RACISM DANGEROUS   73

Chapter 5: RETRENCHMENT AND TAKEOVERS   **75**

RETRENCHMENT – THE DUTY TO CONSULT   75

POTENTIAL RETRENCHEES ENTITLED TO REPRESENTATION   77

WHAT IS A FAIR REASON TO RETRENCH?   79

RED TAPE BEDEVILS URGENT RETRENCHMENTS   81

BEWARE OF RETRENCHMENTS FOR POOR PERFORMANCE   83

EMPLOYERS CAN DROWN IN THEIR REDUNDANCY POOLS   85

CONTRACTORS MUST OFTEN TAKE OVER STAFF IN OUTSOURCING DEALS   87

SECOND GENERATION OUTSOURCING: CAN YOU RETRENCH?   89

Chapter 6: MANAGING WORKPLACE CONFLICT   **93**

STRIKES CAN MEAN DISASTER FOR EMPLOYERS   93

WORKPLACE REBELLIONS CAN WREAK HAVOC   95

IS WORKPLACE VICTIMISATION PROHIBITED?   97

GET THE @#&*!!Ä€» OUT OF MY FACE!   98

STAFF UNHAPPINESS IS NOT INCOMPATIBILITY   100

DON'T SUSPEND EMPLOYEES IN ANGER   102

TREAT WORKPLACE DISRUPTIONS WITH CARE   104

Chapter 7: WHAT MAKES A DISMISSAL AUTOMATICALLY UNFAIR? AND
    WHAT ARE THE CONSEQUENCES?   107

    MANAGEMENT SICK OF ABSENTEEISM   107
    EMPLOYEES WHO BLOW THE WHISTLE ARE PROTECTED   109
    DISMISSING ALCOHOLICS/ADDICTS CAN BE COSTLY   111
    EMPLOYERS MUST CHANGE THEIR ATTITUDES TO GENDER REASSIGNMENT   112

Chapter 8: DISCIPLINE – HOW TO BALANCE LABOUR LAW COMPLIANCE
    WITH BEST PRACTICE   115

    DON'T BYPASS YOUR OWN DISCIPLINARY POLICIES   115
    POOR CONDUCT CAN MEAN POOR MANAGEMENT   117
    INVESTIGATING MISCONDUCT IS A MUST   119
    DON'T DELAY IN DISCIPLINING EMPLOYEES   121
    UNFAIR DISCIPLINE CAN CAUSE CONSTRUCTIVE DISMISSAL   123
    THE VALIDITY OF PRIOR WARNINGS IS A VEXED ISSUE   125
    FAULTY SUSPENSIONS CAN HANG EMPLOYERS   127

Chapter 9: UNDERSTANDING WHAT FAIR DISMISSAL PROCEDURE IS   131

    WHEN IS A FORMAL DISCIPLINARY HEARING NECESSARY?   131
    PRESIDING OFFICERS MUST BE UNBIASED   133
    LAWYERS MAY BE ALLOWED AT DISCIPLINARY HEARINGS   135
    DOUBLE JEOPARDY MEANS DOUBLE WHAMMY FOR EMPLOYERS   137

Chapter 10: WHAT IS A FAIR REASON FOR DISMISSAL UNDER THE LAW?   141

    WHEN IS DISMISSAL FAIR?   141
    'SHOOT FROM THE HIP' EMPLOYERS ARE BREACHING PROBATIONARY LAW   143
    TWELVE REASONS FOR EMPLOYERS TO BE CAUTIOUS   145
    YEARS OF SERVICE A MITIGATING FACTOR   147
    APPLY YOUR WORKPLACE DISCIPLINE CONSISTENTLY   148
    FIRING THE LOT COULD PUT YOU IN A SPOT   150
    BEWARE DISCIPLINING EMPLOYEES FOR OFF-SITE MISCONDUCT   152
    BRING PROOF THAT TRUST HAS BEEN DESTROYED   154
    EXTERNAL PRESSURE DOES NOT JUSTIFY DISMISSAL   156
    INTOLERABLE EMPLOYMENT RELATIONSHIP PIVOTAL TO JUSTIFY
        DISMISSAL   157
    TRAPPING AND ENTRAPMENT NOT THE SAME   159
    BEWARE CANCELLING CONCLUDED EMPLOYMENT CONTRACTS   161

Chapter 11: WORKPLACE MISCONDUCT AND ITS CONSEQUENCES   165

INSUBORDINATION NOT ALWAYS DISMISSIBLE   165
MANAGERS PROHIBITED FROM BITING SUBORDINATES   167
CONFLICT OF INTERESTS   168
EMPLOYEES SHOULD NOT FALSELY ACCUSE EMPLOYERS   170
EMPLOYERS MUST PROVE DERELICTION OF DUTY CHARGES   172
DISHONESTY WON'T ALWAYS MERIT DISMISSAL   174
FALSIFICATION OF CREDENTIALS NOT ALWAYS DISMISSIBLE   176
POOR PERFORMANCE DOES NOT AUTOMATICALLY MERIT DISMISSAL   178
DEAL CAUTIOUSLY WITH ABSENTEEISM   180

Chapter 12: HOW TO MANAGE FAIR DISCIPLINARY HEARINGS   183

DISCIPLINARY HEARINGS – BE PREPARED   183
HEARSAY EVIDENCE CAN RENDER DISMISSALS UNFAIR   185
WITNESSES ARE KEY AT HEARINGS   187
ALLOW EMPLOYEES TO ATTEND THEIR DISCIPLINARY HEARINGS   188
CRACK DOWN ON DISRUPTIONS OF DISCIPLINARY HEARINGS   190
CROSS-EXAMINATION IS A RIGHT   192
DISCIPLINARY HEARINGS MUST BE HONEST   194

Chapter 13: EMPLOYERS MUST KNOW THEIR RIGHTS AND OBLIGATIONS   197

WHO WILL GUIDE YOU THROUGH THE LABOUR LAW MINEFIELD?   197
EMPLOYEES HAVE A FIDUCIARY DUTY TOWARDS THE EMPLOYER   199
LABOUR LAW TRAINING PUTS MANAGEMENT BACK ON TRACK   201
EMPLOYERS MUST PROTECT THEMSELVES   203
LACK OF DISCIPLINARY EXPERTISE CAN PROVE COSTLY   205

INDEX   208

ABOUT THE AUTHOR

Ivan Israelstam is the Chief Executive Officer of Labour Law Management Consulting. He is known as a leading practitioner in labour law and pragmatic labour relations management with many years' experience in corporate industrial relations management. He has an honours degree from The University of the Witwatersrand and an IPM diploma in Personnel Management and in Training.

Ivan is a regular labour law columnist for a number of newspapers and journals including the *SA Labour Guide, HR Pulse* and *Skills Portal*. He is the author of *Walking the New Labour Law Tightrope, Labour Landmines: 99 Ways to Succeed at the CCMA, Labour Law for Managers Practical Handbook, Making Workplace Forums Work* and *The Gold Future or the Cold Future*.

Ivan was, for four years, a part-time commissioner with the Commission For Conciliation, Mediation and Arbitration (CCMA). He has also been chairperson of the Labour Affairs Committees of the South African Chamber of Commerce and Industry and of the EXCO of the Randburg Chamber of Commerce and Industry. His chamber background places him at the cutting edge of business decision making on labour issues.

Ivan Israelstam speaks on television and radio and is a regular speaker at conferences and seminars on subjects including labour relations, labour law, affirmative action, discipline, dismissal, union negotiations and conflict management.

In recognition of his contribution in this field Ivan has been featured in the book *Who's Who in Southern Africa*.

Ivan is currently working on the establishment of the Gold Future Group, a movement for turning around South Africa's economy and for bringing social justice and national unity to South Africans.

INTRODUCTION

There are few, if any, countries in the world that have labour dispensations that are more fraught with heavy restrictions on employers, with industrial conflict, with fast-changing labour law statutes and with conflicting case law decisions than those in South Africa.

Our country is also at a stage in its history when international economies are in a state of flux, labour-intensive investment is weak and jobs are very scarce.

The above-mentioned aspects of our labour dispensation and of our labour economic context make the outlook for many employers and employees in South Africa uncertain, hazardous and insecure.

There appear to be no immediate prospects that government and/or NEDLAC will be taking effective measures to correct this parlous situation and to turn our labour economy around. Therefore, for the time being, it is up to the parties at each workplace themselves to make their businesses or organisations the best they can be for the good of all stakeholders.

This book aims to inform employers, employees and their representatives of key legal provisions prevailing in South Africa and to suggest how the parties can best manage within these parameters. The author also deals with macro issues such as the circumstances at NEDLAC.

CHAPTER 1

SOUTH AFRICA'S LABOUR DISPENSATION – HOW IT AFFECTS THE STAKEHOLDERS

South Africa's economy is a capitalistic one in that anyone can own and run a business and make profits from the labour of the business's employees. However, South Africa's labour legislation has a strong socialistic basis. That is, our laws very strongly protect employees and, in the interests thereof, very strongly constrain the way in which employers treat and utilise the labour of their employees. For example, the law controls what employers must pay employees, forces employers in many industries to provide employee benefits and heavily dictates the processes that employers must use when disciplining and dismissing employees. It also imposes on many employers the legal obligation to implement affirmative action.

This chapter acquaints stakeholders with the legal dispensation within which South African employers have to operate their organisations.

EMPLOYEES – AN EXPENSE OR AN INVESTMENT?

The most important reason for employing people is the need for their skills. The question is whether the money expended in order to acquire and retain these employee skills should be seen as an expense or as an investment. Most frequently, employers consider the money spent on employment as an expense. This expense is most often amongst the biggest, if not the very biggest one. Employment expenses include, amongst others, recruitment costs, training expenses, salaries and commissions, employment benefits such as employer contributions to medical aid and retirement schemes, leave costs, absenteeism and perks such as motor vehicles.

Aside from these traditional employee costs there are other expenses that are not always included in the employment budget. These include legal costs related to labour issues such as the legal fees for fighting CCMA and Labour Court cases, the payment of compensation orders made at these forums and back pay associated with reinstatement orders.

There is not necessarily a right or wrong answer to the question of whether employees should be seen as an expense or as an investment. This is because the answer depends on whether the employer sees the employee as a 'necessary evil' or as an asset. Employers that use proactive measures aimed at minimising unnecessary cost and avoiding the need for costly legal battles tend towards the mentality that employees are an asset.

However, employers must add to the above-mentioned hard expenses the unquantifiable costs associated with the time needed for preparing for and attending CCMA and Labour Court hearings. When all the quantifiable and non-quantifiable costs are taken into account it is no wonder that many employers see employees as an expense rather than as an investment.

The laws of South Africa contribute to the employee expense mentality. Our laws promote minimum wage levels, negotiated pay increases, compulsory benefit contributions in some industries, in certain cases paid sick leave for employees who have no doctor's certificates, skills levies, unlimited back-pay amounts for dismissed employees and compensation/damages orders that can greatly exceed 24 months' remuneration.

In *Parry v Astral Operations Ltd* (2005, 10 BLLR 989) the Labour Court found that the employee had been unfairly retrenched. The Court awarded the employee:

- Contractual damages
- Relocation costs
- Share options
- Accrued profit shares
- Notice pay
- Salary for time worked
- Severance pay
- Compensation equal to 12 months' remuneration
- Punitive scale legal costs.

In *Evans v Japanese School of Johannesburg* (2006, 12 BLLR 1146) the Labour Court found that the employee had been automatically unfairly dismissed. The employer was therefore ordered to pay the employee compensation and damages well in excess of two years' remuneration. The amount came to R406 668.

In *Allpass v Mooikloof Estates (Pty) Ltd* (2011, 5 BLLR 462) the employee, a manager on a short fixed-term contract, was dismissed for dishonestly failing to disclose that he was HIV positive during his pre-employment process. In the Labour Court the employer submitted evidence that the employee's HIV condition would hamper the carrying out of his job responsibilities and that, when they attempted to discuss this problem with the employee, he refused to participate. The Court decided that the employer's true motive for the dismissal was the fact of the employee's HIV status and not that he had failed to disclose this fact. This constituted an automatically unfair dismissal.

The Court ordered the employer to pay the employee compensation equal to 12 months' remuneration as well as the legal costs incurred by the employee for the services of two advocates.

Looked at from this point of view it is difficult to see employees as anything but a source of great expense. However, employers cannot ignore the value that employees can add to the business or other organisation. Employers that wish to convert their employment expense from what is often an expensive nightmare into an investment need to:

- Develop a mature and mutually respectful relationship with employees
- Inform themselves of the skills of their employees
- Train their employees towards optimal competency
- Avoid ignoring employee misconduct and poor work performance
- Discipline employees firmly and swiftly but only where the proven facts justify it
- Utilise the skills of a reputable labour relations expert so as to ensure that they know when they can and cannot demote, retrench, fire or otherwise discipline employees.

EMPLOYERS CANNOT HIDE BEHIND THE CORPORATE VEIL

Many employers try to evade the law by closing down one business and opening another. However, this ploy has become less and less likely to succeed. Especially where the employer opens the same business under a different name and/or in a different place, the new business could be found liable for the compensation payment award made against the old business.

The new business might be registered as a separate company or close corporation from the old one which would normally, in terms of the Companies Act, protect it from liability for any legal obligations of any other entity. However, arbitrators at the CCMA and bargaining councils as well as judges in the Labour Court may be willing to ignore this corporate protection where they deem it appropriate. This practice of ignoring the Companies Act protection is known as 'piercing the corporate veil' because it breaks through the protective shield behind which the employer is hiding. This the courts and arbitrators might do where:

- They believe that the employer is purposely switching businesses in order to evade labour law compliance
- There is a clear and close connection between the old and new business
- The employee could lose out if the corporate veil is not pierced.

For example, in the case of *Marllier v G7 Technologies cc & Another* (2004, 4 BALR 480) the employer retrenched its production manager while the owners of the employer were still running other similar profitable businesses. The CCMA found that:

- The first cc had not been closed down for genuine operational reasons but rather for the convenience of the owners
- The employer had failed to consult with the employee before retrenching him
- The business of the second cc was so intertwined with that of the first one that they could be regarded as a partnership
- The owner's reliance on the juristic personality of the second cc as a means of avoiding liability for the employee's retrenchment justified the piercing of the corporate veil
- The dismissal was unfair
- The employer had to pay the employee six months' remuneration as compensation for the unfairness.

In the case of *Domingo v Ad-Bag Advertising CC* (2008, 7 BALR 646) the arbitrator found that the dismissal was unfair and awarded the employee nine months' remuneration in compensation. However, the arbitrator pierced the corporate veil and found the two owners of the business personally liable for the payment of this compensation despite the fact that officially the employer was a close corporation. This was because the owners lied during the hearing and because there was a danger that the business might not pay the compensation amount due to its impending closure.

In the light of these decisions it is most important for employers to:

- Act cautiously before moving their business operations from one company or cc to another
- Ensure that any such move is carried out for legitimate reasons
- Ensure that the rights of employees will not be unduly prejudiced by the transfer of the business operations
- Avoid misusing the ownership of other companies in order to get rid of employees.

Employers must also ensure that when considering retrenchments:

- There are truly no viable alternatives to the loss of jobs
- Potential retrenchees are properly consulted
- The whole process is managed under the guidance of a labour law expert.

LABOUR BROKERS UNDER SEIGE

The January 2015 amendments to the LRA have affected many hundreds of labour brokers and temp. agencies in South Africa. These agencies employ hundreds of thousands of people in South Africa and are referred to in the LRA as "temporary employment services" (TES). Many of these employers have not fully realised that, in addition to the new TES laws, the old labour laws that still apply to other employers also apply to them. Such legislation provides as follows:

- Strict procedures for firing and retrenching employees
- Many employers are required by law to register with industry-specific bargaining councils which then dictate the terms and conditions of employment in the sector
- There is no legally viable quick and easy way of dealing with strikes
- Trade unions can force employers to allow them access to the workplace
- Deduction from employees' remuneration of money owed to the employer is very difficult to achieve due to the legislation protecting employees and their pay
- All employees are entitled to paid annual leave, sick leave and family responsibility leave
- It is compulsory to pay minimum wages, limit hours of work and pay a premium for overtime work
- Affirmative action is compulsory for a great many employers.

In addition to having to comply with this legislation the cost of fighting CCMA and bargaining council disputes can be very heavy.

The TES provides to the client company staff to do the work that company employees would normally do. The TES thus frees the client from many labour law responsibilities in return for a fee. While employment agencies and labour brokers can make profits from this business they often pay a very high price for taking over the labour law risks involved. This is because:

- Becoming an employer in South Africa is fraught with legal dangers whether you are a TES or not

- Agencies and brokers are often at the mercy of their business clients who may mistreat the TES staff and thus incur legal liabilities for the TES
- Many employment agencies and brokers neither understand our labour laws pertaining to TESes nor understand how to protect themselves from the legal liabilities imposed on them due to their client's actions.

Where labour brokers and employment agencies fail to treat their employees according to the law they are likely to lose at the CCMA or bargaining council. For example, in the case of *Smith v Staffing Logistics* (2005, 10 BALR 1078) the client informed the labour broker that it no longer needed the services of the employee. The broker therefore removed the employee from the client's premises and placed him on indefinite standby without pay. At the bargaining council the employee alleged that this constituted unfair dismissal and the reason for the termination was a disagreement that the employee had with the client. The employer denied this but the arbitrator found that:

- Even though the employment contract gave the broker the right to terminate the employment at the client's behest the dismissal was unfair
- The broker's claim that the employee's assignment had been completed was not proven. The employee's version that the termination was due to his disagreement with the client was more likely
- The broker could not evade its duty as an employer by projecting the role of employer on to the client
- Placing an employee on unpaid standby constitutes unfair dismissal
- The employer had to pay the employee 14 months' remuneration in compensation.

These principles have been confirmed in the cases of *NUMSA obo Daki v Colven Associates Border cc* (2006, 9 BALR 877) and *NUMSA obo Mahlangu and others v Abancedisi Labour Services cc and another* (2006, 1 BALR 29).

Labour brokers are currently under siege by the trade union movement which is determined to close labour brokers down. The unions gleefully use the non-compliance of labour brokers as ammunition when pressuring their ANC alliance partner to ban labour brokers. In the light of this pressure and the legal traps highlighted above labour brokers and employment agencies need to use labour law experts to:

- draw up legally compliant TES contracts with clients and workers
- develop policies and procedures in line with labour law provisions and the employer's operational requirements
- train managers to implement these policies and procedures properly

- ensure that their employees are hired, disciplined and/or dismissed via fair, legally sound and effective strategies and procedures.

USING LABOUR BROKERS AND TEMP AGENCIES NOT ALWAYS KOSHER

Employers use alternative and temporary labour sources for numerous reasons including:

- Permanent employees are away on annual leave, sick leave, maternity leave or other leave and the remaining staff cannot cope with all the work
- Work volumes have increased temporarily and more staff are needed
- The agency or labour broker employs staff with specialised skills that the employer needs
- Avoidance of having to deal with trade unions, discipline, grievances and other labour problems
- The mistaken belief that, where there are problems relating to pay, benefits and working hours the agency/broker employee will take the blame and the company or organisation requiring the agency/broker staff will not be legally liable.

Such employment agencies and labour brokers are referred to in the Labour Relations Act (LRA) as "temporary employment services" (TES).

Previously the TES was legally able to take on many labour law responsibilities from its client in return for a fee. Trade unions, who find this arrangement to be a thorn in their sides, call it 'Atypical Employment' and have successfully launched a campaign to halt it. This culminated in the Labour Relations Act amendments effective 1 January 2015. Even before that date the campaign against misuse of labour brokers and temp. contracts was being bolstered by CCMA and Labour Court decisions made against labour brokers and against their clients.

For example, in the case of *Sibiya & others v HBL Services cc* (2003 7 BALR 796) the employees were employed by a labour broker to provide work to a client. The employees refused to change to a new shift system introduced by the client. When the employees arrived for work the next day to render services under the old shift system, the broker's client locked them out and they referred an unfair dismissal dispute to the CCMA.

The arbitrator found that the employees had been dismissed for refusing to work under the new shift system. As the employees were entitled to refuse the change and as no proper dismissal procedures had been implemented the arbitrator ordered the broker to reinstate the employees with full back pay.

In the case of *NUMSA obo Mahlangu & others v Abansedisi Labour Services and Another* (2006, 1 BALR 29) the employees were employed by a labour broker to render services to a client. The employees were fired by the labour broker because the client no longer required their services due to their poor performance. The arbitrator found that:

- The broker was not entitled merely to take its client's word that the employees were performing their work badly
- The dismissal was unfair and the broker was required to pay the employees compensation.

In the case of *Springbok Trading (Pty) Ltd v Zondani and Others* (2004, 9 BLLR 864) the company wanted to transfer a number of its own employees into the employment of a labour broker. Those employees who refused to take the transfer were retrenched. The Labour Court found the dismissal to be unfair, so the employer took the decision on appeal to the Labour Appeal Court. The Court found that:

- The employer's stated reason for wanting to implement the transfer was not good enough to justify the retrenchment of those employees who refused the transfer. That is, the employer's alleged wish to avoid the burden of payroll administration did not justify the loss of employees' jobs
- It was unlikely that the trade union would have agreed to the retrenchment of its members
- Consultations on the retrenchments were neither completed nor properly conducted
- The retrenchments were unfair.

The employer's appeal was therefore dismissed with costs.

The trade unions' success in curtailing the use of temporary employment services employers means that employers have lost a key method of relieving their heavy labour legislation burden.

BEWARE THE USE OF
FIXED-TERM CONTRACTS

You can inadvertently guarantee a temporary employee further employment.

According to sections 193 and 194 of the Labour Relations Act (LRA) the awards and orders that can be made against the employer for unfair dismissal are as follows:

- The LRA requires the CCMA or Labour Court to reinstate the employee. This means that the employer must give the employee his/her job back and undertake to pay the employee all remuneration calculated back to the date of the dismissal. The employer must also reinstate all the employee's benefits retrospectively.
- The LRA also permits the CCMA or Labour Court to order re-employment instead of reinstatement. This means that, while the employer must take the employee back, it might be under new terms and conditions.
- Even if the employer does not have to take the employee back at all it may still have to pay compensation up to a maximum of 12 months' remuneration calculated at the employee's newest rate of remuneration.
- If the dismissal is deemed to be automatically unfair, the maximum compensation that may be awarded is 24 months' remuneration.
- Such compensation is payable in addition to all other payments due to the employee. These could include notice pay, leave pay and even payment for the unexpired portion of the employee's contract. The Labour Court and CCMA have the powers to make such additional awards by virtue of section 195 of the LRA and section 74(1) of the BCEA. Furthermore, the Labour Court has jurisdiction, in terms of section 77(3) of the BCEA, to determine any matter relating to a contract of employment.

Therefore, in an attempt to circumvent all this onerous legislation, employers attempt to avoid having to dismiss undesirable employees by hiring workers on fixed-term contracts. Then, if the employee is seen as unsuitable, the employer merely allows the contract to lapse at its expiry date and says goodbye to the employee. However, this is a dangerous tactic because labour law has closed this loophole.

The main purpose of a fixed-term contract is supposed to be the filling of a temporary job. That is, the right time to hire an employee on a fixed-term contract is when the job itself is expected to come to an end at a specific time. It can be very dangerous to employ an employee on a fixed-term contract when the job itself is permanent (unless the temporary employee is merely standing in for the permanent incumbent who is away on leave or who has temporarily been deployed elsewhere). The reason for this danger is that, according to the LRA, if the employer (even inadvertently) gives the employee a "reasonable expectation" that the contract will be renewed on expiry, the CCMA or bargaining council could force the employer to renew the contract. In addition, employees may claim to have reasonable expectations that their employment will be made permanent.

However, the LRA does not define what constitutes a "reasonable expectation". This confuses employers and allows arbitrators to make their own decisions as to what does and does not constitute a "reasonable expectation".

In the case of *King Sabata Dalindyebo Municipality v CCMA and Others* (2005, 7 BLLR 696) the employer made a habit of regularly renewing fixed-term contracts. But then it allowed the last contracts to lapse even though there was still available work for the terminated employees. The Labour Court found that the employees had a reasonable expectation of having their contracts renewed again and forced the employer to renew the contracts.

In the case of *Pretorius v Sasol Polymers* (2008, 1 BALR 10) Ms Pretorius was appointed on a fixed-term contract to act in place of the permanent incumbent. When Ms Pretorius's contract expired the employer advertised the post to be filled on a permanent basis and refused to renew Ms Pretorius's contract. She referred an unfair dismissal dispute to the bargaining council because she claimed to have had a reasonable expectation that her contract would be renewed. The arbitrator found that:

- The employer had a policy that required a fixed-term employee occupying a permanent post to be made permanent if management approved
- The fact that management had advertised the post constituted management approval
- This policy gave the employee a reasonable expectation of renewal of her contract
- The employer's failure to give the employee the permanent post constituted an unfair dismissal and the employee was retrospectively reinstated.

The above shows that employers should not take a chance when dealing with the initiation and termination of employment contracts. Instead they should obtain expert advice from a genuine and reputable labour law expert.

NEDLAC PROCESS BESET
BY CONFLICTING AGENDAS

'NEDLAC' stands for the National Economic Development and Labour Council. This is a high-level forum where, amongst other things, legislation regarding labour and economic development issues is debated and formed in preparation for enactment in Parliament. This body therefore has a major responsibility to arrive at proposals for legislation that will promote economic development and a healthy labour economy.

The parties represented at NEDLAC include Government, labour unions, business and community. Their deliberations aim to achieve goals such as legal protection for workers and reversing unemployment. However, two key factors bedevilling the success of this forum are the severe conflicts between the above two goals of NEDLAC and the hugely disparate agendas of groups represented on the forum.

The two goals of protection of employee rights on the one hand and of reversing unemployment on the other hand need not necessarily be conflicting goals. However, in the current South African situation they do seriously conflict with each other. Thus, because the more the unions and government conspire to tighten up labour laws in the "interests of employee welfare", the more employers are reluctant to employ people in South Africa.

The current labour laws impose strong impediments to termination of employment for operational, misconduct and poor performance reasons. The law thus provides limited flexibility for employers and imposes very heavy obligations on them. Again, the more that employers suffer under this yoke the more reluctant they are to employ people. Thus, the very laws that are designed to protect employees have the effect of reducing their employability. The burden of the labour law yoke is felt all the more by smaller employers who do not have the resources to manage the labour law burden but who represent the great majority of businesses in South Africa.

Business owners and aspirant business owners, in response to this problem are:

- Cutting back on existing labour
- Resisting the need to hire people
- Turning to mechanisation
- Looking for non-labour-intensive opportunities
- Keeping their businesses small

- Closing their factories and moving them to the far east, thus exporting South African jobs to the orient
- Choosing not to open new businesses here
- In the case of potential foreign investors (with a few exceptions), finding other countries to do business in.

Those few foreign businesses such as Walmart that are willing to open up here are not always welcomed by the unions.

All of this shows that strong elements in the labour movement do not see job creation as the number one priority for South Africa. Ironically, our government is well aware of the serious damage that our labour laws are doing to the creation of jobs. This is proven by the admission by former Minister Trevor Manuel who said, before he left the cabinet, that our labour laws are hampering the creation of employment. Against the backdrop of the then President Zuma's highly ambitious goal of creating 11 million jobs by 2030 Minister Manuel's statement is hugely significant. A major concern is that, even in the unlikely case that the 11 million job target is achieved, it will not be nearly enough to solve the unemployment problem in SA. This is because of the many millions of school leavers that will be entering the job market over the next 15 years.

The four new labour law amendments introduced in 2014/2015 are highly unfriendly towards employers and thus unconducive to job creation. With these laws in place our labour dispensation is so tight as to choke the life out of employment creation by the private sector.

At the same time the government is making it very easy for Zimbabwean citizens to work in SA, thus reducing job opportunities for South Africans even more. When South Africans complain they are criticised and labelled as xenophobic.

The four new Acts are inflicting severe damage on employers. For example:

- Fixed-term employees will be able to take employers to the CCMA if they have a reasonable expectation of being offered permanent employment
- Employers will have the primary legal responsibility for the rights of people placed with them by temporary employment agencies and labour brokers
- Employers will be unable to terminate the employment of employees unwilling to meet changing operational requirements
- Employers that fail to pay employees doing jobs of equal value the same amount can be accused at Labour Court of unfair discrimination. Employers therefore need to implement job grading systems in order to comply with these new legal requirements.

NEW LABOUR LAWS WEAKEN EMPLOYERS AND STRENGTHEN JOB LOSSES

The government has more than once over the years undertaken to address the internal factors that are weakening our economy and deterring businesses from creating jobs. However, this unfulfilled undertaking has been made against the backdrop of a flood of labour legislation that is bedevilling employers and creating unemployment. For example, the 2015 LRA amendments provide that:

- Members of two minority unions acting jointly might be able to elect shop stewards
- Labour broker employees are able to exercise their trade union rights at the premises of the broker's client
- Employers falling under bargaining councils will fund dispute resolution
- The CCMA is empowered to regulate the rights of employers to be represented in proceedings before the Commission
- Arbitration awards certified by the Commission can be presented to the Deputy-Sheriff without the involvement of Labour Court writs
- The need to have an arbitration award for reinstatement made an order of the Court before contempt proceedings can be commenced be removed
- The operation of an arbitration award may only be suspended if financial security is provided by the applicant for a Labour Court review
- Employees engaged for a fixed term could claim dismissal on expiry of the term whether they have a reasonable expectation of continued temporary or permanent employment
- Section 187(1)(c) of the LRA now prohibits the dismissal of employees for reason of their refusal to accept a demand on a matter of mutual interest (e.g. a change in working hours)
- Labour brokers will not, in most cases, be able to assign their employees to clients for longer than three months unless the broker's employees are hired temporarily to replace the client's absent employees
- Lower-income employees of labour brokers will, in most cases, become employees of the client for purposes of the LRA if they are employed to perform work over a period in excess of three months and be paid the same wages and benefits as the client's other employees who are performing the same or similar work
- Employers may not employ staff on fixed-term contracts for longer than three months unless the nature of the work for which the employee is engaged is of a limited or definite duration or the employer can demonstrate any other justifiable reason for fixing the term of the contract. The LRA sets out a non-exhaustive list of nine justifiable reasons for fixing the term of a contract

- If a fixed term of longer than 24 months can be justified under the law, the employer must, on expiry of the contract, pay the employee one week's remuneration for each completed year of the contract
- Contractors and their clients have joint and several liability for any failures to comply with the LRA or any employment law.

The new BCEA amendments have the effect that:

- the Minister may issue an "umbrella" sectoral determination covering employers and employees who are not covered by any other sectoral determination or by a bargaining council collective agreement and may prohibit the subcontracting of work, prescribe minimum pay increases and set a threshold of representativeness for a registered trade union to have the organisational rights of access to employer premises and deduction of trade union subscriptions
- bottlenecks and delays in the labour law enforcement process are removed.
- the rights of the employer to lodge objections with the Director General and to appeal to court against a compliance order are removed from the Act.

The EEA effectively:

- places much heavier obligations on the employer to implement affirmative action. To take this even further the proposed new amendments provide for the Ministry of Labour to set affirmative action targets for employers
- forces employers to implement job grading systems that take 'effort' into account
- requires employers to be able to prove that they pay equal remuneration to employees doing similar level jobs even where the jobs are entirely different; and
- where such employees are not being paid equally, requires employers to be able to prove that there is a fair and objective reason for the differentiation.

The National Minimum Wage Act that came into law on 1 January 2019 is likely to win votes for the governing party from its labour allies in the 2019 elections but it is more than likely to place intense pressure on the countless businesses in South Africa that are struggling to survive and cannot afford to pay the prescribed minimum wages.

All of this is being imposed on employers without any real assistance to them to thrive and to be able to create jobs.

FOCUS OF SOUTH AFRICA'S LABOUR LAW DISPENSATION NEEDS TO BE BROADENED

It is widely agreed that labour legislation is essential in order to protect employees from exploitation and other mistreatment at the workplace and to right the wrongs of the past. The development, maintenance and enforcement of decent working conditions are not only right and fair to employees, they are essential for ensuring the workplace harmony necessary for a productive and profitable business. All of these needs are of crucial importance.

There is however another equally important priority. Employees who have work need to be secure in their jobs. If employees lose their jobs they and their families lose their livelihoods and often their ability to survive. Section 11 of South Africa's Constitution gives everyone the right to life. This is the most basic of all rights in our Constitution. Yet the lives of many millions of South African workers are being threatened by unemployment; and the proportion of the unemployed is approaching 40 percent of those able to work. This translates into a great many more millions of South Africans who are indigent because, for every worker who loses his/her job, there are normally family members who depend on him/her for survival. The more people who are retrenched the more unemployed family members there are who depend on the ever-reducing number of family members who do have jobs.

This means that, even if an employee receives a pay increase, the benefit of it is eroded because he/she has more mouths to feed due to our retrenchment epidemic. In many cases pay increases, enforced by law, are followed by retrenchments because the employers need to offset the cost of statutory pay increases by reducing the number of employees on the payroll. Thus, the unintended consequence of such labour laws is to impoverish the very employees they are intended to benefit.

This does not necessarily mean that laws protecting employees must be abolished. Rather it means that the planning of labour legislation must fully and carefully take into account all relevant factors, needs and consequences. This will enable the law makers to create a labour dispensation that does not prejudice its intended beneficiaries.

To use an example, further amendments to the Employment Equity Act (EEA) are at an advanced stage of development and all of these amendments are rightly aimed at improving the lot of South African workers. Included in these proposed amendments are provisions for the Ministry of Labour to set affirmative action targets for employers instead of allowing employers to continue setting their own targets. In addition, the proposals are that employers will now need to align their workplace demographies with both provincial and national demographic make-ups. I accept that the intention of these changes is to speed up the implementation of affirmative action, which is a positive intention.

However, the focus of the legislation is too narrow because it ignores the likely unintended consequences of placing these additional obligations on employers. Where an employer is forced to spend extra money on creating positions for affirmative action candidates, head hunting qualified candidates and training people to learn the job, this is essentially a good thing. However, where an employer, just keeping its head above water, does not have the money necessary to advance affirmative action, the imposition of affirmative action targets could be fatal to the business.

Thus the EEA amendment proposals ignore the extremely weak economic circumstances under which employers are currently operating. Many smaller employers (below 100 employees) are struggling to continue employing people at all and a great many larger employers are reducing their workforces.

This means that we must broaden our planning of labour legislation to avoid its disastrous unintended consequences. For example, at the same time as considering ways of advancing affirmative action, we have to devise ways of strengthening employers so that they will be able to implement the new legislation without being weakened or even closed down.

An example of measures to strengthen the finances of employers and thus their ability to comply with labour legislation is the implementation of Shareism. That is, legislation should be negotiated and agreed that motivates and empowers employers and workers to cooperate in jointly creating and jointly sharing in the profits of the company.

This will not only improve the ability of employers to afford the costs of labour law compliance, it will also vastly improve the quality of industrial relations in South Africa.

FOREIGN EMPLOYERS CAN'T ESCAPE SOUTH AFRICAN LABOUR LAW

South African labour law strongly protects people employed in South Africa. Furthermore, our courts do not easily give up jurisdiction to foreign courts. When a foreign embassy is situated in South Africa it is in fact, according to law, based on foreign soil. A South

African working at a South Africa-based foreign embassy would therefore be subject to the labour law of that foreign country. However, a branch of a foreign company based in South Africa is not considered to be on foreign soil and is therefore subject to South African law.

For example, in the case of *August Lapple (SA) v Jarrett & others* (2003, 12 BLLR 1194) the dismissed employee had been the managing director of the South African subsidiary of a German company. He referred his dismissal to the Bargaining Council for the Motor Industry in South Africa. However, the employer disputed the council's jurisdiction as it claimed that it had been the company's head office in Germany that had dismissed the employee. The arbitrator ruled that the bargaining council did indeed have jurisdiction. The employer therefore referred the jurisdiction ruling on review to the Labour Court which found that:

- Although the employee had been employed by the German parent company, the employee had also been employed by the South African subsidiary
- The bargaining council did have jurisdiction to hear the matter
- The employer was to pay the employee's legal costs.

Even South Africans working outside South Africa can, in certain cases, refer labour disputes to the South African dispute resolution system. For example, in the case of *Kleinhans v Parmalat SA (Pty) Ltd*. (2000, 9 BLLR 879) the employee was retrenched after having worked in Mozambique. The Labour Court decided that:

- An agreement by the parties as to where jurisdiction lies does not bind the Court.
- South African law was "impliedly" incorporated into the employment contract and this gave the South African courts jurisdiction
- The contract was concluded and cancelled in South Africa
- The employee's salary was paid in South Africa and was paid in rands
- The termination letter was written by the employer who considered the Mozambican operation as its own
- The Court therefore did have jurisdiction to hear the case.

In the case of *Parry v Astral Operations Ltd*. (2005, 10 BLLR 989) the employee was retrenched after having worked in the position of general manager of the employer's operations in Malawi. The Labour Court decided that:

- Both parties were based in South Africa
- The parties had agreed that the employer's (South African) policies would apply
- The employer had not approved the contents of Malawian law

- Both parties had, when signing the contract, been under the impression that they were concluding it under South African law
- The Labour Court therefore had jurisdiction
- The employee was entitled to damages for breach of contract, balance of relocation costs, share options, accrued profit shares, salary, notice pay, severance pay and compensation equal to 12 months' remuneration. In addition the employer had to pay part of the employee's legal costs.

In the light of these cases, employers should not assume that they can hide behind foreign incorporation or foreign workplaces. That is, they should not assume that they need not follow South African law merely because foreign elements exist in the working situation. Instead, employers should first obtain expert labour law advice before taking any action against employees regardless of where the employee works or where the employer is based.

CHAPTER CONCLUSION

South Africa has a capitalist economy that is controlled by labour legislation that has strong socialist tendencies. On the one hand this ensures that the rights of employees are very well protected. On the other hand it often makes running a business problematic. Those businesses that are not geared up for working within these legal constraints will struggle to survive.

South Africa has a capitalist economy that is controlled by labour legislation

CHAPTER 2

UNDERSTANDING SOUTH AFRICA'S LABOUR DISPUTE SYSTEM

The primary aim of South Africa's labour law dispensation to protect the rights and interests of employees is based on the section 23 Constitutional provision that "Everyone has the right to fair labour practices". It is significant that the focus of South African labour law and its application by the courts interpret the word "Everyone" in this provision to exclude employers when it comes to the referral of labour disputes.

Our labour dispensation in general and our dispute resolution system in particular focus on levelling the playing fields between assumedly powerless employees and assumedly powerful employers.

While employers are not entitled to refer disputes of right to forums of the dispute resolution system such as the Commission for Conciliation, Mediation and Arbitration (CCMA) employees have the full right to refer disputes as long as the relevant forum has jurisdiction. One example of this imbalance is that, if an employee terminates his or her fixed-term employment contract before its expiry date, the employer cannot take the employee to the CCMA in order to get restitution for this unfair act. However, the CCMA does have jurisdiction to deal with a premature termination of an employment contract perpetrated by the employer.

In this chapter we examine the mechanisms of our dispute resolution forums such as the CCMA, bargaining councils and the labour courts.

THE LABOUR DISPUTE SYSTEM – HOW IT WORKS

The Labour Relations Act of 1995 (LRA) makes it very easy for employees to challenge alleged unfair dismissals and other unfair practices at private or statutory dispute resolution forums. Such disputes may, by agreement, be dealt with via private (non-statutory) dispute resolution forums such as ArcelorMittal South Africa (AMSA), Arbitration Foundation of Southern Africa (AFSA), Tokiso Dispute Settlement and others. On the other hand, the statutory dispute resolution forums established by the LRA include:

- The dispute resolution arms of bargaining councils (BC) in certain industries including, for example, the metal and engineering, motor, public service and chemical industries
- The Commission for Conciliation, Mediation and Arbitration (CCMA) for those industries that do not have their own bargaining councils (e.g. retail, IT, security, financial services and others)
- The Labour Court
- The Labour Appeal Court.

The process is that:

- The aggrieved employee must start off by completing a dispute referral form and lodging it with the relevant BC or with the CCMA
- A conciliation meeting is set up where a mediator is appointed to attempt to facilitate an out-of-court settlement
- If this is successful the employer and employee sign a contract setting out the terms of their settlement agreement and the matter is then closed
- If conciliation fails to resolve the dispute the employee may refer it to the next level which, depending on the nature of the dispute, will either be an arbitration tribunal (similar to a junior court) or to the Labour Court (the more senior dispute resolution forum). The matter will go to the Labour Court instead of to arbitration if the dispute relates to matters such as multiple retrenchment, strike dismissals or automatically unfair dismissals. The arbitration or Labour Court hearing would normally take place at a later date
- Alternatively, the CCMA may set the matter down as a conciliation/arbitration (con/arb). In such a case, unless one of the parties objects, the arbitration would take place immediately that conciliation fails
- At arbitration or Labour Court the arbitrator or judge hears evidence from the employer and employee and decides whether the dismissal or other act was fair or not
- Once an arbitrator has communicated his/her decision to the parties either of them may, if dissatisfied, apply for a review at the Labour Court. For example, should either party have evidence that the arbitrator accepted a bribe, was biased, ignored relevant evidence, refused to listen to relevant evidence, assisted the other party unduly or otherwise acted wrongly, it may apply to the Labour Court to set aside the arbitrator's decision
- Any decision of the Labour Court may be referred to the Labour Appeal Court and could be referred even higher to the Supreme Court of Appeal and to the Constitutional Court as occurred in the case of *Sidumo v Rustenburg Platinum Mines Ltd.*

When a dismissal dispute is referred to arbitration or Labour Court the employee only has to prove that he/she was, in fact, dismissed. Then the employer has to prove that the dismissal was both procedurally and substantively fair. And the employer normally has to provide such proof before hearing the employee's evidence as to why he/she has alleged that the dismissal was unfair.

This means that the employer is assumed guilty of unfair dismissal until it proves itself innocent; but also has to present its case first. Thus the employer is in a seriously disadvantaged position.

At conciliation the employee may be represented only by himself/herself or by a union official. The employer may represent itself or be represented by an official of an employer's organisation.

At arbitration lawyers may be allowed if:

- the dispute is not a matter of misconduct or incapacity; or
- the arbitrator allows lawyers due to the legal complexity of the matter or to 'uneven playing fields'.

Employers are therefore advised to join registered employers' organisations in order to avoid the uncertainty of being allowed representation.

CON-ARB AT CCMA HAS PROS AND CONS

Employers and employees need to look very carefully at notices to attend the CCMA in order to see what type of process has been set down. No party wants to arrive at CCMA thinking that they will only be facing a mediation process and then find that the court case (arbitration hearing) occurs on the same day.

The CCMA is constantly overloaded with cases, hearing in excess of 170 000 cases a year. This can result in backlogs and delays in resolution of disputes. As a consequence the Labour Relations Act (LRA) as amended in 2002 provides for a speedier dispute resolution process called con-arb which stands for conciliation-arbitration. This hybrid process is most frequently used and the old system of conciliation now and arbitration later is seldom applied in the normal course of events.

Regardless of whether the old or the new system is applied, the process always begins with conciliation. This is a peace-making process whereby a CCMA or bargaining council

(BC) mediator tries to assist the employer and employee to reach an out-of-court agreement. It is an exercise that is intended to end in a settlement agreement. The commissioner has no authority to make an award (judgment).

On the other hand, arbitration is a judicial-type process that usually occurs if a conciliated settlement is not achieved. That is, it is Step 2 in the process if Step 1 (conciliation) fails to resolve the matter. At arbitration the employer and employee do not negotiate an agreement. Instead, they bring and present evidence as in any court case. Then the arbitrator, after hearing all the evidence, makes a finding as to which party was in the wrong.

Con-arb is when, instead of scheduling the arbitration for a later date, it is held on the same day, the very MINUTE that conciliation fails! The employee is not required to apply for arbitration; it occurs automatically the very moment the conciliator declares that conciliation has failed. Thus, the parties have no time after the conciliation meeting to prepare their evidence and arguments for the arbitration!

Con-arb is not compulsory for all types of dispute. It is compulsory when the dispute concerns:

- The dismissal of an employee for any reason relating to probation
- Any unfair labour practice relating to probation.

In addition, if neither party objects to con-arb then con-arb is likely to take place even if probation is not involved, provided that the dispute concerns:

- A non-strike dismissal for conduct or capacity
- Constructive dismissal
- The employer's failure to substantially preserve the employment conditions of employees when transferring them in terms of section 197 of the LRA
- An employee who does not know the reason for the dismissal
- An unfair labour practice.

Therefore, on receiving any con-arb notice a party who does not want con-arb must lodge a formal objection at least seven days in advance of the set hearing date. However, such an objection will not be valid if the dispute concerns an unfair dismissal relating to probation or an unfair labour practice relating to probation.

It is essential for employers and employees who receive con-arb notices to:

- Realise straight away that it is a con-arb that has been scheduled
- Understand what con-arb means for them in practice
- Begin immediately with preparations for the con-arb.

This is particularly so because the parties seldom get more than 14 days' advance notice of a con-arb. The parties need to enter into intensive preparations the moment they receive a con-arb notification because 14 days is very little for purposes of preparation. Included in these preparations should be:

- The preparation of the witnesses of truthful, relevant and accurate testimonies
- Collecting and preparing documentary and other evidence
- Responses to anticipated evidence that the opposing party could bring
- Preparation of case arguments and case law.

CCMA GUIDELINES ON MISCONDUCT CRUCIAL

The CCMA has updated its guidelines on misconduct dismissal arbitrations in terms of the provisions of the Labour Relations Act (LRA). Despite the fact that these guidelines have been in existence since January 2012 many employers are still not familiar with them.

The stated purpose of these guidelines is to "…promote consistent decision making in arbitrations dealing with dismissals for misconduct." The guidelines spell out in detail the procedures that arbitrators are to use when arbitrating cases where unfair dismissal on the grounds of misconduct has been alleged. The guidelines also set out some basic principles and factors that arbitrators are to take into account when deciding on whether a dismissal is procedurally and substantively fair. The gazetted document states that the guidelines constitute CCMA policy but is silent as to whether or not the guidelines apply to arbitrators outside of the CCMA. That is, the document does not state whether arbitrators on the panels of bargaining council dispute resolution centres and of other dispute resolution forums accredited by the CCMA are obliged to follow these guidelines. It would make sense for all bodies accredited by the CCMA to arbitrate dismissal disputes to be required to follow the policy of the institution with which they are accredited. As the document does not define its scope the result could be inconsistency between CCMA and non-CCMA arbitrations in the way that they are handled and in the awards themselves.

The LRA contains a large number of very big and crucial legal gaps. This fact, together with the fact that the concept of what is and is not 'fair' is heavily influenced by the views of each arbitrator, has historically rendered the labour law jungle an extremely dark, uncertain and dangerous place for employers to be. It is therefore high time that a document was put together to clear up these uncertainties. While the CCMA Guidelines do not entirely fulfil this function they do go some way towards clearing up some uncertainties as regards the law of fair misconduct dismissal.

The document does indicate, at least in part, that the guidelines represent CCMA policy and should thus be applied by commissioners in carrying out arbitrations. However, a factor that could detract from the good intentions of the guidelines, is that item 4 thereof allows Commissioners to depart from this CCMA policy where they have "… good reason for favouring a different interpretation to that which is represented in the guidelines." However, this licence to be inconsistent is balanced by the requirement that arbitrators are to set out their reasons for adopting an approach different to CCMA policy as reflected in the guidelines.

The guidelines further require commissioners to interpret and apply the LRA and other legislation in accordance with judicial decisions that are binding on the CCMA and that the most recent binding decisions of the highest court must be followed by Commissioners. These include decisions of the Constitutional Court, the Supreme Court of Appeal, Labour Appeal Court, High Court and Labour Court.

Item 10 of the guidelines makes it compulsory for arbitration awards and rulings to be lawful, reasonable and procedurally fair. This item of the guidelines draws directly on the provisions of Section 33 (1) of South Africa's Constitution which gives everyone the right to administrative action which is lawful, reasonable and procedurally fair. It appears that this has paved the way for parties taking arbitrators to the Labour Court on review to do so on the basis that the arbitrator failed to comply with these Constitutional provisions.

The guidelines deal with a wide spectrum of aspects relating to misconduct dismissal cases. These aspects include, amongst others, the manner of conducting the arbitration hearing, the nature of the arbitration, requirements for different stages, explanation of the inquisitorial approach as opposed to the adversarial approach, rules for the assessment of evidence by arbitrators, the components of substantive and procedural fairness, the role of the employers' disciplinary procedure and code and discipline of trade union representatives. The guidelines also reinforce the principle that the legal onus is on the employer to prove the fairness of the dismissal.

It still remains to be seen whether the "consistent decision making" desired by the CCMA will be achieved and whether fewer reviews at the Labour Court will be successful. However, I am optimistic that if these guidelines are taken seriously by Commissioners, arbitration awards will begin to be more consistent and less reviewable.

THE AWARDS OF ARBITRATORS
MUST BE RATIONAL

I often receive calls from angry employers who, having been certain of success at arbitration, have received notice that they have lost the case. The reasons that this might happen include, amongst others:

- The case of the employer concerned was weak without him/her realising it
- The employer's case was strong but he/she failed to present it in an understandable and/or convincing manner
- The employer presented a strong case in a proper manner but the arbitrator nevertheless failed to make a decision properly based on the case put forward.

It is the third of these three reasons that is unfair to the employer. However, in such a case the disappointed party has the right to challenge the arbitrator via a review at the Labour Court on the grounds that, amongst others, the arbitrator took a bribe, was biased, ignored pertinent evidence or failed to arrive at a properly reasoned award.

Wayne Hutchinson, who has many years of experience as a CCMA arbitrator, has stated that the arbitrator is required to "... weigh up and consider all the evidence, both oral and documentary, prior to embarking upon the process of making factual findings" (May 2007, CLL page 107). In his article Hutchinson cites the decisions of senior judges that reinforce the arbitrator's requirement to provide a properly reasoned award. Specifically he cites the cases of *Crown Chickens v Kapp* and *Rustenburg Platinum Mines v CCMA*.

As per Hutchinson's report the Court, in the Crown Chickens case, found that the award of an arbitrator:

- must not be arbitrary
- must be arrived at by a reasoning process as opposed to conjecture, fantasy, guesswork or hallucination
- must have applied his mind seriously to the issues at hand
- must have conclusions that are justifiable and defensible and logical.

In the Rustenburg Platinum case, the Court found that "...the Promotion of Administrative Justice Act (PAJA) applied to CCMA arbitration proceedings" and that "the PAJA was enacted in order to give effect to the right to administrative action that is lawful, reasonable and procedurally fair."

In effect the PAJA requires the decisions of arbitrators to:

- comply with the law
- be rational
- be properly explained via the giving of reasons for the decision.

Thus the arbitrator must not only have logical and legal reasons for his/her decisions but must also give these reasons at the time of rendering the decisions otherwise it may be assumed that he/she did not have good reason. The emphasis has been placed on the actual giving of good reasons because:

- The parties have the right to know why the arbitrator has found against them so they can decide whether and how to challenge the arbitrator's decision
- This requirement deters the making of faulty decisions by arbitrators. That is, an arbitrator who has to explain his actions will be less likely to ignore or misconstrue relevant evidence and to make bad decisions.

The comprehensive furnishing of reasons by the arbitrator enables anyone questioning the decision to better assess whether the arbitrator has:

- considered all serious objections to and all alternatives to the decision he/she has made
- provided a rational connection between the facts of the case and the decision.

The significance of this for employers is that they must:

- themselves have good reason when acting against employees
- provide their good reasons clearly and comprehensively to the arbitrator when called to CCMA hearings.

This will pave the way for the arbitrator to accept the employer's reasoning and to follow the same line of reasoning as did the employer. In this way the employer aids the arbitrator to find in its favour.

The above approach requires of employers that they insist on managerial decisions to be made unemotively, rationally and in line with the law by managers who have been trained in labour law and decision making.

EASIER TO TAKE ERRANT ARBITRATORS TO TASK

The CCMA's policy guideline for misconduct dismissal arbitrations that became effective in January 2012 increases the obligation on commissioners to conduct themselves properly when arbitrating such matters. These guidelines, backed up by the law, pave the way for employers and employees to take the arbitrator's conduct on review to the Labour Court if they are able to prove that the arbitrator, in making his/her award, has materially broken a rule, thereby committing 'misconduct'. This is different to an appeal because an appeal is lodged, not against the arbitrator's conduct, but rather against his/her decision.

Arbitrator 'misconduct' can and does occur in many different forms including, amongst others, bias, interrogation of witnesses, failure to keep records, ignoring of evidence, refusal to allow a party the right to question witnesses or bring evidence, failure to apply his/her mind, misconstruing of evidence, overstepping his/her authority and failure to consider statutory provisions.

In the case of *Prince v CCMA and others* (2005, 2 BLLR 159) the employee was fired for stealing money collected from the car park pay station. The arbitrator found that the employee had been involved in the theft and upheld the dismissal. The employee then applied to the Labour Court for a Review. The Labour Court found that the evidence led by the employer was inadequate as proof of the employee's guilt. There had been other people who could have taken the money.

The Court found that the CCMA commissioner's award finding had not been based on the facts. As it is the duty of commissioners to take proper account of evidence led, the Court found the CCMA award to be both unsustainable and unjustified. The employer was required to reinstate the employee with 44 months' back pay plus interest. The employer was also ordered to pay the employee's legal costs.

In *De Nysschen v General Public Service Bargaining Council & others* (2007, 5 BLLR 461) the employee had been temporarily acting in a post for some time. When an advertisement was distributed for purposes of filling the upgraded post permanently the acting incumbent applied for it. As she was not successful she lodged a dispute at the bargaining council. However, the arbitrator found that the employer had not been unfair in appointing someone else to the position. The employee then lodged a review application at the Labour Court which found that:

- The employer was unable to show that the employee who was appointed to the post was the most suitable candidate

- The interviewing panel had recommended the aggrieved employee, yet she had not been appointed
- The criteria used in deciding against the employee were not the criteria that were advertised with the job advertisement
- The successful applicant had been a black male. However, the employer did not claim that it had used affirmative action criteria to fill the post
- The criteria used by the employer to fill the post were therefore incorrectly accepted by the arbitrator whose award was therefore overturned.

The employer was ordered to appoint the employee into the disputed post with retrospective effect.

In an unreported case (Number JR 1606/04) the employee was reprimanded by a manager for failing to phone in while absent from work. The employee left his employment, went to the CCMA and claimed that he had been dismissed. At the CCMA the employer denied that the employee had been dismissed and brought substantial evidence to show that the employee had been instructed to return to work.

During the arbitration hearing the commissioner frequently cross-examined the employer's witnesses and made remarks deriding the evidence of those witnesses. The arbitration award, which was in favour of the employee, failed to take into account the evidence brought by the employer. The employer's manager later saw the employee and the arbitrator shaking hands.

The employer took the arbitrator on review to the Labour Court claiming that the award failed to take the facts into account and that the arbitrator was biased. The Court found in favour of the employer and found the dismissal to be both procedurally and substantively fair.

Parties therefore need not give up if they truly believe that, on the proven facts, they were short changed due to irregular conduct on the arbitrator's behalf.

However, even if the aggrieved party has evidence of arbitrator 'misconduct' it is difficult to persuade a court judge that this evidence amounts to solid proof meriting the overturning of the award. In the unreported case described immediately above the employer used proper labour law expertise in order to prove its case. Failure to use such expertise would most likely have resulted in the employer losing the case.

WHAT POWERS DO THE LABOUR COURTS HAVE?

The Labour Relations Act (LRA) gives the Labour Court and Labour Appeal Court numerous and strong powers to make decisions relating to labour disputes. Section 158 of the LRA gives the Labour Court the power to make, amongst others, orders:

- Granting urgent relief and interdicts
- Remedying wrongs and determining disputes
- Clarifying legal circumstances (declaratory orders)
- For compensation and damages
- For legal costs to be paid by the loser to the winner of a case
- Enforcing compliance with the provisions of the LRA
- Enforcing arbitration awards
- Condoning the late filing of disputes or documents with the Court
- Reviewing decisions made or acts performed by the State
- Reviewing awards and rulings made by CCMA and bargaining council arbitrators.

These orders may deal with various dispute types including unfair dismissals for misconduct, poor performance, illness and operational requirements.

In addition, the Basic Conditions of Employment Act (BCEA) gives the Labour Court the power to determine disputes relating to employment contracts. And the Employment Equity Act (EEA) empowers the Labour Court to make orders relating to unfair discrimination disputes.

The Labour Appeal Court, being senior to the Labour Court, has higher powers than the Labour Court and can hear appeals against the decisions made by that court. In addition, it has the power, when required, to deal directly with any of the matters normally dealt with by the Labour Court under the LRA.

It is clear that, between them, these two courts have very substantial powers. And they are not normally reluctant to exercise their powers strongly even if it results in a very severe financial burden to the party on the receiving end. For example, in the case of *Evans v Japanese School of Johannesburg* (2006, 12 BLLR 1146) the Labour Court found that the employer had unfairly dismissed and unfairly discriminated against the employee. The Court therefore ordered the employer to pay the employee compensation and damages totalling R377 000. Some years ago the Labour Court awarded a one million rand compensation amount against the Ministry of Labour.

While these courts have extensive powers they do not seem to be sure of the exact extent thereof. That is, there seems to be strong disagreement between the different courts as to the maximum amount they may award to unfairly treated employees.

It is necessary to explain the difference between two types of awards the Labour Court may make. That is, the Court may make compensation awards and it may make back-pay awards. Compensation awards are made where the unfairly dismissed employee is not reinstated. The Court then awards the employee financial compensation for the loss of his/her job. However, under the LRA the Court is required, where feasible, to reinstate the employee rather than award compensation. When reinstatement is ordered the Court usually requires the employer, in addition, to pay the employee for the period between the dismissal and the date of the reinstatement order. This is to make up for the employee's loss of earnings prior to reinstatement.

The LRA specifically lays down the maximum amount that the Court may award by way of compensation when the dismissed employee is not reinstated. This limit is 24 months' remuneration in the case of an automatically unfair dismissal and 12 months' remuneration in all other unfair dismissal cases. However, the LRA is silent as to whether there is any maximum limit on the amount of back pay the Court may award in tandem with a reinstatement order. It has, for a very long time, been assumed that the amount of the back pay is only limited by the number of months between the date of dismissal and the date of the reinstatement. In 2005 the Labour Appeal Court upheld this view. For example, in the case of *Kroukam v SA Airlink (Pty) Ltd* (2005, 26 ILJ 2153 as reported in CLL January 2007) the Labour Appeal Court held that the amount of back pay could be calculated back to the date of dismissal even if this exceeded the limits for compensation payments.

However, soon after the Kroukam decision, in *CWIU & Others v Latex Surgical Products (Pty) Ltd* (2006, 27 ILJ 2018 as reported in CLL January 2007) the Labour Appeal Court held that the amount of back pay ordered must be subject to the same limits as are laid down for compensation orders. Then, in *SACCAWU and others v Primserv ABC Recruitment (Pty) Ltd* (2006, 27 ILJ 2162 as reported in CLL January 2007) the Labour Court held that the amount of back-pay orders is not limited to the maximums set for compensation orders. It should further be noted that, in the Kroukam case, one of the three judges on the Labour Appeal Court bench disagreed with the majority finding.

It is most disturbing that there is so little agreement within the courts as to the law, as this makes decisions for employers very unclear. In the light of this confusion the only solution for employers is not to end up in the labour courts. They can only achieve this by ensuring that, before they take any decision affecting employees, they get labour law and practical strategic advice from a reputable labour law expert.

INTERDICTS, DISCIPLINARY HEARINGS AND REPRESENTATION

Section 158 of the Labour Relations Act (LRA) gives the Labour Court the power to issue interdicts preventing employers, employees or trade unions from proceeding with threatened or current actions.

A distinction should be drawn between an interdict and a writ. This is because a writ is issued by the Court in order to ensure that something gets done rather than to prevent an action. For example, the Court may issue a writ in order to ensure that an employer pays an employee the amount of a compensation order made by the CCMA.

On the other hand, the Court has the power, via interdicts to prevent or halt:

- Industrial action
- Retrenchments
- The removal of remuneration or benefits
- Disciplinary proceedings
- Other employment or workplace-related actions.

Normally, the applicant party requests an interdict in order to prevent an opposing party from proceeding with actions that the applicant sees as undesirable. Sometimes, such an application is brought merely as a tactic to frustrate the opposition rather than because there is any real urgency or prejudice to the applicant.

However, the courts are quite miserly with their interdicts and are inclined to grant these only where the applicant can prove that:

- There is a genuine urgency in the need to interdict the targeted action
- A grave injustice would occur if the interdict were not issued
- The applicant's labour law rights would be seriously infringed should the interdict not be granted
- He/she has done all that is reasonable to obtain relief from the alleged injustice.

In the case of *Nyathi v Special Investigating Unit* (2011, 12 BLLR 1211) the employee was dismissed for refusing to undergo a polygraph test. Prior to the dismissal the employee applied for an interdict to prevent the termination. However the employer convinced the Court that:

- The employee had signed an employment contract agreeing to undertake polygraph tests
- This agreement to take such tests was a material term of the contract in the context of the type of unit the applicant worked in
- Dismissal would be a just response to a breach of such a material term
- There was no grave injustice attached to the dismissal.

In the case of *Mahlalela v Office of the Pension Fund Adjudicator* (2011, 6 BLLR 587) the Court found that the applicant employee had shown that there was an urgency resulting from pending disciplinary proceedings but had neither raised his objections before the hearing's presiding officer nor shown that a grave injustice would follow should the interdict not be ordered.

In the case of *Volschenk & another v Morero NO & others* (2011, 3 BLLR 313) the Labour Court refused to issue an interdict halting a disciplinary hearing at which two employees were accused of committing financial irregularities. The employees claimed that the disciplinary proceedings should be stayed until they could obtain legal representation. They claimed that it was their right to have lawyers at the enquiry because:

- the employer was represented by a legal practitioner
- the alleged offence could result in criminal action
- there were legal complexities in the case.

The Court turned down the interdict application because the employees had failed to show:

- that they were entitled to legal representation and
- that their trade union could not be trusted to represent them.

The Court found further that the employer's policy went beyond the requirements of the LRA and allowed trade union representation. The employees therefore had no grounds to claim that they were entitled to use lawyers instead of the trade union at their disciplinary hearing.

This decision conflicts to an extent with that in the case of *Molope v Mbha* (2005, 3 BLLR 267) where the Court stated that every employee has the right to be represented by a person of his choice whether it be a union official or a lawyer.

While employers can take some heart from these decisions they are likely to find interdict decisions going against them should they fail to interpret properly the principles of justice in the labour law context.

CHAPTER CONCLUSION

South Africa's labour dispute resolution system exists primarily to enable employees to challenge the actions of employers. The CCMA, bargaining councils and labour courts all accept complaints from employees but not from employers. This means that employers need to develop their own internal rules of conduct, communicate these clearly to their employees and empower management to implement these rules properly. This is necessary for workplace harmony and productivity and in order to avoid falling foul of the dispute resolution process.

South Africa's labour dispute resolution system exists primarily to enable employees to challenge the actions of employers

Employees have more rights than responsibilities

CHAPTER 3

EMPLOYEES HAVE MORE RIGHTS THAN RESPONSIBILITIES

South Africa's labour statutes give employees the right to join trade unions, to go on strike, to minimum pay, leave, restricted working hours, safe working conditions, fair disciplinary decisions and procedures, freedom from unfair discrimination, affirmative action, employment benefits and many others.

On the other hand our statutes give employees few responsibilities. Employees are required, under statute, to behave safely at their workplaces but the labour acts impose very few other specific obligations on employees. However, common law does require employees to serve their employers loyally, honestly and diligently.

Due to the relative dearth of legal obligations on employees many employers use employment contracts and internal policies in an effort towards ensuring that employees behave in line with the employer's requirements. However, the content and operation of these internal policies are strongly limited by labour law.

This chapter explains the wide spectrum of rights that employees have and the ways in which employers need to comply therewith while at the same time managing their operations effectively.

WHEN DOES A JOB APPLICANT BECOME AN EMPLOYEE?

You can be an employee before you start work!

Case law makes it very dangerous for an employer to sign employment contracts before it is certain that there is definitely a job for the applicant and before the employer is certain that it wishes to employ the job applicant.

The Labour Relations Act does not deal with the situation where a job applicant has been offered the job but, before starting work, is told that he/she has no longer got the job. This is a serious gap in the legislation for a job applicant who may have resigned from his/her old job on receiving the offer of the new job. On hearing that the new job is no more he/she will have lost both the old and new jobs and be without a livelihood.

Neither the Basic Conditions of Employment Act (BCEA) nor the EEA nor the Labour Relations Act (LRA) shed any light on the recourse of a person who finds him/herself in this unenviable situation. Historically, the view has been that one is not an employee until he/she starts working and can therefore not use the labour dispute resolution system to take the employer to task.

One therefore had to rely on the law of contract. That is, when an employer offers a position to an applicant and the applicant accepts, then a contract has been concluded. Such a contract is legally binding whether it is in writing or not. Therefore, if the employer then refuses to let the employee start work, the employer is in breach of contract and can be sued in civil court.

There is little if any dispute as to the employee's theoretical right to sue the employer and the employee has a very good chance of succeeding with his/her suit if he/she can prove breach of contract. However, in practice, many employees do not have the substantial resources necessary to fight such a case in civil court. Secondly, it could take years for the employee to get his/her pound of flesh should the case go ahead.

It is possibly for this reason that Labour Court Judges and CCMA arbitrators have more recently become willing to broaden their view of what constitutes an employee.

According to section 213 of the LRA an employee is:

> "(a) any person, excluding an independent contractor, who works for another person or for the state and who receives, or is entitled to receive, any remuneration; and
>
> (b) any other person who in any manner assists in carrying out or conducting the business of an employer..."

This definition seems to make it clear that a person only gains the status of 'employee' when he/she begins working for the employer. That is, the definition strongly implies that the employer's legal obligations begin on the day that the employee physically begins work.

In the case of *Wyeth SA (Pty) Ltd v Manqele and others* (2005, 6 BLLR 523) Wyeth and Manqele signed an employment contract. Before Manqele began working a dispute arose between the parties as to Manqele's company car. As a result the employer terminated the employment contract on the grounds that the parties to it had been unable to agree to one of its terms (relating to the company car). Manqele took the employer to the CCMA for unfair dismissal. The employer contended that the CCMA had no jurisdiction to hear the matter as Manqele had not been an employee. It based this claim on the fact that Manqele had not yet begun work and that the legal definition of an employee includes the provision that an employee is someone who "works for another person". However, neither the CCMA nor the Labour Court was prepared to accept this argument. Wyeth therefore took the matter on appeal to the Labour Appeal Court which rejected the literal interpretation that Wyeth had put on the definition of an employee. The Court found that Manqele had become an employee the moment the employment contract was signed by the parties. The Court therefore dismissed the employer's appeal and required the employer to pay the employee's legal costs.

In *Solidarity obo Nortje v Xtrata Lydenburg Works* (2009, 7 BALR 673) the employer repudiated the contract before the job applicant began work. The employer had offered Nortje a contract post in Lydenburg which he accepted. After he relocated to Lydenburg but before he took up his post the company told Nortje that it would not take him into service because he had failed to pay the company money owed to them in respect of a previous period of employment. At arbitration the company denied that their action constituted dismissal. The arbitrator found that the employment relationship had begun once the contract was finalised and that the company's refusal to allow Nortje to commence work constituted a dismissal. As a proper procedure had not been followed the dismissal was unfair.

The above case decisions make it clear that employers should not enter into employment agreements with job applicants before all the terms and conditions of employment have been fully agreed and until all possible reasons for not employing the applicant have been fully considered.

TRAINEES COULD BE SEEN TO BE EMPLOYEES

Section 213 of the Labour Relations Act (LRA) provides that an employee is anyone, other than an independent contractor, who works for another person or who assists in conducting the business of an employer. This definition omits only service providers who are external and/or truly autonomous.

Section 200A of the LRA states that, unless the contrary is proven and regardless of the form of the contract, a person is presumed to be an employee if any one of the following circumstances exist:

- The manner in which the person works or his/her hours of work is/are subject to the direction or control of another person
- The person forms part of the organisation
- The person has worked for the other person for an average of at least 40 hours per month for the last 3 months
- The person is economically dependent on the other person
- The person is provided with tools of the trade by the other person
- The person only provides services to one person.

This law applies to government, business, welfare, NGOs, religious and all other employers except perhaps the Secret Service, National Intelligence Agency and Defence Force.

It could be argued that anyone doing work as a means of receiving training in their trade or profession would be defined as a learner and not as an employee. For example, the Skills Development Act and the Manpower Training Act appear to provide for special circumstances where people are signed up for learnerships and apprenticeships purely for purposes of advancing their learning and qualifications. Work contracts that clearly fall under the jurisdiction of either of these two acts may well not qualify as employment contracts.

In *Mokone v Highveld Steel and Vanadium* (2005, 12 BALR 1245) the arbitrator found that the applicant had done some work for the respondent while he was completing studies financed by the respondent. Despite this the arbitrator found that the applicant had not been an employee in terms of the LRA and that the Council therefore did not have jurisdiction to hear the case.

However, in the case of *Andreanis v the Department of Health* (2006, 5 BALR 461) Ms Andreanis was appointed as an intern at a state hospital. Four years later she was told to vacate her post as her internship period had come to an end. She claimed unfair dismissal as she believed that she was an employee and that the end of her internship was irrelevant to her employment status.

The employer claimed that:

- Ms Andreanis was a trainee and not an employee

- The CCMA had no jurisdiction to hear a case brought by a non-employee
- In any case Ms Andreanis had not been dismissed as her appointment had expired automatically when her internship period expired.

The arbitrator found that:

- Ms Andreanis was an employee in terms of the definition in Section 213 of the LRA
- She also qualified as an employee in terms of all but one of the seven criteria in section 200A of the LRA
- Section 200A gave arbitrators no discretion at all to find that a person was not an employee if any one of the seven criteria in section 200A applied. (This is a puzzling finding as section 200A clearly leaves room for discretion via its proviso "Unless the contrary is proved...")
- The Department of Health had been attempting to hide behind Ms Andreanis's internship
- The dismissal was unfair
- The employer was to reinstate the employee with full back pay.

Employers are advised, in the light of the above, to ensure that all trainees are treated fairly.

FORCED CHANGES TO EMPLOYMENT CONDITIONS NOT ON

An employee is entitled, in terms of Section 77(3) of the Basic Conditions of Employment Act, to ask either the civil courts or to the Labour Court to determine any matter concerning a contract of employment. As a contract can be enforceable even if it is not in writing, the employee can even take a dispute relating to an oral or tacitly agreed contract to these courts. In addition, the employee, if dismissed for refusing to accept changes to his/her employment conditions, can sue the employer for automatically unfair dismissal.

There is a problem for employers because their operational circumstances often create the genuine need to change the employment conditions of employees.

Modern-day production pressures lead senior managers to transfer such pressures for change on to line management. Line management in turn attempts to relieve the pressure by trying to force the changes through as quickly as possible. This often results in severe employee relations problems and contraventions of the law. That is, labour law severely restricts the employer's right to make such changes without the employee's consent. Specifically, under the Labour Relations Act (LRA):

- It is not a disciplinary offence for an employee to disobey an unreasonable instruction. And it would not normally be unreasonable for an employee to refuse to work according to new terms and conditions unless this has been agreed to by the employee or his/her representative
- In a takeover of a going concern the employer is compelled to retain the terms and conditions of employment of the employees concerned
- Unfair acts on the part of the employer as regards employee benefits are prohibited
- Section 187(1)(c) of the LRA prohibits the employer from firing employees who refuse to agree to changes in terms and conditions of employment. Specifically, this section provides that:

"A dismissal is automatically unfair if an employer, in dismissing the employee, acts contrary to section 5 or if the reason for the dismissal is …. a refusal by employees to accept a demand in respect of any matter of mutual interest between the employer and employee…". This applies where the employer threatens the employee that, if he/she does not agree to a change in terms and conditions of employment, the employee will be dismissed. If the employee then refuses to agree to the change and is consequently dismissed this could be seen to be automatically unfair.

However, what if the employer needs to change the work circumstances due to its operational requirements? That is, what if, for example, client work circumstances are such that a new shift system is required but the employees are not willing to agree to the change? Is the employer entitled to go into a retrenchment process with a view to hiring employees willing to accept the new terms and conditions of employment?

In the case of *CWIU and others v Algorax (Pty) Ltd* (2003, 11 BLLR 1081) the employer needed to switch to a new shift system but the employees refused to accept this. The employer then retrenched its employees but consistently said that it would re-employ them if they would change their mind and agree to the new shift system. The Labour Appeal Court found that:

- The retrenchments could have been avoided or minimised if the employer had got rid of a number of contractors
- The employer's firm and consistent statements that the employees would be taken back if they agreed to the new shift system showed that the employer had ulterior motives

- The dismissals were not genuine retrenchments but were instead a ploy to get the employees to agree to a change in their conditions of employment
- The dismissal was therefore automatically unfair in terms of section 187(1)(c)
- All the employees were to be re-employed with effect from the date of the court order.

In the case of *Pedzinski v Andisa Securities (Pty) Ltd* (2006, 2 BLLR 184) the employer informed the employee that, if she did not agree to extend her working hours to full day she would be retrenched. When she was retrenched, she took the employer to the Labour Court where it was decided that:

- The employee had been threatened with retrenchment in order to coerce her into extending her working hours
- Her dismissal was automatically unfair
- The employer was to pay the employee compensation equivalent to 24 months' remuneration as well as the employee's legal costs.

While the making of such changes is often justified, employers need to be extremely careful as to how they go about this.

JAILED EMPLOYEES STILL HAVE RIGHTS

Dismissing employees who have been arrested can be dangerous.

It seems obvious to employers that, if an employee is arrested by the police he has 'dismissed himself'. However, this mistaken belief is born from wishful thinking. Reasons for such wishful thinking may include:

- The employer fears having a criminal at the workplace
- Employers do not wish the names of their businesses or organisations to be associated with criminals
- The employer's disciplinary code might state that a criminal conviction merits dismissal.

While this approach was often successful pre-1996, the new labour dispensation makes it much more difficult for an employer to get rid of an undesirable employee. The philosophy that labour law must protect the jobs of employees has been taken to heart by CCMA and bargaining council arbitrators.

A number of case decisions reflect this liberal philosophy to differing degrees. In the case of *Langa v CBC Laser Fab Engineering* (2007, 6 BALR 526) the employee was given a prison sentence. After his release it was some time before he returned to work. He was sent home and told that there was no longer a job for him. After he referred a dispute to the bargaining council his employer reinstated him and held a disciplinary hearing. There he was fired for absence without leave. The employer argued that, while the employee had been unable to attend work while in jail he could have returned to work immediately on his release. His failure to do so constituted absence without leave. The arbitrator found that:

- The employee should have been forgiven for failing to return to work because serving a jail term "could be disruptive" to him
- The employee's absence had not caused any inconvenience for the employer
- The employment relationship had not been seriously harmed by the employee's conduct
- The disciplinary enquiry had been a sham and had been held in an attempt to justify the original dismissal
- The dismissal was unfair and the employer was required to reinstate the employee with retrospective effect.

In *Samancor Tubatse Ferrochrome v MEIBC & others* (2010, 8 BLLR 824) the employee was arrested and held in police custody on suspicion of having been involved in an armed robbery. After six months the employer dismissed him via a letter. Four months later, after the employee was released from custody, a post-dismissal hearing was held where the dismissal was confirmed on grounds that this was the second time that he had been unable to perform his duties due to having been arrested. The arbitrator, and later the Labour Court, found the dismissal to be both procedurally and substantively unfair. The Labour Appeal Court (LAC) found that:

- The employee was dismissed after six months of absence by the employer who had no way of knowing when the employee would be released
- The employer had specific and valid operational reasons for needing the employee to be able to perform his duties
- The employer could not be expected to wait indefinitely for the employee's return
- The employee's arrest had incapacitated him so that he could not perform his duties
- The cause of incapacity that results in dismissal does not have to be confined to ill health
- The dismissal was therefore substantively fair
- It may have been impracticable for the employer to convene a hearing while the employee was in police custody

- However, the employer had dismissed the employee before giving him the opportunity to state his case
- The dismissal was therefore procedurally unfair.

The employer was ordered to pay the employee six months' remuneration in compensation.

While the above case shows that it can be substantively fair for employers to dismiss arrested employees this can only be done if the employer understands the complex legal principles prevailing, particularly as regards legal procedure. In the words of the Labour Appeal Court (LAC) the fairness of a dismissal for incapacity "depends on the facts of each case".

TERMINATING FIXED-TERM CONTRACTS A HEADACHE

It is very easy to employ a worker on the basis of a fixed-term contract. However, it is when you want to end the employment relationship that the pain begins.

The employer's need to terminate the contract could have a number of different reasons. For example, during a retrenchment exercise, the employer may need to terminate all temporary contracts so that it may give preference to saving the jobs of the permanent employees.

There could be a variety of factors contributing to the need for operational requirement dismissals (retrenchment). These include:

- Faulty or archaic equipment or technology, ineffective management systems or underskilled/demotivated employees can reduce productivity, increase financial losses and affect jobs
- Employers may need fewer employees due to labour-saving devices or technology
- A desire to evade labour legislation might result in the contracting out of work instead of giving it to employees
- Bankruptcy or losses caused by mismanagement or misappropriation of funds
- Strikes and lockouts that weaken your company and chase customers and work away
- A drop in sales due to economic factors such as the strengthening of the Rand
- Rationalisation to shed "surplus" employees resulting from buy-outs or mergers. Beware, retrenchments for reasons related to a takeover as a going concern will be automatically unfair.

However, the above factors will not automatically render a retrenchment fair. For example, the courts have traditionally taken into account four key factors when deciding whether a retrenchment is fair. Viz:

- Was there a sufficient operational reason for the retrenchment or was the retrenchment a sham?
- Was a fair criterion used for choosing the employees to be dismissed or should other employees have been retrenched instead?
- Before deciding to retrench did the employer consult properly with the employees or trade union on measures to avoid or reduce the number of retrenchments as well as on numerous other issues related to the retrenchment?
- Did the employer give the employees or union all the information relevant to the retrenchment and to the consulting process?

However, a fifth factor has been brought into play.

In the landmark case of *Buthelezi v Municipal Demarcation Board* (2005, 2 BLLR 115) the Labour Appeal Court found that retrenchment of an employee prior to the expiry of his/her fixed-term contract was unfair. In this case Mr Buthelezi had a five-year fixed-term contract with the Demarcation Board but was retrenched one year after commencement. Prior to retrenchment he was invited to apply for an alternative post but was unsuccessful. The Labour Appeal Court found that the employer did not have the right to terminate the fixed-term contract before its natural expiry date.

The Court's startling decision means that:

- As regards retrenchment, a temporary employee with a fixed-term contract has stronger rights than a permanent employee
- The practice of terminating the contracts of temporary employees in a retrenchment exercise as a means of saving permanent jobs needs to be urgently reviewed
- The terms and wording of fixed-term contracts need to be radically revised.

It is clear that employees on fixed-term contracts are extremely well protected. This is due not only to the above but also to the new labour law amendments which now enable many employees on fixed-term contracts to force the employer to make them permanent.

AUTOMATIC TERMINATION
CLAUSES DANGEROUS

It has become a practice by employers to insert automatic termination clauses into employment contracts for reasons including the following:

- The employer and employee might agree that, should the employee cease to be a shareholder or a director, his/her contract of employment would automatically cease
- The employer might insert into the employment contract a clause providing for automatic termination in the event that the employer's funding dries up
- The employer may be a contracting firm that is dependent on its client's willingness to continue the contract
- The employer may be a labour broker or contracting firm that is dependent on its client's willingness to allow the individual employee to continue in his/her role.

Whatever the circumstances, where factors outside the employer's control are at play, it makes perfect sense for the employee and employer to sign a contract allowing for automatic termination of employment should the potential obstacle to employment become reality. This principle was confirmed as being acceptable by the Labour Court in the case of *Sindane v Prestige Cleaning Services* (2009, 12 BALR 1249). Thus, until and including 2009, the courts have accepted such automatic terminations of employment not as dismissals but as mutually agreed terminations of the employment. This is fair and just:

- because of the employer's lack of control of the problem factor,
- because the employee is aware of this lack of control and
- because the employee has consequently agreed, with his/her eyes wide open, to the automatic termination provision of the employment contract.

However, more recently, these goalposts have shifted away from a focus on operational rationality and towards protection of employees' jobs.

In the case of *Mayo and another vs Global Cleaning Services* (2011, 10 BALR 1051) the two employees had been assigned by the cleaning company to clean at the Tshwane University of Technology. When the employer lost this contract the employees were told that their employment had come to an end automatically in terms of their employment contracts. However, the commissioner held that the Prestige Cleaning Services decision was outdated and declared the termination of the employment of Mayo and his co-applicant to have constituted a dismissal.

In *Mahlamu vs CCMA & others* (2011, 4 BLLR 381) the employer was a security company that employed a guard on the basis that his contract would end automatically on termination of the contract between the firm and its client or if the client no longer required the guard's services for any reason. When the client cancelled the security contract the employer invoked the automatic termination clause and ended the employment. The CCMA found that, because the employee had signed the contract containing the automatic termination clause, the employee had failed to prove that he had been dismissed.

The Labour Court disagreed with the CCMA commissioner and said that the automatic termination clause was tantamount to the parties contracting out of the fair dismissal requirements of the Labour Relations Act (LRA). The employer had to prove that the automatic termination clause was fairly triggered in order to render the dismissal fair. This, together with the fact that contracting out of the law is prohibited, was the basis for the Court's decision that the termination constituted a dismissal. In my view, with respect, this reasoning is fatally flawed as it is based on a specious, circular argument which is itself based on flawed assumptions. Firstly, the Court has made its decision based on the assumption that the employer must prove the dismissal to be fair. While this is true and correct, the Court is not entitled to require the employer to do so until the employee has proven that he was dismissed. However, the Court heard no evidence to that effect. That is, Section 186(1)(a) of the LRA defines dismissal as meaning that an employer has terminated a contract of employment. Nothing in this case shows that the employer did so. On the contrary, the parties had agreed to the termination on signing the contract and such agreement took the termination out of the realm of dismissal. Secondly, the parties had not contracted out of the law (as the Court incorrectly decided) as neither the LRA nor any other law prohibits such agreements.

In *SA Post Office v Mampeule* (2010, 10 BLLR 1052) Mampeule was appointed as both the CEO and member of the board of directors of the Post Office. The contract expressly provided that termination of board membership would automatically lead to termination of Mampeule's appointment as CEO. More than two years after Mampeule's appointment the board approved a motion by the Minister to terminate Mampeule's membership of the board. He was also informed that his employment as CEO had ceased. Both the Labour Court and (later) the Labour Appeal Court found that the automatic termination clause was in conflict with the employee's right not to be unfairly dismissed. The Labour Appeal Court found that the employer had used the automatic termination clause in order to evade its obligations under the LRA. It therefore dismissed the appeal and awarded costs against the employer.

This clear shifting of the goalposts should serve as a warning to employers that the content of their employment contracts, even if such content is rational and willingly agreed upon, may be viewed by the courts as unfair.

LABOUR LAWS PROTECT NEW MOTHERS

Pregnant employees are strongly protected under South African law. There are no fewer than six pieces of legislation that require employers to treat pregnant and post-pregnant employees with the greatest of care. One of these pieces of legislation is the Code Of Good Practice On The Protection Of Employees During Pregnancy And After The Birth Of A Child (The Code).

The Code, issued in terms of the Basic Conditions of Employment Act (BCEA), is aimed at protecting pregnant and post-pregnant employees, and obliges employers to:

- Encourage women employees to inform the employer of their pregnancy as early as possible so as to ensure that the employer can assess risks and deal with them
- Evaluate the situation of each employee who has informed the employer that she is pregnant
- Assess risks to the health and safety of pregnant or breast-feeding employees within the workplace
- Implement measures to protect pregnant or breast-feeding employees
- Supply pregnant or breast-feeding employees with information and training regarding risks to their health and safety and measures for eliminating and minimising such risks
- Maintain a list of jobs not involving risk to which pregnant or breast-feeding employees could be transferred.

Employers should note that, even where an employee who has already given birth is 100% well, the illness of the newborn baby entitles the employee to time off to look after the child. In the case of *De Beer v SA Export Connection cc t/a Global Paws* (2008, 1 BLLR 36) the employee gave birth to twins and took one month's maternity leave by agreement. As the babies were both ill by the time the one month's maternity leave period was up, the mother applied for another month off. The employer granted her only two more weeks' leave and, when she did not return to work, she was dismissed.

The employee referred the matter to the Labour Court claiming that the dismissal was automatically unfair because she had been fired for reasons related to her pregnancy. That is, Section 187 of the Labour Relations Act (LRA) classifies a dismissal as automatically unfair if the reason for the dismissal was related to the pregnancy of the dismissed employee. The employer argued that the illness of the children did not relate to the pregnancy. That is, it argued that the phrase in the LRA "reasons relating to pregnancy" refers to the mother herself and not to the newborn children.

The Labour Court decided that:

- The phrase in the LRA "reasons relating to pregnancy" refers not only to the mother herself but also to the newborn children and to the mother's right to nurture them
- The agreement entered into by the parties limiting the maternity leave to one month was null and void
- The employee was legally entitled to take the remainder of her maternity leave to look after her babies
- The dismissal was automatically unfair
- The employer was to pay the employee 20 months' remuneration in compensation plus the legal costs of the employee.

In the De Beer case it is possible that the employer believed that it had been generous enough in giving the employee substantially more leave than the three days allowed under the family responsibility leave section of the BCEA. However, the Court found that the employee did not need specific permission to be off work because looking after newborn babies falls under maternity leave (not under family responsibility leave or any other type of leave), and that working mothers are automatically entitled to four months' maternity leave.

Due to the substantial legal protections of pregnant employees employers cannot afford to treat them as they believe is fair. Instead, employers need to utilise the services of labour law experts to devise and implement detailed strategies for ensuring the welfare of working mothers and for minimising the effect of motherhood on workplace productivity without breaking the law.

EMPLOYMENT OF SEX OFFENDERS REGULATED

Certain employers could be prosecuted for employing sex offenders.

In order to protect vulnerable persons in society the employment of certain sex offenders was regulated some years ago under chapter 6 of the Criminal Law Amendment Act 32 of 2007 (CLAA). The Act prohibits certain employers from hiring or continuing to employ sex offenders. For the purposes of this law "employers" are defined as those that employ staff who, directly or indirectly, deal with or come into contact with children or mentally disabled persons (MDPs) in the course of their work.

Employers therefore need to understand all the provisions of the CLAA, to comply with all their legal obligations under this act and to do so in such a way that they do not infringe labour legislation protecting the rights of employees (whether they are sexual offenders or not).

The purpose of this legislation is to prevent employees from committing sexual acts against children or MDPs as members of these two population groups are normally unable to protect themselves from offences such as rape, sexual molestation and other sex-related infringements. It appears that the promulgation of this legislation is a reaction to reports of such offences having been perpetrated in South Africa.

The scope of this legislation is not entirely clear but it appears that employers to be affected would include those who employ staff such as nurses, psychologists, doctors, teachers, airline staff, domestic workers, church employees and officials, scoutmasters, social workers, crèche staff, child counselling centre workers and other employees dealing with children or MDPs.

The term 'sex offenders' apparently means, for purposes of this legislation, people who have, or who are officially alleged to have, committed sex offences against children or MDPs. The CLAA requires the establishment of a Register of such sex offenders. Employers, as defined above, may not employ persons whose names are on the Register or persons who have failed to disclose to their employers, convictions against them for sexual offences against children or MDPs.

This section requires the employers in question to screen all job applicants and not to employ them if they are sexual offenders as defined. Furthermore, employers must screen existing employees and terminate the employment of those who they are not allowed to employ in terms of the CLAA. However, the employer may not terminate the employment if it is possible to transfer the sex offender to a post where there is no risk of him/her committing a sexual offence in terms of the CLAA. The employer is required to apply to the Registrar for a certificate stating whether or not he/she is on the Register of offenders.

Where the employee claims that his/her registration as a sex offender is erroneous or has lapsed the employer should give the employee a chance to apply for his/her name to be removed from the Register. This may require a suspension from duty of the employee for the period necessary to have the name removed. The CLAA does not clarify what happens if the employee's registration as a sex offender lapses. That is, where the employment continues due to the lapsing of the employee's offender registration and the employee then commits a sexual offence against a child or MDP, it is unclear what degree of liability, if any, the employer will have. Employers are therefore advised to obtain indemnities and insurance against such liability.

Employers are further advised, before deciding to terminate such a sexual offender's employment, to first hold a hearing to give the employee the opportunity to show why he should not be dismissed. Employers, as is so often the case, are in a tight position. On the one hand the CLAA requires them to terminate or refuse the employment of such sex offenders. But, on the other hand, the Labour Relations Act (LRA) prohibits employers from terminating employment without good reason and without following fair procedure. The employer is therefore the meat in this legislative sandwich.

In view of the above dangers affected employers should obtain expert advice However, the employer should not delay in getting such advice as any delay could result in the employee committing a sexual offence at work which will put the employer in serious hot water. The CLAA provides for a fine and/or a prison sentence of up to seven years for employers who do not comply with section 45 of the CLAA. Added to this could be the damage and even ruin of the employer's reputation resulting from the sensational media coverage that is likely to ensue in cases of sexual offences committed against the children and MDPs who the employer is supposed to be looking after.

ILLEGAL WORKERS ARE PROTECTED

Lack of awareness of Constitutional and labour law protections of employees from foreign countries has prompted many employers to mistreat illegally employed staff. That is, employers have paid illegal immigrants low wages, deprived them of employee benefits and have dismissed them at will. They have based their actions on the assumption that their so called 'illegal employees' are unable to use the law to take the employer to task. However, this type of employer is labouring under a dangerous misapprehension.

In the case of *Discovery Health Ltd v CCMA & others* (CLL Vol. 17 April 2008) a Mr Lanzetta, an immigrant, obtained a temporary residence permit and later a work permit to work for a business called MPCS. He later joined Discovery Health as a call centre agent before his work permit was renewed. He claimed that Discovery had delayed giving him the documents he needed to renew his work permit which then expired. Discovery then terminated his employment on the grounds that his continued employment would breach section 38(1) of the Immigration Act that effectively prohibits persons from employing foreigners whose status does not authorise their employment.

Lanzetta then referred a dispute of unfair dismissal to the CCMA. Discovery then contested the CCMA's jurisdiction to consider the dispute on the grounds that his employment contract had been voided by his illegal status and that Lanzetta was therefore not an employee. It is law that the CCMA does not have jurisdiction over cases referred by people who are not employees. The CCMA decided that, as long as an employment relationship existed, it did have jurisdiction to deal with the matter. The employer, dissatisfied with this jurisdictional finding, took it on review to the Labour Court.

The Court found that:

- Although Lanzetta's employment status may have been illegal he was resident in South Africa legally
- It had been the employer and not Lanzetta who had contravened the Immigration Act because the wording of that act prohibited employers from employing certain foreigners rather than prohibiting the foreigners from accepting employment
- Section 23 of the Constitution provides that 'everyone' has the right to fair labour practice and there is no indication in the Constitution or in the Immigration Act that illegally employed foreigners are excluded from this constitutional right
- The Immigration Act's prohibitions against the employment of so called 'illegal' foreigners does not void the employment contract of such a foreigner
- The definition of an employee as per the Labour Relations Act (LRA) does not require there to be an employment contract in order for a person to be an employee
- Neither does section 23 of the Constitution require the existence of an employment contract
- International law and ILO Convention 87 supports this principle
- The definition of employee does extend to people who work without the existence of a contract
- The Court therefore agreed with the CCMA that Lanzetta was an employee in terms of labour law and that the CCMA did have jurisdiction to consider his dispute.

It is important to note that this most important court decision did not include a finding that Lanzetta had been unfairly dismissed. The Court was merely asked to decide whether the CCMA was entitled to hear Lanzetta's matter. This ruling only allows the CCMA process to get going. It is still to be decided whether it was unfair of the employer to dismiss Lanzetta due to the fact that his continued employment breached the provisions of the Immigration Act. Nevertheless, employers need to take heed of the warnings that stem from the Lanzetta case. That is, employers should not:

- employ people whose employment is illegal
- delay in assisting foreign employees to obtain the documents they need to maintain the legality of their employment

- treat foreign or illegal employees any differently from other employees
- in dealing with the problem of illegally employed staff members, terminate their employment without following legal procedure
- become the meat in the sandwich between the provisions of the Immigration Act on the one hand and the requirements of the LRA on the other. Instead, employers should obtain expert advice before taking any decisions or any action in this regard.

SANGOMAS NOT YET REGISTERED TO PROVIDE MEDICAL CERTIFICATES

Confusion abounds as regards whether employers are required to accept medical certificates from traditional healers. The causes of this confusion are as follows:

- Firstly, the Traditional Health Practitioners Act No. 22 of 2007 was signed into law in 2008
- Secondly, the Traditional Health Practitioners Council (THPC) constituted in terms of this Act has already been set up
- Thirdly, the Supreme Court of Appeal's decision in the Kievits Kroon/Mmoledi case discussed below has given the impression that employers reject traditional healer certificates at their peril.

In January 2019 Mr Petrus Mokoena of the Department of Health explained that:

- The THPC has not yet begun registering traditional healers
- The THPC will be able to begin with such registrations after the training programme for traditional healers, currently underway, has been completed.

In the case of *Kievits Kroon Country Estate (Pty) Ltd v Mmoledi and others* [2014] 3 BLLR 207 the Supreme Court of Appeal pronounced unfair the dismissal of an employee who left work to go and train as a traditional healer.

In this case the employee, a chef with supervisory status, was granted one week's unpaid leave to undergo a traditional healer's course. The employee furnished the employer with a certificate from a traditional healer indicating that the employee needed to attend the course due to her own unwell mental state.

The employee did not return to work at the end of her week of leave and was dismissed. A CCMA Commissioner found that the employee was genuinely ill and ruled the dismissal unfair. On review, the Labour Court agreed.

On appeal the LAC found that:

- It was apparent from the records of both the disciplinary inquiry and of the arbitration hearing that the employee believed she was ill
- Management understood the cultural significance of the employee's condition
- It was beyond dispute that the employee's beliefs are part of the culture of about 80% of the country's population, and many resort to traditional healers for their physical, spiritual and emotional wellbeing
- The courts are equipped to deal with conventional medicine, but not with religious doctrine and cultural practices
- The employee's claim that she would suffer some serious misfortune if she did not undergo the training had gone unchallenged by the employer
- Absence from work without authority, even if contrary to an employer's express instruction, is excusable if the absence was justified and reasonable
- Management could have discussed with the employee some alternative to accommodate her.

The appeal was dismissed with costs.

It is clear that this finding causes severe problems for those employers unable or unwilling to grant leave to employees for reasons related to traditional medicine. However, it is my view that the Kievits Kroon/Mmoledi decision did not focus on the issue of whether employers must accept traditional healer certificates. With respect, the Court evaded the question of the validation of the traditional healer's ability to diagnose illness and, instead focused mainly on the arguments that the employee genuinely believed she was ill and that the employer should have recognised this as a satisfactory reason for her absence.

The employer lost the case not because of any finding that traditional healer certificates must be accepted, but rather because the courts were convinced that the employee believed she was ill and therefore did not deserve to be fired.

The above factors confirm for me that:

- Traditional healers are not yet registered in terms of the Act and are therefore not yet able to issue medical certificates in terms thereof
- The Kievits Kroon/Mmoledi decision does not prescribe that employers must automatically recognise and accept traditional healers' certificates.

In my view employers should:

- Do nothing to give the impression that they or their employment policies accept certificates from any source not proven to be genuine or that does not have the medico-legal competence to diagnose and treat illness
- Base their decisions as regards the recognition of each individual certificate not on whether traditional healing is acceptable in our society but on whether the professed healer has been proven to be competent to diagnose and treat illness
- Give careful consideration, when assessing mitigating circumstances, to whether it accepts that the employee truly believes that he/she was ill or that he/she was in danger
- Be able to support any rejection of any claims made by employees relating to alleged illness or related matters.

REFUSED PROMOTION CAUSES COMMOTION

Employees do not ordinarily have an automatic entitlement to a pay increase or to advancement up the corporate ladder. However, the Labour Relations Act (LRA) does allow employees who have been passed over for promotion to lodge an unfair labour practice dispute at the relevant bargaining council. Should the industry in question have no bargaining council the employee may lodge the dispute at the CCMA.

Where an internal vacancy exists that is senior to the job of the employee concerned and if the employee can prove that he/she has the ability to do the more senior job, the employer has the legal duty to justify why the employee was not given the promotion. While it may be possible to provide such justification this task is not easy.

This is because the employee's ability to do the job is a strong argument in favour of granting him/her the promotion. Should the employer, for example, be able to prove that someone else was promoted into the relevant post and that this person was better qualified for the post than the aggrieved employee, the employer will have a good chance of winning the case. On the other hand, if the successful promotee was less qualified than the aggrieved employee the employer is likely to lose.

Arbitrators are not impressed by reasons for refusing promotions that stem merely from bureaucratic rules or unsubstantiated claims relating to the employer's financial constraints. For example, in the case of *Dedering v University of South Africa* (CLL Vol. 17 February 2008) the employee applied for promotion to the position of associate professor but was appointed to the position of senior lecturer instead. That is, the employee's new post was below that of the one he wanted.

It appears that the employee was well qualified for the post of associate professor. That is, he published extensively, was an internationally acclaimed researcher, delivered papers at conferences and fulfilled his teaching obligations. The employer admitted that the employee's qualifications exceeded the requirements for an associate professorship.

Despite the employee's glowing qualifications and undoubted suitability for the job the employer's rules prevented him from being granted the promotion. That is, the employer's rules prohibited 'rank jumping'. That is, a lecturer must become a senior lecturer before moving higher up the ranks. The employer's reason for this was that there was a limited budget for such promotions and rank jumping would have prematurely exhausted this budget.

When the employee was interviewed after submitting his application, he was not told that the interview was for the senior lecturer post. He was told that the university had received a number of promotion applications that would entail rank jumping and that this was problematic. However, it was established that another employee had been allowed to jump rank.

It also appears that the budget was big enough to withstand a reasonable amount of rank jumping and that the university may not have done its homework. That is, it appears that the university may have made its decision based on a concern in principle for the budget without doing the necessary calculations. This omission removed the rationality necessary to justify the decision not to grant the associate professorship. As a result the CCMA arbitrator declared the failure to promote the employee an unfair labour practice and ordered the university to promote him to that post. In addition the employer was ordered to make up the shortfall between the salaries of the two posts and to pay the employee's legal costs.

The above finding acts as a warning to employers that:

- While the concept of management prerogative still exists, such prerogative is not unfettered. Management decisions that affect employees must not only be legal, they must also be fair
- In order to be fair they must be justifiable
- In order to be justifiable management decisions must be based on proven facts that are rationally connected to the decisions made.

It is a very common problem that managers struggle to base their decision-making purely on facts and rationality. The reasons for this may include the facts that:

- Managers' decisions are often hampered by feelings of anxiety about the employer's finances. Often these feelings result in irrational reactions instead of in analysis of the facts
- Managers are not properly aware that their management prerogative or right to use management discretion is limited by the law
- Managers sometimes assume that the employees concerned will not dare to question their decisions because 'might is right'.

UNPLEASANT CCMA SURPRISES FOR EMPLOYERS

A while ago I received a panic phone call from an employer who had received an unfavourable arbitration award in respect of a CCMA case they never knew existed. That is, the employer had never received a summons to appear at the CCMA. The award required the employer to pay tens of thousands of rands to an ex-employee. This can happen for a number of different reasons including:

- The employer's clerk received the summons via fax, email or post but did not give it to the relevant person at the employer's address
- The employee gave the CCMA the wrong address for the employer
- The possibility that the CCMA did not ensure that the notice of the arbitration hearing reached the employer.

It can also occur that an employer loses a case because the presiding commissioner was incompetent. Fortunately, not all CCMA commissioners are incompetent. I have had the pleasure of presenting cases before some highly competent arbitrators. However, there are too many case decisions made at the CCMA that are overturned by the Labour Court.

Uncertainty as to whether or not you will have a competent arbitrator is bad enough. However, if you also arrived at the CCMA without labour law expertise you are doubly weak. That is, if the arbitrator is weak and you are strong in labour law you may well be able to help the arbitrator see that light. But if your own knowledge is also lacking you are a sitting duck for your opposition's legal representative.

Due to the fact that ignorance of the law is no excuse, employers who do not know the law normally come off second best at the CCMA. Why do employers, twelve years after the creation of the new Labour Relations Act (LRA), still not know the law? There are many reasons:

- The LRA has been badly written in parts and is therefore confusing to employers. That is, many sections of the LRA are very general and broad, leaving too much room for interpretation or abuse.
- CCMA rules dealing with how the parties must proceed with matters get struck down by the courts as legally unacceptable. For example, in the case of *Premier Gauteng & another v Ramabulana NO and others* (CLL Vol. 17 February 2008) the Labour Appeal Court recently struck down CCMA Rule 30 that allows commissioners to dismiss cases where employees fail to arrive for conciliation meetings.
- The vast difference in interpretation of the LRA by arbitrators and judges adds to the confusion amongst employers. It frequently occurs that findings by one arbitrator/judge is overturned by another and then overturned again.
- Even those laws that are reasonably clear and less subject to interpretation are very complex and numerous. For example, it is clear and unambiguous that an employer must give an employee a hearing before firing him/her for misconduct. However, how that hearing must be conducted is complicated.
- Employers are unwilling to spend the time and money necessary to train their managers on how to discipline and otherwise treat their employees. It is only when employers lose a case at the CCMA that they realise the value of legal expertise.

For some time, parties will not know what level of expertise they will find in the arbitrator who hears their case. The best a party can do, in view of this uncertainty, is to ensure that they spare no expense in going properly equipped to the CCMA. Becoming properly equipped to go to the CCMA is best achieved via a strategy including the following steps:

- Recognition by top management that labour law presents an extremely dangerous minefield for the employer
- Training of all managers, supervisors and HR/IR professionals in the labour statutes and case law
- Acquisition of the services of an expert in labour law implementation to help deal with disciplinary, grievance, retrenchment, merger, CCMA, bargaining council, trade union and other labour matters.

Properly equipped employers will be able to:

- Distinguish between good and bad arbitrators
- Tactfully point out to the arbitrator where he/she might be erring
- Recognise which acts of the arbitrator, if any, need to be taken on review
- Gain a firm grasp of the LRA and of the laws of evidence
- Manage their employees productively and effectively while remaining within the law.

DON'T MISS THE ARBITRATION HEARING!

It may well continue without you.

Where the employer fails to attend an arbitration hearing the arbitrator is entitled to continue without the employer unless the arbitrator is aware of an acceptable reason for the employer's absence. As the arbitrator has little or no way of testing the truth of the employee's evidence he/she will most often accept the employee's version and find against the absent employer. This is called a default judgment.

Whose fault is it when CCMA notices of any kind do not reach the parties? At times the CCMA has been unable to provide proof that it has sent notices to the proper addresses of the parties. On other occasions, the CCMA has been able to provide proof that it has properly sent notices to the parties, but one or other party claims not to have received its notice. This would be due to a problem or error occurring after the notice leaves the CCMA but before it reaches the party concerned.

What can you do if you receive a default judgment in such circumstances? Your first step is to apply for a rescission (or cancellation) of the default award. There are strict rules and time deadlines for such applications.

A rescission application is normally made to the same arbitrator who made the original arbitration award on the grounds that the award was made erroneously. Such application might be granted if it is properly put together and valid proof is submitted of factors such as illness, or failure of the CCMA/bargaining council effectively to serve the notice of set down on the party concerned.

In the rescission application and in any opposition papers the main issues argued are the applicant's reasons for absence and the applicant's prospects of succeeding with the case if the rescission is granted.

Should your rescission application be turned down you can take the arbitrator on review to the Labour Court. Here, the party who is unhappy with the award or rescission ruling asks the Labour Court to set the ruling or award aside on the grounds that the arbitrator, in making the ruling/award, 'misconducted himself/herself'. That is, the review application is not a direct appeal against the arbitrator's decision but rather a claim that the arbitrator:

- committed misconduct in relation to his/her arbitration duties
- committed a gross irregularity in the conduct of the arbitration proceedings

- exceeded his/her powers or
- made the award improperly.

In the case of *Northern Province Local Government Association v CCMA and Others* (2001, 5 BLLR 539) the Labour Court found that Commissioners are not entitled to regard fax transmission slips as definitive proof that the party received the notice of the arbitration hearing.

In the case of *Total Facilities Management (Pty) Ltd v CCMA & others* (2008, 1 BLLR 73) the employer missed the arbitration hearing because the CCMA unwittingly sent the notice of the hearing to the computer of an official of the employer who had left the company. As nobody else had the computer's access code the employer was unaware of the notice and of the date of the arbitration. The CCMA continued with the hearing and made a default award in favour of the employee. The employer then applied for rescission of that award. The CCMA arbitrator accepted that the employer was not at fault for failing to attend the arbitration hearing but still turned down the rescission application. The arbitrator based her ruling on the employer's alleged failure to show that, should the rescission be granted, the employer had reasonable prospects of winning its case.

The employer then took this ruling on review to the Labour Court which overturned the arbitrator's ruling. The Court found that the arbitrator had erroneously based her ruling on the evidence given by the employee at the arbitration hearing. However, the arbitrator was supposed to have based her ruling on the submissions made by the employer in its rescission application. In its application the employer argued that the dismissal had been based on a fair procedure and that the employee had admitted committing the offence. As the Court found this to be sufficient grounds for prospects of success of the employer's submission, it overruled the arbitrator and granted the employer's rescission application.

These judgments should not make employers complacent. Due to the fact that fax transmission reports are generally accepted as proof of legal service of notices, any argument as to why such fax reports should not be accepted needs to be very well argued. While the use of emails for this purpose is increasing, proof that the intended person from the other party received the email is problematic. Also, the reason for the employer's absence at the hearing as well as the employer's prospects of success need to be very carefully worded, well argued and backed up. In the absence of this the CCMA is likely to turn down rescission applications. The employer is then left to take the matter to Labour Court. There are three reasons that this should be avoided. Firstly, you may not win. Secondly, going to Labour Court is expensive. Thirdly, if you lose you may have to pay the other party's legal fees. It is therefore obviously better to ensure that you win the rescission application first time.

DIRTY HANDS WILL BE CANED AT CCMA

In common law employers and employees have the obligation to treat each other fairly and within the law.

For its part, the employer is required to pay the employee the agreed remuneration by the normal pay date. The employer is also required to employ the employee in reasonable working conditions and to avoid rendering the employment circumstances intolerable. Failing this, the employee is entitled to seek legal remedy.

The employee has the obligation towards the employer to refrain from misrepresenting his/her qualifications and to carry out his/her work to the best of his/her ability. The employee is also obliged to behave in an honest and reasonable manner, to serve the interests of the employer and to refrain from rendering the employment relationship intolerable. Failing this, the employer has a right to legal remedies including discipline, dismissal and even court action.

While both parties have legal recourse against the infractions of the other they must beware of the dangers of taking such action. That is:

- Legal action can be extremely expensive. Many lawyers charge high fees for representing parties at the CCMA, bargaining councils or at Labour Court.
- Sometimes, legal fees are paid to attorneys or advocates for representation services at the CCMA but the arbitrator, on the day of the case, evicts the lawyer from the hearing because the case in question does not, in the discretion of the arbitrator, require a legal mind. As such, arbitrator discretion does not apply to union representation and more and more employers are joining employers' organisations (unions for employers) in order that they can be represented at arbitration by an employers' organisation official.
- The judge or arbitrator sometimes orders the losing party to pay the legal costs of the winner even if the loser's case was a reasonable one. It appears that this practice may be carried out as a means of deterring parties from taking cases to court.
- Should it be found in court, at the CCMA or at bargaining council that a party has referred a frivolous or vexatious case, that party is likely to be required to pay the legal costs of the winner. In this context, a frivolous case is one that is devoid of seriousness, sense or worth. A vexatious case is one that is brought more to cause annoyance than because it has valid grounds.
- A party may also be punished for bringing a case to the CCMA with 'dirty hands'. This means that the party bringing the complaint has broken a rule or transgressed the law. For example, an employer may be accused by the employee at the CCMA

of retrenching him unfairly. However, the employer may be able to show that the employee's disloyal or malicious behaviour was the cause of the financial backslide and the need to cut back on staff. This misbehaviour of the employee would then mean that he has come to the CCMA with dirty hands. This is likely to count against him/her at the arbitration.

Alternatively, where the employee claims unfair dismissal at the CCMA, but is proven to have committed the misconduct for which he/she was dismissed, his/her 'dirty hands' are likely to disqualify him/her from the right to relief from the CCMA even if the employer was partly at fault. For example, in the case of *Simani v Coca Cola Fortune* (2006, 10 BALR 1044) the employee was dismissed for dishonesty. The arbitrator found that the employee, well aware of his guilt, nevertheless approached the CCMA. This was unacceptable as it was not a genuine dispute. The employee came to the CCMA with dirty hands and, in addition to having his case dismissed, was ordered to pay the respondent's costs resulting from the losses that he had caused.

In *SACCAWU obo Haliwell v Extrabold t/a Holiday Inn Sandton* [2012] 3 BALR 286 (CCMA) the applicant employee had refused to obey an instruction from the respondent's general manager. She then filed a grievance against the GM and posted derogatory comments about him on her internet Facebook page. The applicant was called to a disciplinary hearing and dismissed for "gross insubordination" and "disrespect".

The commissioner noted that the respondent had done its best to resolve the applicant's complaints about the GM. After concluding that she could no longer work with him, management had decided that she should be transferred to another department. Her response to this suggestion was an uncivil email to the manager who had communicated that decision. The commissioner also rejected the applicant's claims that she had written the Facebook messages in a fit of anger, and that her privacy had been invaded.

The commissioner also rejected the applicant's claims that she had not understood the charge sheet and that she had not given evidence in mitigation when invited to do so because she did not understand the meaning of that term. The email and Internet communications were written in English, and contained phrases more sophisticated than "mitigating factors".

The applicant's dismissal was ruled substantively and procedurally fair. The arbitrator found that she had no justification for having made the public derogatory comments about her GM and for having disrespected him. She had come to the CCMA with 'dirty hands' and was ordered to pay the costs of the arbitration.

In the light of all the dangers of the dirty hands principle discussed above parties should:

- Think carefully before taking legal action
- Avoid making the decision to go to CCMA or court merely because they are angry
- Avoid misusing the CCMA as a means of extorting money from the other party
- Ensure that they have valid reasons for the legal action they take
- Gather solid proof of their allegations
- Check that their own hands are clean before pointing a finger at the other party.

CHAPTER CONCLUSION

Employees have the responsibility for looking after their employer's best interests but not at the cost of their own labour law rights. Thus, every employee needs to strike a balance between protecting his/her own rights and ensuring that the employer's business is not jeopardised by his/her actions or inaction. In the interests of this, both parties should work together to ensure that employees know what their rights and duties are and how to balance the two.

Dirty hands will be caned at CCMA

CHAPTER 4

EMPLOYMENT EQUITY LAWS –
ANTI-DISCRIMINATION AND
AFFIRMATIVE ACTION

Colonialism in South Africa, culminating in the apartheid era that spanned three and a half decades, brutally removed the rights of non-white South Africans in general and at the workplace in particular. While black workers were paid, employers were effectively free to exploit them by paying minimal wages and treating these employees, in many cases, as little more than slaves.

After the new democratic government came into power in 1994 it prioritised the drastic reform of labour legislation. However, it was only six years after the apartheid government was replaced that the Employment Equity Act number 55 (EEA) came into effect. This act prohibits unfair discrimination at the workplace and requires designated employers (larger employers) to implement affirmative action. This effectively requires affected employers to normalise the racial, gender and disability profiles of their enterprises so as to mirror the population profile of South African society.

In this chapter we examine the EEA and its subsidiary legislation, and discuss how the courts expect employers to implement it.

EMPLOYMENT EQUITY
OBLIGATIONS MUST BE MET

Fines of up to R2 700 000 await defaulting employers.

Some time ago a major airline operating in South Africa was reported to have been fined R900 000 for failing to comply with the Employment Equity Act (EEA). This penalty highlights the seriousness with which the Department of Labour (DOL) takes non-compliance and shows that they will not hesitate to bring the maximum penalty against defaulters.

If you are a designated employer you are required to submit your Employment Equity Report before mid-January of each year. Designated employers are those that either:

- have more than 50 employees; or
- have fewer than 50 employees but have an annual sales turnover that exceeds the threshold for their sector.

The Department of Labour is now enforcing a strict policy prohibiting their acceptance of late submissions. This means that employers will no longer receive a slap on the wrist for late submission but will rather be liable for a fine of up to two million, seven hundred thousand rand. Employers are warned that, while submitting the EE Report in time is crucial, this is not enough. Employers are also legally bound to ensure that the Report's contents are true and correct and that they can show that they have made sufficient progress with affirmative action as required by the EEA. It is clear that prosecutions in the Labour Court and potentially bankrupting fines can result if employers fail to comply.

This means that designated employers will have to:

- Shift from merely putting together 'impressive looking' reports for the DOL.
- Do a detailed Employment Equity (EE) Analysis.
- Set affirmative action targets that are achievable on the one hand but substantial enough on the other hand to satisfy the Director General of Labour.
- Prepare and implement a detailed EE Plan. This is a comprehensive strategy for recruiting, 'accommodating' and developing members of designated groups. That is, each employer must devise an action plan aimed at ensuring that it has the right proportion of black, coloured, Indian, female and disabled people working in all departments and at all levels of the organisation including the very top. For example, if you have fifty members on your board of directors then you must aim to have approximately 35 black, 5 coloured, 4 Indian and 5 white directors. Of these, 25 should be female and 2 should be disabled.
- Ensure that these plans are implemented effectively and in tune with the EEA's procedural requirements.
- Consult with a full cross-section of their workforce and representative trade union on the devising and implementation of the above-mentioned analysis, report, plan and target.
- Make available to employees all the documents referred to above.
- Make special arrangements to ensure that black, coloured, Indian, female and disabled employees are able to remain with the organisation, cope with their duties and work environment, fit into the organisation and to advance in the organisation.
- Eliminate barriers to employment of members of designated groups.

While none of these requirements are impossible they will be very much more difficult to achieve with the DOL inspectors breaking down your door. It is important to bear in mind that, once you have set up your EE system based on your own level of resources and circumstances, the task of EE compliance becomes very much easier.

While potential investors are being deterred by South Africa's labour law requirements, the Director General is charged with implementing the law as regards affirmative action. He therefore has no option but to police employers that do not comply and to prosecute those that do not heed his instructions to implement affirmative action meaningfully.

Unfortunately the EEA does not sufficiently take into account the fact that the number of jobs available in South Africa is falling. This makes it extremely difficult for you to increase your numbers of employees from designated groups even if you want to. However, as long as you can prove that you are doing everything possible to normalise the demographics of your organisation and that you have been completing the compulsory analyses, reports and plans, the DOL is unlikely to take action against you.

CHINESE EMPLOYEES QUALIFY FOR AFFIRMATIVE ACTION

The Employment Equity Act (EEA) makes it compulsory for designated employers to implement affirmative action (AA). This means that most employers are required to employ, train and retain the services of employees belonging to previously disadvantaged population groups being black, female and disabled people. The EEA defines black people as "Africans, Coloureds and Indians". Based on this definition Chinese people do not qualify under the heading of affirmative action employees. This is illogical and unfair because, under the apartheid regime, Chinese people were severely discriminated against and are therefore previously disadvantaged.

It is therefore not surprising that the Chinese community took this issue to court. *The Star* reported on 19 June 2008 (page 5) that the Pretoria High Court decided that Chinese South Africans are to be included in the definition of black people for purposes of BEE legislation and the EEA.

Also, in its favour, this decision corrected an injustice. That is, as Chinese people were unfairly discriminated against historically their omission from the legislation appears to have been more for political than for reasons of logic or justice.

The EEA requires designated employers to strive to ensure that the demography (population ratios) of their organisations mirrors the demography of the society in which the organisation operates. For example, if the population of Gauteng is 80% black then designated employers need to do everything possible to ensure that there are 80% black people at every level of their organisations including top management.

While the law does not expect employers to fire all their able white males from key positions to make way for designated groups the EEA does expect employers to fill vacancies with black, female and disabled people until the required demographic levels have been achieved.

While chapter 2 (prohibition of unfair discrimination) and chapter 3 (requirement for AA) of the EEA have similar goals, the way in which each of the two chapters are to be enforced differ. That is, where an employee or job applicant felt unfairly discriminated against he/she could sue the employer in the Labour Court. However, where employees feel that the employer is failing to implement AA they could report the employer to the Director General of Labour.

This apparently clear division of recourse for aggrieved employees has been reinforced by the Labour Court's decision in the case of *Dudley v City of Cape Town & another* (February 2004 Vol. 13 No. 7 Contemporary Labour Law page 1). In this case Dudley had been appointed to the post of Interim Manager: Health Services. Later on Dudley applied for a more senior post (Director: City Health) advertised by the municipality. The City appointed a white male to the post despite the facts that Dudley was qualified for the job and the City had the obligation, in terms of its own policies, to implement affirmative action.

Dudley, who was a black female, referred an unfair discrimination dispute to the Labour Court on the grounds that the employer's failure to implement AA constituted unfair discrimination. The Court found against this claim because, in its view:

- Failure to implement AA is a matter for the Director General of Labour (DGL) to deal with and not the Labour Court (unless the DGL refers the matter to the Labour Court after having implemented his/her own enforcement mechanisms)
- AA is a group-based obligation and not an individual right
- Both SA's Constitution and the EEA distinguish between AA and unfair discrimination.

However, in the case of *Harmse v City of Cape Town* (February 2004 Vol. 13 No. 7 Contemporary Labour Law page 1) the Labour Court found that an individual employee did have recourse directly to the Labour Court on the grounds that failure to implement AA constituted unfair discrimination. This is yet another instance where the courts are unable to agree with each other on key legal issues. In the light of this uncertainty employers are advised to ensure that they implement AA responsibly, that their AA policies are in line with the EEA and that these policies are realistically implementable.

The decision of the Pretoria High Court including Chinese South Africans as AA employees gives employers more opportunity to achieve their AA targets. This decision will therefore be welcomed not only by Chinese people and by those who believe in justice, but also by those employers forced by law to implement affirmative action. As maximum fines for failure to submit these reports exceed one million rand for a first offence, employers need to get moving now with their AA projects.

EQUAL PAY FOR WORK OF EQUAL VALUE NOW COMPULSORY

The new section 6(4) of the Employment Equity Act (EEA) effective from 1 August 2014 classifies as unfair discrimination differing terms and conditions of employment where:

- this difference is based on the grounds for unfair discrimination listed in the EEA; and
- the employees affected are doing work of equal value.

It is stressed that this provision is already in effect, and non-compliant employers are currently liable for prosecution at the CCMA. The DOL has designed a code on equal pay for work of equal value which came into effect on 1 June 2015.

The Code, read together with section 6(4) of the EEA, requires all employers, including the State, to implement very specific measures to achieve this goal, including job grading, pay comparison and explanation of pay differentials.

Scope and Meaning of the Equal Pay Code

What is "work of equal value"?

This refers to two or more *jobs that may be entirely different* but have the same rating value as each other. For example, it is possible that the job of a sales rep. and that of a machine operator could be at the same grade level in terms of job evaluation criteria that cut across different jobs.

NB: It is not the employee who is graded; it is the demands of the job that are evaluated whether the post is occupied or vacant.

What is remuneration and how must its fairness be monitored?

The term "remuneration" as defined in the EEA and other labour legislation includes any payment in money or in kind, or both, made or owing to any person in return for working for another person, including the State. The statutory concept of remuneration includes deferred remuneration, commission and other forms of variable compensation or pay. Employers must, therefore, examine all aspects of their remuneration policies, procedures and practices to ensure compliance with the principle of equal remuneration for work of equal value.

Practical necessity requires that all employers establish Remuneration Committees which should:

- annually review all remuneration and benefits received by employees to ascertain whether they are legally compliant, appropriate and competitive and
- assist senior management in setting up and administering a remuneration policy.

The Code provides three steps to determine compliance with section 6(4):

The first step requires a determination of whether the jobs being compared are the same, substantially the same or of equal value in terms of an objective assessment. This means that the Code does not prescribe which job grading system is used but only that an objective measure is required.

What criteria must be used to assess and compare the value of different jobs?

The Code provides for the following three factors: the responsibility demanded by the work, the skills and qualifications required for the work, and the physical, mental and emotional effort required to perform the work. The weighting attached to each of these factors may vary depending on the sector, employer and the job concerned.

The second step requires a determination of whether there are any differences in terms and conditions of employment, including remuneration of the employees in the jobs that have to be graded and compared.

The final step requires the employer to determine whether the differences identified are justifiable on fair and rational grounds. Differences are justifiable if they are based on any of the following grounds:

- the individual's seniority or length of service
- the individual's qualifications, ability or competence
- the individual's performance or quality of work
- whether the employee has been demoted for any legitimate reason but draws a salary still fixed at a higher level than employees in his/her new job category until their remuneration reaches that level
- where an individual is temporarily in a position for the purpose of gaining experience or training
- a difference in terms and conditions due to the existence of a shortage of relevant skill in a particular job classification.

Implementation of job grading system

The size and intricacy of the task of implementing the above requirements in a practical, operationally effective and legally compliant manner requires the use of experts versed in labour law and in the implementation of job grading systems.

EMPLOYERS HAVE CLOSE SHAVE
WITH RELIGIOUS DISCRIMINATION

Section 6 of the Employment Equity Act (EEA) prohibits unfair discrimination against an employee on arbitrary grounds One of these grounds is that of religion. This means that no employer is entitled to discriminate against an employee or applicant for employment purely on the grounds of the employee's religion. For example, it would be discriminatory for an employer to:

- turn down a job applicant because he/she was Christian, Jewish, Muslim or a believer in any other religion
- decide that only employees belonging to a specific religion will be allowed to go to their place of worship during working hours
- require employees only of certain religions to work on public holidays.

However, while all of the above are examples of discrimination they will not necessarily always constitute unfair discrimination. Whether such discrimination is unfair or not will depend to an extent on whether or not the discrimination makes objective sense. For example:

- Turning down a Jewish person for the position of Pope would not be unfair
- Refusing to employ an atheist as a priest would be seen as fair
- It would not be unfair to allow only Muslims to go to mosque.

A key contributing factor as to whether discrimination at the workplace makes sense is whether or not it is based on the inherent requirements of the job. For example, forcing employees to stop wearing emblems of their religion might be unfairly discriminatory, especially if such emblems are worn under the clothing. This is because the wearing of such emblems is unlikely to affect the employees' work circumstances in any way.

However, should employees working with machinery insist on wearing their religious emblems on chains dangling freely around their necks the employer would obviously be entitled to prohibit this on the grounds of safety. Such prohibition would then not constitute unfair discrimination unless employees of certain religions were allowed to wear the dangling chains and others were not. Hence, consistency also plays an important part in establishing the fairness of discrimination.

It is important to note that each case must be evaluated in terms of general principles such as consistency, the need for good sense and the inherent requirements of the job, as applied to the circumstances of each case.

In the case of *Dlamini and Others v Green Four Security* (2006, 11 BLLR 1074) the employees, who were all security guards, belonged to the Nazarene religion. They had received an order to shave or trim their beards but refused on the grounds that the Nazarene religion forbade them to do so. As a result they were dismissed and claimed that the dismissal was automatically unfair as it involved unfair discrimination against them due to their religious beliefs.

The employer argued that:

- Bearded guards looked untidy and that a tidy and clean-shaven appearance was both an inherent requirement of the job as well as a necessity of the image of the company
- The employees had contractually agreed to be clean-shaven
- The employees had been clean-shaven when they were employed.

The Court found that:

- The employees had failed to prove that cutting of beards was a central tenet of their religion and that they would have to suffer a harsh penance should they breach such tenet

- The employees worked on Sundays despite the fact that their religion forbade it. This indicated that the church applied its rules flexibly
- The employees had been selective about which religious rules they chose to follow
- The rules requiring guards to be clean-shaven had been applied consistently by the employer
- Grooming is an important factor in all security establishments
- The employees had not been unfairly discriminated against.

Employers are warned that this finding does not mean that they will always win cases concerning alleged unfairness relating to religion or to the appearance of their employees.

SEXUAL RELATIONSHIPS HARASS EMPLOYERS

The Employment Equity Act (EEA) prohibits sexual harassment of employees by other employees and holds the employer liable in such cases even if the employer does not know that the sexual harassment is going on. The courts have upheld this provision. For example, in the case of *Christian v Colliers Properties* (2005, 5 BLLR 479), two days after the complainant started work, the owner of the business invited her to dinner and to sit on his lap. He also kissed her on the neck. After she objected to the owner's conduct she was dismissed with two days' pay and referred a sexual harassment dispute.

In a default judgment the Court decided that:

- The employee had been dismissed for refusing the owner's advances
- This constituted an automatically unfair dismissal based on sexual discrimination
- Newly appointed employees are as deserving of protection from sexual harassment as are their longer-serving colleagues.

The employer had to pay the employee:

- 24 months' remuneration in compensation
- Additional damages
- Interest on the amounts to be paid
- The employee's legal costs.

The above finding might lead employers to believe that, in order to protect themselves, they need to dismiss any employee found guilty of sexual harassment. However, this is not always so. For example, in the case of *SABC Ltd v Grogan* (2006, 2 BLLR 207) a regional sales manager was dismissed for (amongst other things) sexual harassment after he had allegedly kissed a junior female colleague several times, given her love literature and had physical contact with her in his car. An arbitrator later found that, while he was guilty of sexual harassment, the level of seriousness of his conduct did not merit dismissal. This was largely because the alleged victim had not seemed to mind his advances very much and had said she thought he should not be dismissed. The arbitrator therefore ordered the employer to reinstate the employee. The employer took this decision on review to the Labour Court but lost again as the Court pronounced the arbitrator's finding to have been properly thought out and justified.

In the case of *Moboea v AVBOB Mutual Assurance Society* (2010, 5 BALR 524) a district manager was dismissed for sexually harassing a subordinate. He was found guilty of having had sexual relations with her and then threatening to fire her if she reported it. It was further alleged that the district manager's wife, who was also a manager at the company, also threatened to dismiss the subordinate after discovering that she had been having sex with her husband. The arbitrator ruled that:

- The district manager and his subordinate had been having consensual sexual relations for some time
- There was no proof that the subordinate had been threatened
- The dismissal was unfair
- The district manager was to be reinstated with full retrospective effect.

The above case findings show that:

1. Employers cannot ignore sexual harassment of their employees and must act swiftly
2. However, this neither means that every allegation is genuine nor that dismissal is appropriate in every case
3. Employers need to acquire the expertise necessary in:

   ◦ Deciding what the appropriate action should be in each individual case of sexual harassment
   ◦ Designing a comprehensive sexual harassment policy
   ◦ Ensuring that every owner, manager and employee knows and understands the severe consequences of committing such acts
   ◦ Communicating to all concerned that such misconduct will result in severe penalties including possible dismissal
   ◦ Ensuring that all employees feel entirely free to report sexual harassment
   ◦ Training all employees in the above listed issues as well as in what does and does not constitute sexual harassment, how to deal with it, where to report it and the company's supportive policy towards sexual harassment victims.

FALSE ACCUSATIONS OF RACISM DANGEROUS

The movement to end racist behaviour in South Africa has recently gathered new momentum. This, together with the strict set of laws and policies against racism, renders extremely foolish any employee who behaves in a racist manner. However, despite this, the biases and discrimination that characterised the 'old South Africa' still exist in the hearts and minds of many people. Such unfair discrimination could include, but is not limited to, discrimination on arbitrary or subjective grounds such as race, gender, family responsibility, religion, age, disability, opinion, and trade union affiliation.

Where discrimination takes place for purposes of promoting affirmative action, such discrimination would not normally be unfair.

However, in the case of *Coetzer and Others v the Minister of Safety and Security* (2003, 2 BLLR 173) the Labour Court voted against (alleged) racial discrimination despite the fact that it had been perpetrated in the name of affirmative action.

Coetzer and his colleagues were all members of the police force's (SAPS) explosives unit. They complained that it was unfair for them to be refused promotions due to the fact that they were white males and therefore did not belong to groups designated for affirmative action. The SAPS claimed that it was merely carrying out its employment equity plan (EE Plan) in accordance with the law.

The Court noted however, that the SAPS had also undertaken not to erect absolute barriers against advancement of employees from non-designated groups. Also, no applications from members of designated groups had been received. The SAPS was therefore ordered to promote the white males.

In the case of *Oerlikon Electrodes SA v CCMA and others* (2003, 9 BLLR 900) the Labour Court was asked to review an award made by a CCMA commissioner relating to the dismissal of an employee for using racist language. The arbitrator had found the dismissal to be unfair partly because the employer's disciplinary code did not provide for dismissal on a first offence of using racist language. The employee was consequently reinstated with retrospective effect. The Labour Court found that:

- The employee had admitted to calling a repairman of a service provider a "Dutchman" and had further admitted that this was a derogatory term
- The employer's disciplinary code did require two warnings before dismissal could be implemented. However, the employer was not required to follow its disciplinary code rigidly

- The term "Dutchman" was racist in the sense that it connoted white supremacy. While this might not be seen as being as serious as terms such as "kaffir" it was still unacceptable
- The employer had the right to deviate from its disciplinary code when circumstances called for this
- The CCMA commissioner had improperly interfered with the employer's right to impose discipline
- The dismissal was fair.

From this judgment it is clear that:

- The Courts will not allow employers to practise discrimination unless it is done in the name of genuine affirmative action
- Even moderate forms of racism will not be tolerated in South African workplaces
- Employees may, under certain conditions, be fired even if the employer's disciplinary code does not provide for dismissal.

However, employees must avoid making false accusations of racism as this could put them in hot water. In the case of *SACWU and another v NCP Chlorchem (Pty) Ltd* (2007, 7 BLLR 663) the employee was attending a meeting when he unjustifiably accused a colleague of racism and threatened to call for his dismissal. The employee was then dismissed for having made a false allegation of racism. He then referred a dispute of unfair dismissal to the bargaining council where the arbitrator upheld the fairness of the dismissal. The employee then took the matter to the Labour Court where it was decided that:

- Falsely accusing a person of racism threatens racial harmony at the workplace
- It is racially offensive, abusive and insulting
- Such accusations therefore deserve strong discipline.

CHAPTER CONCLUSION

The Employment Equity Act (EEA) was introduced in the year 2000 to undo the workplace gross inequalities of the past. This was done as part of the broader goal of normalising and transforming South African society that had been subjected to apartheid legislation. As a result the courts take the application of the EEA extremely seriously and employers must therefore make sure that their policies, procedures and practices avoid the type of legal liabilities reflected in the cases discussed above.

CHAPTER 5

RETRENCHMENT AND TAKEOVERS

South Africa is currently experiencing a long-term and severe economic downturn. With the exception of the civil service, employers are cutting back on costs, and the biggest cost is employment.

Over the past seven years we have experienced a tidal wave of retrenchments the size of which appears to be increasing in proportion to our shrinking economy. While our legislation strongly protects employees from unfair retrenchment it cannot protect them from the tens of thousands of fair retrenchments carried out every year.

The focus of section 189 of the Labour Relations Act (LRA) is on obligating employers to seek ways of avoiding retrenchments. Employers that carelessly ignore this requirement or that purposely misuse retrenchment to get rid of 'undesirable' employees experience the wrath of the courts.

This chapter highlights the way in which the law regulates retrenchment practices and penalises recalcitrant employers.

RETRENCHMENT – THE DUTY TO CONSULT

When an employer contemplates retrenching employees it is required by the Labour Relations Act (LRA) to first consult about this prospect before making any decision to retrench. Where the relevant employees belong to a trade union the employer is required to consult with that union on a number of issues, the most important of which is any means of avoiding job losses.

Should the employer choose not to engage in proper pre-retrenchment consultations and the employees are forcibly retrenched this will normally result in an unfair dismissal finding against the employer. However, where the employer has, in vain, made every effort to consult, it may possibly not be blamed for any failure to consult.

There are a number of reasons that retrenchment consultations may fail to take place or may fail to comply with the requirements of the LRA. These include:

- The employer was unaware of its legal obligation to consult with the employees/union. Some employers are aware of the requirement to consult but are not aware of the role of the union or of the extent of the consultation requirements. It can also happen that the employer is not aware of the fact that the employees have joined a union. It is not likely that any of these reasons will suffice as an acceptable excuse for the employer's failure to consult. This is because employers are required to find out about what they do not know.

- The employer may have urgent reasons for needing to retrench such as:

  a. Dire financial circumstances threatening the immediate survival of the business
  b. A pressing need to get rid of employees pending a hastily arranged takeover by another entity. The prospective buyer may have set a very tight deadline for the date of the takeover and may have made it a condition of the deal that workforce numbers be reduced before the conclusion of the sale
  c. The employer may have no money to pay salaries during a consultation exercise (which exercise may be very protracted especially where the employer has more than 50 employees). The employer may therefore need to curtail retrenchment consultations.

Once again, none of these reasons will be accepted by the courts as an excuse for failure to consult fully and properly.

- Where the employer has truly exhausted every effort to locate and contact the union without success it may consider the possibility of consultation with the employees/shop stewards directly. The question arises as to whether the employer should, after being forced to give up on a recalcitrant trade union, consult directly with the employees. In the case of *Numsa v Ascoreg* (CLL Vol. 12 July 2008) the Labour Court found that the employer could consult directly with the employees where the union refused to consult. However, the employer will need solid proof of such trade union refusal as consultation with employees instead of their union is forbidden under normal circumstances.

- The trade union may be purposely delaying the consultation process. If a court finds that the union unreasonably delayed the consultation process by making unreasonable demands or failing to participate in consultations the courts may well refuse to find against the employer despite the implementation of retrenchments without proper consultations. In the case of *Simelane and others* v *Letamo Estate*

(CLL Vol. 17, July 2008) the Labour Court found that the trade union has a duty to cooperate and participate in the consultation process.

However, the law clearly gives the employer the onus of ensuring, as far as it possibly can, that proper consultations take place. Therefore, despite difficulties in getting the union to cooperate, the employer must do everything in its power to gain the union's cooperation. It is only where the employer has proven that the union has been unreasonably uncooperative despite the employer's best efforts that the courts may excuse the employer for retrenching without union consultations.

The employer's duty to consult before retrenching lies at the heart of the employer's duty to ensure procedural fairness. Despite the numerous and varied obstacles to the achievement of proper consultations the employer is likely to find that failure to consult (or to consult properly) is extremely costly from a legal point of view. On the other hand, where the retrenchments are delayed due to hold-ups in consultations this could be equally costly from a salary bill point of view. Employers are therefore advised to obtain advice from a reputable labour law expert on:

- The requirements of the law regarding retrenchment consultations
- How to prepare for and conduct retrenchment consultations
- How to overcome obstacles to legally compliant consultations without unduly delaying the completion of the retrenchment exercise.

POTENTIAL RETRENCHEES ENTITLED TO REPRESENTATION

The law requires employers to have very good reasons when retrenching employees. Reasons for retrenchment that are not acceptable include the employer's personal dislike of the employee, a desire to replace the employee with a family member, the employee's misconduct, poor performance, population group, state of pregnancy or trade union affiliation. Acceptable reasons for retrenchment may, depending on circumstances, include financial problems of the employer, lack of work, technological changes or restructuring of the business.

In addition to requiring a good reason for retrenching, the law requires the employer to consult with the potential retrenchees or with their representatives before deciding to retrench. The primary purpose of such consultations is to give the parties the opportunity to find ways of avoiding the contemplated retrenchments.

Another important function of the consultation process is to enable the employees and their representatives to check whether the reasons for retrenchment given by the employer are genuine and valid. This should prevent employers who want, for example, to get rid of an undesirable employee, from using financial problems as a false pretext for retrenchment.

Section 189(1) of the Labour Relations Act (LRA) gives potential retrenchees the right to be represented in such retrenchment consultations. This is because lay employees are often out of their depth in terms of understanding retrenchment law, of understanding their rights, of picking up underhand tactics of employers and of effective consultation and negotiation skills.

Despite the fact that the law gives potential retrenchees the right to such representation employers often refuse to allow the employees to bring external representatives to the consultation meetings. This can happen for a variety of reasons including:

- The employer is aware that its reason for wanting to retrench is not legally acceptable. The employer is therefore nervous that the representative will be able to detect its impure motives
- The need to retrench is extremely urgent as the employer's business is in immediate danger of going insolvent. The employer may then be concerned that the involvement of employee representatives could cause the process to be dragged out for too long and result in the demise of the business
- The employer may be concerned that the employee representative may be able to identify alternatives to retrenchment that the employer would rather not implement
- The employer may not be aware that the employees have the right to be represented.

However, whatever the employer's motive for trying to prevent employee representation, this tactic is likely to land the employer in hot water. This is because, if the employer breaches the provisions of the LRA allowing such representation, the courts or CCMA will punish the employer. Section 189(1) provides that potential employees are entitled to be represented by their workplace forum or trade union. Where the affected employees are not members of such organisations they are entitled to be represented by representatives nominated by the employees for purposes of retrenchment consultations.

Many employers do allow trade union representation at retrenchment consultations but a few allow non-unionised employees to bring lawyers, consultants or other external representatives. The most common reason given for this is that the matter is an internal and private one and that therefore only internal representatives should be allowed. However, section 189(1) of the LRA does not confine such representation to internal parties. On the contrary, the section allows external representation in the form of trade union officials. So why should non-unionised employees be barred from bringing external representatives? This issue is a contentious one with many employers still intent on barring external representation. In the light of the above this is a risky approach.

In the case of *Workers Labour Consultants obo Petros Khoza & others v Zero Appliances cc* (1999, 11 BLLR 1225) the retrenched employees took the employer to Labour Court on a number of grounds. Included in their grounds was the employer's refusal to allow their external labour consultant to represent them at retrenchment consultations. The Court found this to be unfair and ordered the employer to pay each employee the equivalent of 12 months' remuneration in compensation.

As the law appears to be clear in allowing employees external representation employers should comply with the law. They should then deal with their concerns of being outmanoeuvred by such employee representatives by hiring their own labour law expert to represent the employer.

WHAT IS A FAIR REASON TO RETRENCH?

The number of retrenchments occurring in South Africa is still increasing. The law requires that:

- The employer follows a fair procedure aimed at an attempt to find alternatives to retrenchment. This involves good faith consultations with the employees concerned or with their representatives
- Fair or agreed criteria are used to decide which employees should be targeted for retrenchment
- There is an acceptable reason for the need for retrenchments.

Section 213 of the LRA indicates that the reasons for retrenchment may be based on the economic, technological, structural or similar needs of the employer. It is necessary to look at each of these reasons more closely.

- Typically, economic reasons given for the need for retrenchment include the ability to make money or to retain sufficient funds to continue operations. Such reasons need not be confined to the current financial situation but could include the company's projected financial circumstances. The courts are divided on whether the desire to increase profits is a fair reason for retrenchment.

- Technological reasons advanced for the need to retrench often include the introduction of new chemical formulas, equipment, computer packages, electronic systems and techniques that might reduce the need for labour.
- Structural reasons advanced for the need to retrench include the need to flatten the management structure or to switch from a functional corporate structure to a project-based structure.

The question that is left without a clear answer is: 'What does the LRA definition mean when it refers to "…. or similar needs of an employer"?' That is, what other operational needs (similar to economic, technological or structural needs) would be acceptable in law as reasons to justify retrenchments? The case of *Tiger Foods Brands Limited v L Levy* (CLL May 2007 page 102) provides an inkling as to a possible answer to this question. In this case the employer wished to introduce a system whereby employees would work on public holidays. The employees embarked on a strike in protest against this move. During the industrial action a large number of strikers attacked replacement workers with knobkerries. Also, a manager was shot and several other received death threats. As the company was unable to identify the perpetrators it concluded that it was unable to continue managing the workplace. It therefore decided to consider retrenching several employees. The union disputed the CCMA's jurisdiction to facilitate the retrenchment consultations on the grounds that the reasons for the proposed retrenchments did not fall under the definition of operational requirements in section 213 of the LRA. The CCMA agreed with the union, stating that retrenchment is supposed to be based on no-fault dismissals. The employees targeted for retrenchment had already been suspended for reasons related to misconduct.

When the company took this ruling to the Labour Court the Court found that the CCMA was wrong. It found that the CCMA arbitrator had, amongst others, made the error of ignoring the last part of the LRA's definition of operational requirements that says: "or similar needs of an employer". The Court decided that the company's need to protect its managers and to manage the business fell under the definition of "operational requirements" as they affected the viability of the business. These were grounds "similar to economic, technological or structural needs".

In my view this finding makes sense. It seems that the legislators' decision to include in the definition "economic, technological or structural needs" was based on the intention to give examples of what operational requirements entail rather than to consider this list of three needs as exclusive. The inclusion of the phrase "or similar needs" makes it clear that the definition should be interpreted broadly rather than narrowly. It would make no sense to include some types of operational requirements and to exclude others arbitrarily.

Employers are warned not to interpret this finding as a licence to invent their own reasons for retrenchment. Should the reasons given for retrenchment be found by the courts to be bogus or not to constitute operational requirements the employer will lose the case. Losing a case where a number of employees have been retrenched is likely to be extremely costly for employers. This is more so because a likely remedy for the unfair retrenchments will be the reinstatement with full back pay of all the retrenchees.

For example, it would be folly for an employer to retrench employees on the basis of its operational requirement for "employees who perform their work well". While the need for good work performance can well be argued to be an operational requirement there is a separate legal procedure prescribed in Schedule 8 of the LRA for dealing with poor performance. In the case of *NEHAWU v Medicor (Pty) Ltd* (2005, 1 BLLR 10) the Labour Court forced the employer to reinstate 67 unfairly retrenched employees with full back pay. This was because the employer had used the retrenchment process to get rid of alleged poor performers.

RED TAPE BEDEVILS URGENT RETRENCHMENTS

The provisions of the Labour Relations Act (LRA) make the implementation of retrenchment difficult and turn large-scale retrenchments into a nightmare for employers. Section 189 of the LRA lays down a number of strict requirements, the breach of which would normally place the employer in hot water. These provisions require that the employer must:

- Have a good reason for the need to retrench
- Use fair criteria in deciding which employees are to be retrenched
- Follow an intricate consultation procedure aimed primarily at seeking ways of avoiding retrenchment. This process is started off with a section 189(3) notification to employees that the employer is contemplating retrenchments. The intricate requirements of this procedure make speedy retrenchments extremely difficult, if not impossible.

Despite the existence of these restrictions section 189A of the LRA [read together with section 64 (10)(a)] contains additional far-reaching provisions that further delay the completion of the retrenchment process. Section 189A applies only where the employer has more than 50 employees and:

- where there are up to 200 employees employed, the employer contemplates retrenching at least 10 employees

- where there are up to 300 employees employed, the employer contemplates retrenching at least 20 employees
- where there are up to 400 employees employed, the employer contemplates retrenching at least 30 employees
- where there are up to 500 employees employed, the employer contemplates retrenching at least 40 employees
- where there are more than 500 employees employed, the employer contemplates retrenching at least 50 employees.

The number of retrenchments is calculated by adding the number of retrenchments over the previous 12-month period to the number of retrenchments currently contemplated.

Section 189A allows employees wishing to dispute the fairness of the retrenchments to either challenge them in court or to go on strike. The section also requires that the CCMA must provide a facilitator to help with the retrenchment consultations should either party request this.

Whether or not a facilitator is requested, the employer is not entitled to finalise the retrenchments before 60 days from the date on which it gave the employees the section 189(3) notification.

While section 189A has been written in a very confusing and unclear manner it appears that, where the employees have neither lodged a dispute with the CCMA nor applied for a facilitator, the employer must either lodge a dispute in terms of section 64(1) of the LRA or apply for a facilitator. However, this can only be done 30 days after the 189(3) notification has been issued. It seems (although there is no clarity) that this needs to be done even if the parties are in full agreement on all aspects of the retrenchment.

Case law appears to have confirmed some, but not all, of these complex, confusing and extremely peculiar legal provisions.

In the case of *NUM v De Beers Consolidated Mines (Pty) Ltd* (September 2007, CLL Vol. 17 No. 2) the Labour Court found that, if the employer wanted to complete the retrenchment process within 60 days of the date of issue of the section 189(3) notification, it would need to lodge a dispute to the CCMA itself as soon as the law allowed it to do so.

In the case of *De Beers Group Services Ltd v NUM* (2011, 4 BLLR 319) the Labour appeal Court found that in a section 189A retrenchment situation the employer is required:

- either to appoint a facilitator and wait 60 days from the date of issuing its initial section 189(3) notification before finalising retrenchments and issuing notices of termination
- or, if no facilitator is appointed, to strive to reach consensus for 30 days, and, if no consensus is reached, to refer a dispute to the CCMA and wait another 30 days before finalising retrenchments and issuing notices of termination.

It appears that the law relating to large-scale retrenchments is not only complex but is also incomplete. This is because it does not specify whether a dispute must be referred even if the parties are in full agreement on all issues. The result is that employers will end up either lodging disputes where there are none just in order to err on the side of caution, or leaving out this step and taking the risk of being penalised for committing a procedural irregularity.

Due to the onerous, complex and dangerous nature of the requirements of the LRA, employers should not take any steps towards retrenchment before obtaining advice from a labour law expert.

BEWARE OF RETRENCHMENTS FOR POOR PERFORMANCE

The legal procedures that an employer is required to follow in implementing dismissals for misconduct, retrenchments and poor work performance are all different. For instance, it is not normally acceptable to use the procedure laid down for retrenchments in order to deal with poor work performance.

However, while retrenchments and poor performance terminations should not be 'mixed and matched', there are circumstances where these two legal concepts might overlap in practice.

Firstly, when considering possible retrenchments employers are required to use fair and objective criteria in deciding which employees should be retrenched and which should retain their jobs. While last-in-first-out (LIFO) is the criterion that unions prefer, the law allows the employer to consider using other fair and objective criteria. This is why employers sometimes prefer to use work performance as the retrenchment selection criterion. However, employers are warned that, while the retrenchment code of good practice does not specifically outlaw this, it also does not specifically permit it. Also, implementing performance measurement in a fair and objective manner can be very tricky. For these reasons employers should be extremely careful before even considering the use of work performance as a retrenchment selection criterion.

Secondly, an employer may perceive the poor performance of one of its departments as justification for a retrenchment exercise. The rationale might be that the poor performance is causing loss of clients or loss of profits. If these losses are in conflict with the employer's operational requirements they may be seen by the employer as a reason to retrench.

However, as a rule, such an approach is dangerous, especially where the employees are being blamed for the department's poor performance. On the other hand, poor performance retrenchments are somewhat less dangerous in cases where the fault lies with the efficiency of the department as a whole due to factors such as work organisation, outdated techniques, organisation structure or inefficient production methods. Put another way, where the cause of the poor performance is seen not as systemic but rather as the slackness of one or more employees, this problem should be dealt with via a performance correction procedure rather than via retrenchments.

One case that appears to contradict this principle is that of *FAWU and others v Ruto Mills (Pty) Ltd* (CLL Vol. 17 No. 6 January 2008). In this case the employees were retrenched due to their collective poor work performance. The Labour Court found the retrenchments to be fair. It appears that this unusual decision was made for a combination of reasons including:

- The employer proved that the poor performance resulted in a genuine and serious operational need to meet production targets
- The employees knew of the required performance standards
- The employees had been warned of possible dismissal should they fail to meet these targets
- The production targets were achievable and reasonable
- The employer had made every reasonable effort to correct the problem
- The employer had given the employees ample opportunity to correct their performance levels.

Despite the fact that the employer won in this case employers should not see this as a licence to get rid of poor performers via retrenchments. In the case of *SA Mutual v IBSA & others* (2001, 9 BLLR 1045) the Labour Appeal Court found that the retrenchment of the employees was in fact a disguised dismissal of the employees for poor work performance.

In 2005 a similar finding was made in the case of *NEHAWU vs Medicor* (CLL Vol. 17 No. 6 January 2008). And in *South African Airways v Bogopa & others* (2007, 11 BLLR 1065) the employer retrenched some employees after it discovered inefficiencies in one of its departments. The Labour Appeal Court found the retrenchments to be unfair. One of the reasons for this decision was that the employer used the retrenchment procedure to solve problems relating to poor performance.

It frequently occurs that groups of employees are performing below standard and that this causes operational problems such as production shortfalls, reduction in orders or loss of clients. However, instead of using retrenchments to resolve these problems employers should obtain expert assistance in resolving the performance problem.

EMPLOYERS CAN DROWN IN THEIR REDUNDANCY POOLS

Due to the fact that some employers are unskilled in dealing both effectively and legally with poor performance or misconduct they look for other ways of getting rid of 'troublesome employees'. However, the law has made it clear that employers must use laid-down corrective/disciplinary processes in such cases and are not allowed to misuse other methods such as retrenchments.

Many employers cull undesirable employees by declaring jobs redundant and placing the incumbent employees in a 'redundancy pool' or 'redeployment pool'. The employer then requires the pooled employees to apply for vacant posts but turns down the applications of the targeted 'undesirables'. The practice of 'pooling' might succeed if the employer can prove that the pooling and the redundancies are legally justified in the prevailing circumstances, that there are no hidden agendas and that the employees concerned have agreed to the pooling option. However, this approach bears so many pitfalls and is so open to misuse that I strongly advise employers to avoid it.

A case that illustrates this point is that of *Oosthuizen v Telkom SA Ltd* (2007, 11 BLLR 1013). Oosthuizen was an engineer with 30 years of service. During a staff cut-back exercise his job was made redundant and he was placed in a redeployment pool with the agreement of his trade union. He then applied for 22 vacancies at Telkom but, although he was short-listed for some of them, he was unsuccessful with all of them. When he was retrenched he claimed that this was unfair as the employer had not consulted with him.

The Labour Court found that the employer had no obligation to consult with him as they had consulted with his trade union. The court therefore found the retrenchment to be fair. Oosthuizen therefore appealed to the Labour Appeal Court where it was found/decided that:

- Employers are obliged not to retrench employees if this can be avoided
- The employer had offered to retrain the employees in the redeployment pool but had failed to retrain Oosthuizen
- It is unfair to retrench an employee whose job could have been saved via minimal retraining
- The employer had brought no evidence as to why the employee had been unsuccessful with his 22 job applications
- The fact that the employee had been short-listed for some of the jobs suggested that he had the basic qualifications required for those jobs
- In choosing Oosthuizen for retrenchment the employer had applied the criterion of required skills despite having agreed to apply the criterion of LIFO (last-in-first-out)
- The employer, in deciding to choose the employee for retrenchment had completely ignored his 30 years of service
- The above meant that the employee may have been rejected for the vacant posts on arbitrary grounds
- The employee had belonged to a trade union and therefore would normally not have been entitled to individual consultations with the employer. However, the employer had conceded that the employee was a manager and the employer's normal practice was to consult directly with managers on the retrenchment list even if they belonged to a trade union
- While the employer had entered into consultations with the employee's trade union it had failed to consult on the issue of the criteria for deciding which employees should be placed into the redeployment pool
- No evidence was led to justify the employer's decision to require the employee to apply for new positions alongside colleagues with shorter service than his
- As a result the retrenchment was procedurally and substantively unfair
- The employer was to reinstate the employee with 12 months' back pay
- Should the reinstatement result in an extraneous employee the employer would have to consider retrenching another employee
- The employer was required to pay the employee's appeal costs.

This case reinforces the fact that the courts are now applying a much tougher test than ever before on the question as to whether the employer is entitled to retrench employees. This means that hidden agendas are more likely to be uncovered and punished. Before employers consider dismissing employees under any circumstances they should obtain expert advice in order to ensure both effectiveness and legal compliance.

CONTRACTORS MUST OFTEN TAKE OVER STAFF IN OUTSOURCING DEALS

The takeover of an entity or part thereof by a new owner or new management often causes loss of jobs and employees are often desperate to stay on with the new enterprise. On the other hand, the new owner/management very often already has its own staff and wants to avoid the expense of taking on additional employees.

The law relating to takeovers of going concerns has been expanded and is no longer confined to situations where one business buys another or where two entities merge. The Labour Relations Act (LRA) was amended in 2002 to include a "service" in the definition of an entity that may be taken over as a going concern for purposes of section 197 of the LRA. This has come to mean that:

- A "service" includes even internal services of a business insignificant to the service provided by the business to outsiders (for example, non-core departments such as cleaning and gardening)
- Outsourcing of services (be they internal or external) to contractors normally constitute the takeover of a going concern for the purposes of section 197 of the LRA.

In view of this, section 197 of the Labour Relations Act (LRA) comes into effect when outsourcing occurs and forces the new operator of the service to take over all the labour law obligations of the old undertaking.

However, not all transfers qualify under this legislation because not all are transfers 'as going concerns'. It is vital for employers to know which transfers do and do not fall under this legislation because they need to know:

- whether the new employer will be forced to take over all the old employer's employees; and
- whether the new employer will have to recognise and preserve all the benefits, remuneration, working conditions, years of service and other rights of the employees.

Unfortunately, the statutes are not clear enough to tell the parties whether the new entity must or must not comply with section 197 of the LRA. We have therefore offered below our view as to what circumstances would be likely to characterise a merger or takeover as the transfer of a going concern.

- If the new undertaking continued the running of the business as a going concern in much the same way as it had been run before the takeover, this would point to the takeover of a going concern
- Such a takeover would also be likely to qualify if the new undertaking served the same client market as did the old undertaking.

While the sale of a business as an operating entity has normally been considered to qualify under the heading of a section 197 transfer, it was initially unclear whether the outsourcing of an enterprise to a contractor without selling the entity constitutes the transfer of a going concern.

This uncertainty sprang primarily from the contradictions in court decisions on this issue. For example, in the case of *Schutte & others v Powerplus Performance (Pty) Ltd and another* (1999, 20 ILJ 665) the Labour Court found that the takeover of a company's motor workshop by a contractor did constitute the takeover of a going concern and forced the contractor to take over all the workers attached to the motor workshop employees.

However, in the case of *NEHAWU v University of Cape Town & Others* (2000, 1 BLLR 803) the Labour Court found that the outsourcing of the university's cleaning, maintenance and gardening functions did not constitute the takeover of a going concern because the university did not transfer its equipment and other assets to the contractor and because the outsourcing was not of a permanent nature.

Again, in *SAMWU and others v Rand Airport Management Company (Pty) Ltd & others* (2002, 12 BLLR 1220) the Court found that the transfer of part of an employer's structure that did not comprise a recognisable entity did not constitute the transfer of a going concern.

However, the Labour Appeal Court in *SAMWU and others v Rand Airport Management Company (Pty) Ltd & others* (2005 3 BLLR 241) overturned the earlier Rand Airport case decision, and the Constitutional Court, in *NEHAWU v University of Cape Town & Others* (2003, 24 ILJ 95) overturned the earlier University of Cape Town decision.

The legal pendulum has thus swung far in favour of the view that outsourcing of services constitutes the takeover of a going concern.

Due to the complex nature of the section 197 legislation and the powerful constraints on contractors and other employers, nobody should enter into takeovers or outsourcing agreements before consulting reputable experts.

SECOND GENERATION OUTSOURCING: CAN YOU RETRENCH?

It was for a long time highly contentious as to whether second generation outsourcing falls under section 197 of the Labour Relations Act, the law protecting employees when a business or a part thereof is taken over.

In the case of *SAA v Aviation Union of SA obo Barnes* the airline transferred its Infrastructure and Support service (I & S service) to a company called LGM as a going concern and accordingly transferred the relevant employees to LGM under section 197 of the LRA.

Before LGM's contract with SAA expired, SAA fired LGM and sought tenders from other contractors to take over the service. However, SAA did not include in the tender documents the requirement that the tenderers had to undertake to take over all the LGM staff providing services to SAA. Therefore, before any tender could be considered, the union applied to the Labour Court for orders that, in effect, would prevent any takeover of the services until the LGM employees were first taken over by the new service provider and that would declare any retrenchment of the LGM staff automatically unfair.

The Labour Court refused to grant such orders for reasons including that second generation outsourcing would become untenable and because section 197 of the LRA did not cover second generation outsourcing. This was because section 197 (1), in effect, defines a transfer in terms of this section as a transfer of a business or part thereof "*by*" one employer to another. In a situation where the I & S service of SAA would be transferred to a new contractor (i.e. whichever tenderer won the contract) the I & S service would not be transferred *by* one employer to another because SAA, who 'owned' this service, was not the employer (LGM was) and LGM would be the one to transfer the service to the new contractor.

The Labour Appeal Court (LAC) overturned the LC's decision and found that:

If the LC's interpretation were applied it would directly conflict with the purpose of section 197 which was to protect employees from losing their employment due to a transfer of a business or part thereof. The LAC preferred the purposive interpretation of the meaning of the word "by" which is that, although it would technically be SAA initiating the transfer of the I & S service to the new contractor, the service would effectively be moved by LGM to the new contractor even if this was done via the auspices of SAA. That is, while it would be SAA making the transfer decision, the old employer, LGM would be the one to be effecting the transfer.

Another way of explaining this is that the word "by" in the definition of a transfer of a going concern should, in the view of the Court, be read to mean "from". This would mean that, although it would be SAA who would legally transfer the I & S service to the new contractor, the service would be transferred from LGM to the new contractor, thus rendering the takeover a section 197 transfer.

SAA then took the matter further to the Supreme Court of Appeal which reversed the LAC's decision. It said that the literal interpretation of section 197 should be applied and that applying the LAC's interpretation would require every new service provider to take over the staff of any previous service provider every time the client changed its mind as to who it was going to use.

The union took the matter to the Constitutional Court because the issue of outsourcing and the resultant loss of jobs is very high on the agenda of the labour movement in SA. The Court found in favour of the union.

The effect of this decision is that contractors who win new projects will, in many cases, have to take over the employees of the outgoing contractor. If the outgoing contractor has lost the contract due to worker inefficiency the client will then be saddled with the very same inefficient workers when the new contractor takes over. This will defeat the whole purpose of the firing of the old contractor.

In *Jenkin v Khumbula Media* (2010, 12 BLLR 1295) the applicant was told that his contract had lapsed after the business had changed hands twice. The Court rejected the employer's version that the employee had been a fixed-term contractor and found that the employee had, in effect, been retrenched. It also found that on both occasions of takeover these had been carried out as transfers as a going concern. The employer had conducted only one meeting with the employee and this one meeting was not held in good faith because the employer had not even made its intentions clear. The retrenchment was thus procedurally unfair and the employer was ordered to pay the employee eight months' salary in compensation plus severance pay calculated on the basis of 29 years of service.

Even the judges in the Courts differ with each other as to whether a business or part thereof has been transferred in terms of section 197 or not. Therefore, employers need to get expert advice before effecting any transfer that could possibly be seen as a section 197 takeover. Also, everyone in management and others dealing with employee dismissals must be thoroughly trained in the complexities and requirements of the law.

CHAPTER CONCLUSION

The cases discussed above make it clear that employers may only use retrenchment to terminate the employment of employees where there is no alternative. For example, where it is possible to reduce costs, change working methods, change job functions or transfer potential retrenchees, these alternatives must be used unless the employer can objectively justify their non-use. Where employers fail this test they are likely to have to reinstate retrenched employees.

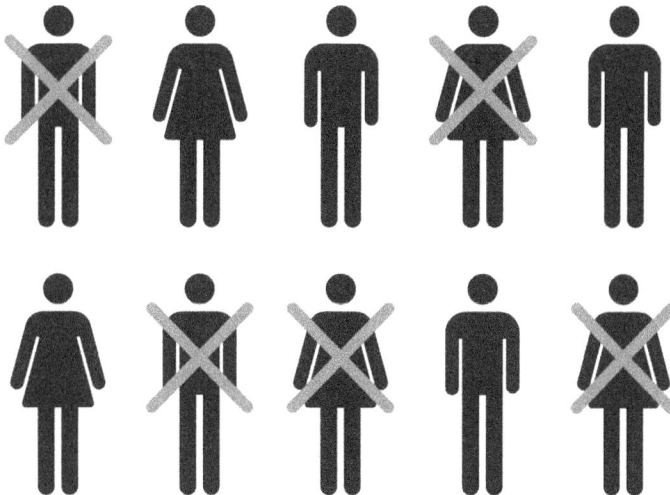

Retrenchment should only be used as a last resort

Managing workplace conflict

CHAPTER 6

MANAGING WORKPLACE CONFLICT

South African workplaces have inherited the legacy of the intense industrial conflict that was born out of our apartheid history. The apartheid era germinated a fierce we-they culture that dominated industrial relations.

After South Africans won a democratic government in the mid-1990s our labour laws were drastically changed to reflect the labour relations policy of the new government. However, while efforts were made to achieve political reconciliation, insufficient processes were put in place to heal the deeply hostile relationship between management and labour.

That is, although institutions such as NEDLAC and the CCMA were established these have taken the role of battlefields between employers and employees instead of places where the parties can truly find each other and make true and lasting peace.

This leaves the parties at their individual workplaces the task of trying to cope with their ongoing conflicts. This chapter looks at how to do this within the constraints of South Africa's labour dispensation.

STRIKES CAN MEAN DISASTER FOR EMPLOYERS

Mid-year brings with it South Africa's strike season. The loss of production and of customers is usually the first consequence of a strike. However, indirect strike costs incurred later can be just as serious. In the case of *NUM and others v Chrober Slate (Pty) Ltd* (2008, 3 BLLR 287) the mine dismissed its quarry workers and factory staff due to an unprocedural strike by the quarry workers. The employer admitted that the factory staff were not to blame for the work stoppage as it had been the quarry workers who had refused to work. The dismissals of the factory staff were found to be unfair and the Labour Court ordered the mine to reinstate the 42 dismissed employees with back pay. In order to avoid the snowballing costs and loss of business that strikes can cause the employer needs to understand:

- What constitutes a strike in legal terms
- The economic effects of a strike for both parties
- The effects of a strike on the employment relationship
- How to resolve constructively the conflict that causes industrial action
- How to minimise the damage caused by a strike
- How to bring a strike to a speedy end.

What Constitutes a Strike?

A strike is any concerted withholding of labour by a group of employees in support of a demand made by them to the employer. Examples of this are work stoppages, go-slows, overtime bans and work-to-rule.

The economic effects of a strike for both parties

The employer is likely to lose money due to delayed service to clients or to lost production time. The employees will lose their pay due to the no work, no pay principle. If the strikers are dismissed they will lose their livelihoods altogether.

The effects of a strike on the employment relationship

Once the strike is over, even if the business has not been closed down by it, the feelings of hostility resulting from the strike can severely damage teamwork, productivity and profitability.

How to resolve constructively the conflict that causes industrial action

Before the conflict gets to the stage of impasse that results in a strike the parties need to utilise the services of an expert in conflict resolution. The CCMA was set up with the purpose of helping the parties to resolve conflict peacefully. However, in practice, the warring parties too often go to the CCMA because the law says they must rather than in a sincere attempt to sort out their differences. In other words, by the time the parties end up at the CCMA the conflict is often beyond the point of no return.

For this reason, during times of industrial peace, employers and employees should identify and agree upon the use of a trained and reputable conflict resolution expert to be called in when the parties are unable to solve the problem themselves.

How to minimise the damage caused by a strike

Employees should allow the business to continue to run in order to avert the likelihood of a closure that could result in job losses. Employers should use the services of a reputable labour broker who can provide alternative labour during the strike. Both parties should behave in a civil and professional manner towards each other.

How to bring a strike to a speedy end

Where the parties are unable to find common ground they should not delay in bringing in the services of their mutually agreed strike resolution expert. An expert in this field will not only have techniques of bringing the parties together but will also be able to see solutions that the emotions of the parties have prevented them from seeing. The expert should also be able to help the parties rebuild their relationship once the strike is over.

WORKPLACE REBELLIONS CAN WREAK HAVOC

Workplace rebellion can bring the company to its knees. The most typical form of rebellion known in South Africa is industrial action. Such rebellion can cripple the business, especially if it lasts for several weeks and if the majority of employees take part.

However, even smaller-scale workplace rebellion or defiance can result in costly damage including:

- Discipline and lost employment for employees
- Damaged management-employee relationships
- Trade unions being brought into the workplace
- Reduced morale
- A strained working atmosphere
- Demotivation
- Slowed production output
- Lack of teamwork and co-operation
- Poor work performance
- Unhappy clients
- Loss of clients and/or loss of orders
- Retrenchments
- Material wastage
- Industrial sabotage
- Increased accidents and injuries

- Go slows
- Outright refusal to obey instructions.

There are two basic reasons why employers need to avoid, or at least quickly resolve, such rebellions:

- Firstly, the above factors are likely to affect profitability.
- Secondly, rebellions have the habit of ending up in the CCMA or bargaining counsil. Neither of these are good places for employers to go. Fighting disputes at such tribunals is time wasting, energy sapping, emotionally draining and financially costly.

In the case of *NUMSA obo Rewu v Borbet SA* (2008, 3 BALR 237) the employee refused to perform quality inspection work because it did not fall within his job description. As a result he was dismissed. The arbitrator found that the work did fall within his job description and that his repeated refusal to do this work constituted defiance. The dismissal was therefore found to be fair. The employer won this case because it was able to show that the employee's defiance was unjustified and that the employer had not done anything unreasonable to provoke the defiant act of Rewu.

However, where it is shown that the employer had been unreasonable in its expectations of the employee, the result could be very different. Also, even if the employer has acted reasonably the reasons for the employee's defiance must be considered carefully before the sanction of dismissal is imposed. In the case of *Petersen v Kost Engineering (Pty) Ltd* (2000, 9 BALR 1068) the employee was fired for refusing to work. His reason for this gross insubordination was that he was unhappy with his pay. The CCMA found in the employee's favour due to mitigating circumstances, one of which was that he had misconducted himself due to the fact that he believed the employer was not paying him a high enough salary.

Thus, while the law does not give employees the right to disobey instructions or to rebel unprocedurally in protest against employer actions, the CCMA still found in the employee's favour. Had it been 50 employees that rebelled this employer would have been in extremely serious trouble. This could mean disaster for the employer especially if the rebels are all reinstated because such reinstated rebels will feel untouchable and could become even more disruptive knowing that they are protected by the CCMA. Therefore, any decision to dismiss such employees should be informed by advice from a reputable labour law expert.

IS WORKPLACE VICTIMISATION PROHIBITED?

There is substantial disagreement, uncertainty and confusion as regards the meaning of certain labour law terms. The reasons for this include:

- There are a large number of labour law statutes and codes and employers do not always have access to all of them
- There are numerous legal terms in labour law that are confusing, unclear, ambiguous and vague
- Many of these terms are not defined in the statutes
- Those terms that are defined in the statutes are sometimes still confusing because the definition is incomplete or unclear and therefore open to interpretation
- Court judges and arbitrators, via their judgments and awards, quite often disagree with each other on the meaning of certain terms and as to how they should be applied
- In view of these legal uncertainties employers, employees and trade unions struggle to understand and agree on the requirements of the law because the meaning of the law is itself a reason for dispute. In practical terms, when labour law is unclear, then employers are unsure of how they should act when legal steps need to be taken and employees are unsure what workplace rights they have and how far their rights extend.

The legal terms and concepts that appear to confuse employers and employees include, amongst many others, the following:

victimisation, reasonable, sufficient, con-arb, unfair dismissal, evidence, going concern, racial abuse, sexual discrimination, accumulated leave, consultation, automatically unfair, desertion and reinstatement.

Victimisation

Labour legislation avoids dealing directly with the concept of 'workplace victimisation'. I have been unable to find this term mentioned anywhere in the LRA. This is most surprising in view of the fact that one of the key purposes of the Labour Relations Act (LRA) is to give effect to the Constitutional provision for the right to fair labour practice.

The LRA does, to an extent, deal with the issue of victimisation in an indirect way. For example, sections 5, 185 and 186(2) of the LRA deal with certain unfair practices (short of dismissal) that could amount to victimisation. And chapter 2 of the EEA also alludes to practices that could constitute victimisation. These sections attempt to define and prohibit the following acts on the part of employers:

- Preventing employees or job applicants from joining trade unions or carrying out lawful trade union activities
- Bribing employees or prejudicing them so as to avoid or halt their lawful trade union activity or to disadvantage employees/applicants due to past trade union involvement
- Prejudicing an employee or job applicant due to his/her legitimate disclosure of information
- Prejudicing an employee or job applicant who has previously or who may exercise any right conferred by the LRA
- Bribing any job applicant not to exercise any right conferred by the LRA
- Unfair promotion, demotion, suspension, discipline, training or provision of benefits
- Unfair conduct on the employer's part in relation to probation or contravention of the Protection of Disclosures Act 26 of 2000
- Unfair discrimination and harassment.

In the case of *Jabari v Telkom SA* (Pty) Ltd (2006, 10 BLLR 924) the employee was ostensibly dismissed for incompatibility. However, the Court found that the true reason for his dismissal was the fact that he had lodged grievances against the employer, challenged its unfair labour practices and refused a separation package. The Court found that this amounted to victimisation. The Court judged the dismissal to have been automatically unfair and ordered the employer to reinstate the employee retrospectively with full back pay.

Employers therefore need to be very careful of doing anything that might resemble victimisation of employees. Section 186(1)(e) does consider a forced resignation as a dismissal (constructive dismissal) and, if the employee can prove victimisation, he/she will have a good basis for a constructive dismissal claim.

GET THE @#&*!!Ä€» OUT OF MY FACE!

When an employer instructs an employee temporarily to vacate its premises and to stop performing his/her duties this is called 'suspension'. The effect of a suspension is that the employee is not allowed to return to work until the employer instructs that he/she may do so. Such suspensions normally occur:

- while the employer is investigating misconduct/poor performance allegations against the employee
- while the employer and/or employee are preparing for a disciplinary hearing
- after the employer has decided that the employee is guilty of misconduct/poor performance.

In our experience the reasons that motivate employers to suspend employees include:

- To remove the employee from the workplace as a means of preventing him/her from causing further harm by repeating the alleged misconduct or poor performance
- To prevent the employee from interfering with the investigation instituted against the employee
- To avoid disharmony at the workplace that could be caused due to the employee's awareness that he/she is being investigated
- As a result of the employer's anger. That is, the employer is so furious with the employee due to his/her alleged actions that the employer wants the employee 'out of my sight!'
- As a means of retribution. The employer wishes to humiliate or demean the employee or otherwise punish him/her for the alleged offence.

Often, especially when the employer evicts the employee in a fit of anger, it is unclear whether the employee has been suspended (evicted temporarily) or whether the employee has been fired. This is because the employer shouts at the employee to 'get the @#&*!!Ä€» out of my face!'

Regardless of whether such evictions are meant as suspensions or dismissals, the affected employees more often than not go to the CCMA or bargaining council claiming unfair dismissal and/or unfair suspension. Especially where the eviction takes place while the employer is in a fit of anger, the employer loses the case.

Labour law does not prohibit employers from suspending employees but does allow employees to challenge the fairness of suspensions. Section 186(2)(b) of the Labour Relations Act (LRA) defines as an unfair labour practice "the unfair suspension of an employee". Section 191(1) allows an employee to refer an alleged unfair labour practice to the CCMA or to a bargaining council. Where the employer has suspended the employee for an unfair reason or in an unfair manner the employer can be forced to pay the employee compensation or lost wages or to lift the suspension.

In the case of *CEIWU obo Khumalo v SHM Engineering cc* (2005, 10 BALR 1009) the employee, a boilermaker, was accused of failing to obey an instruction from his superior and was therefore suspended for six weeks. The employee's excuse for defying his superior was that his superior had screamed at him. The arbitrator found that this was not a sufficient reason for disobeying a reasonable and lawful instruction and that the employee's behaviour constituted gross insubordination. However, the arbitrator found the suspension to be unfair and ordered the employer to pay the employee for the full period of the suspension. The arbitrator's rationale for this was that, while the suspension might have started out as a "holding" measure, it became punitive due to its unreasonably long duration.

In the case of *Sajid v Mohammed NO & others* (1999, 11 BLLR 1175) the employee, who worked as an Imam for a mosque, was suspended from duty. The charges against him included removal of copies of notices, persuading congregants to make false statements and failure to attend prayers. The Labour Court found that there was no evidence to prove that there had been a breakdown in the employment relationship and that the suspension had been unfair. The Court ordered the employer to lift the suspension.

In the case of *MEC for Tourism and Environmental Affairs Free State v Nondumo & others* (2005, 10 BLLR 974) the employee was suspended after being charged with several counts of misconduct. The Labour Court found that the suspension was unfair and ordered the employer to pay the employee compensation and lost pay amounting to R840 000.

In the light of the above employers are advised to avoid suspending employees unnecessarily or due to anger.

STAFF UNHAPPINESS IS NOT INCOMPATIBILITY

The lodging of complaints by staff can be used as grounds neither for alleging incompatibility nor for dismissing employees.

In the case of *Jabari v Telkom SA (Pty) Ltd* (2006, 10 BLLR 924) the Labour Court, in explaining the nature of workplace incompatibility, highlighted three important characteristics of incompatibility. It said that:

1. Incompatibility refers to the employee's "inability or failure to maintain cordial and harmonious relationships with his peers"
2. Incompatibility is a form of "incapacity"
3. Incompatibility is an "amorphous, nebulous concept, based on subjective value judgements".

It is necessary to look more closely at each of these three important characteristics of workplace incompatibility:

1. **Incompatibility refers to the employee's "inability or failure to maintain cordial and harmonious relationships with his peers"**

It is important to note that this description of incompatibility is fairly narrow. It refers to the failure or inability to work harmoniously with "colleagues" rather than with the rules of the employer or with the instructions of the employee's superiors. While both poor relationships with colleagues and refusal to obey instructions can affect work efficiency they are not the same thing.

While the legal meaning of incompatibility can be stretched to include an employee's inability to fit in with corporate culture it cannot be stretched to include the straightforward breaking of the employer's rules. Such failure is a form of misconduct rather than incompatibility.

2. **Incompatibility is a form of incapacity**

As stated, incompatibility itself is not misconduct. It is rather a form of incapacity in the sense that the incompatibility negatively affects work performance. The incompatibility renders the employee unable to do his/her work properly or hinders the work performance of the team.

3. **Incompatibility is an amorphous, nebulous concept, based on subjective value judgements**

That is, whether the employee is truly the cause of the disharmony or whether there really is disharmony is difficult to judge. If the manager dislikes the employee he/she may erroneously allow this dislike to persuade him/her that the employee is at fault and is incompatible whereas the employee may in fact only be exercising his/her legal rights.

In the Jabari case mentioned earlier in this article the employee lodged a grievance and also lodged a dispute with the CCMA for unfair promotional practice. The employee was then fired for incompatibility and lodged a case of automatically unfair dismissal. The Labour Court decided that:

- The employer had neither established that the employee had been at fault and nor that there had been any incompatibility
- The employee had not been given a chance to confront the allegations
- The employee had neither been given counselling nor a chance to remedy the alleged incompatibility

- The employee had been dismissed for having challenged the employer's earlier promotion decision
- This amounted to victimisation and an automatically unfair dismissal
- The employer had to reinstate the employee with full retrospective effect.

It is very difficult to place an employee's behaviour in the incompatibility box for the reasons explained earlier. In addition, even when the employer decides to go the incompatibility route, it still has the onus of proving that:

- There really was incompatibility
- It was the employee's fault
- It resulted in serious consequences for the employer
- The employer had tried to implement remedial measures
- The employee was given the chance to defend his case and to correct his/her behaviour.

In the light of the numerous and dangerous pitfalls and of the extreme complexity of such cases employers are advised to:

- Act with extreme caution when dealing with such employees
- Obtain advice from a reputable labour law expert. Very often, such advice illumines a very much simpler, less dangerous and more effective route to follow in solving the problem.

DON'T SUSPEND EMPLOYEES IN ANGER

Angry employers too often fire employees on the spot for having broken workplace rules, or for doing poor work. This is understandable in circumstances where the employee has seriously messed up a business deal, damaged equipment, lost crucial information, committed a dishonest act, refused to obey an instruction or caused other serious damage. However, there is no place for anger in the implementation of discipline. This is because the law punishes employers who act hastily, and anger very often results in hasty and foolhardy action.

Over time many employers have learned this bitter lesson, often after a traumatic and costly experience at the CCMA, bargaining council or Labour Court. Such employers then often resort to venting their anger on destructive employees by suspending them instead of firing them. However, emotionally motivated and unreasoned suspensions can also result in problems for employers. This is because section 186(2) of the Labour

Relations Act classifies unwarranted suspensions as unfair labour practices. Also, a suspension could constitute a breach of contract and will only be tolerated by law enforcers if it has been implemented via a fair process and for a good reason.

In the case of *Mogothle v Premier of the Northwest Province & another* (2009, 4 BLLR 331) the deputy director general of agriculture, conservation and development was suspended from duty after the publication of a media article alleging his involvement in corruption. He accepted the first month of suspension, but not the employer's decision to extend the suspension indefinitely until the conclusion of the investigation. The employee therefore launched an urgent application to the Labour Court on the grounds that:

- His rights under the Promotion of Administrative Justice Act had been breached
- His contract of employment had been breached
- The employer had failed to comply with the disciplinary code of the Public Service
- He had not been given a hearing prior to his suspension.

The employer opposed the application on the grounds that:

- The matter was not urgent
- The Labour Court lacked jurisdiction to hear suspension matters as such matters were to be dealt with at arbitration
- The suspension had been lawful.

The Court found that:

- The principle of fair dealing established by the Supreme Court of Appeal had to be applied
- Case law did not prevent parties from pursuing contractual disputes relating to employment issues
- Employees have the right to refer contractual disputes to the Labour Court in terms of section 77(3) of the Basic Conditions of Employment Act (BCEA)
- Suspension of an employee prior to a hearing is "equivalent to an arrest" and should only be used when there is reasonable cause to show that the employee will interfere with investigations or pose some other threat
- An employee should not be suspended for preventive reasons unless there are prima facie grounds for believing that the employee has committed an offence that gives rise to objectively justifiable reasons requiring his exclusion from the workplace
- The employer must give the employee an opportunity, before suspending him, to make representations against the suspension

- There was no indication that the employee's presence at the workplace would jeopardise the investigation
- Suspension can have serious personal and social consequences for the employee
- The right to work is linked to the right to dignity
- The matter was urgent and the suspension was a breach of the employee's contractual rights.

The Court therefore required the employer to uplift the suspension.

This finding makes it clear that employers considering suspension need first to ensure that they are able to justify the suspension decision and to follow proper pre-suspension procedures.

TREAT WORKPLACE DISRUPTIONS WITH CARE

Where employees disrupt the workplace the operations of the business can be seriously affected. Employees who behave in a disruptive manner might do so for a variety of reasons including:

- Abuse of alcohol or other substances
- Incompetence – that is, while the employee is not intentionally disruptive, his/her inability to perform properly disrupts the flow of work in the workplace
- Resentment – employees may resent receiving a low or zero pay increase
- Unwillingness to work – there are many employees who would prefer to sponge off their families instead of working. These employees tend to behave disruptively either because they do not care if they get fired or because they are trying to get fired. Then they can tell their families that it was not their fault and go and make some money at the CCMA by complaining about their 'unfair dismissal'
- Having received a warning or other disciplinary action, ill treatment, being overlooked for promotion, resentment that the manager has a fancy car or life in general
- Industrial action – employees trying to pressurise the employer may, instead of going on a fully fledged strike, embark on disruptive behaviour
- Dislike of a colleague or a boss.

Disruptive behaviour at the workplace can be seriously damaging to the effectiveness of business operations and can even result in losses for the employer. For example, disruptive behaviour can cause:

- Bosses to lose their tempers
- The speed of production to slow down
- Legal disputes arising from unprocedural discipline and dismissal
- Service to clients to suffer
- Loss of orders or of clients
- Injury to employees or other people
- The quality of products to deteriorate
- Damage to property
- Clashes between employees and managers or amongst employees.

It is therefore most important that the employer acts swiftly and firmly, yet within the law, in order to minimise the damage and send a strong message that such behaviour will not be tolerated. Especially where an employee's disruptive behaviour is habitual the employer needs to follow the correct disciplinary procedure to prove that the employee is guilty. Otherwise there is a danger of the disruptive employee being reinstated by the CCMA, Labour Court or bargaining council.

In the case of *Mofokeng v Afrikaans Import and Export cc* (2001, 11 BALR 1184) the employee was dismissed for disrupting the workplace after he had been caught under the influence of alcohol and had refused to obey the instructions of a superior. However, the employer reinstated the employee as it wanted to give him one more chance and commuted the dismissal to a final warning. Later, the employee was again dismissed, this time for driving a forklift under the influence of alcohol, damaging the employer's property with the forklift, smashing the windows of the company quarters in which he lived and loudly threatening management while the owner was on an international telephone call. Instead of calling a disciplinary hearing the employer fired the employee on the spot. The CCMA stated that the existence of the final warning did not exempt the employer from holding a disciplinary hearing.

Employees are advised, if they are aggrieved by anything at work, not to disrupt the workplace lest they end up out on the street. Instead, aggrieved employees should lodge formal grievances and/or CCMA disputes.

Employers are advised, when faced with 'disruptive' employees to:

- Avoid losing their tempers
- Use professional advice to help:

  ◦ carefully and thoroughly investigate the cause of the problematic behaviour
  ◦ arrive objectively and unemotionally at the route cause of the problem

- decide upon a legally compliant, practical and effective course of action appropriate to the particular type of disruption and to its specific cause. Such action may vary from a warning to a disciplinary hearing or from counselling to training or treatment.

CHAPTER CONCLUSION

It is often the case that 'bad egg' employees cause conflict in the workplace. And many employers also blame trade unions for shop-floor strife. However, it is employers who are primarily responsible for achieving and maintaining harmony at the workplace; and it is often employers and their managers who cause or fan the flames of conflict by failing to design and implement proper employee policies, failing to listen to employees, failing to deal properly with employee problems, failing to control their feelings of anger when things go wrong and by failing to temper unrealistic expectations amongst employees. In an environment characterised by industrial relations tensions employers need to ensure that management is made responsible for maintaining workplace harmony by avoiding the above-mentioned behaviours that lead to conflict.

'Bad egg' employees cause conflict in the workplace

CHAPTER 7

WHAT MAKES A DISMISSAL AUTOMATICALLY UNFAIR? AND WHAT ARE THE CONSEQUENCES?

Some reasons for dismissing employees are so unacceptable that they render the dismissals automatically unfair. That is, The Labour Relations Act has isolated a number of reasons for dismissal as unjustifiable under any circumstances. For example, it is automatically unfair to dismiss an employee merely due to his or her race because such a dismissal is unjustifiable.

As this type of dismissal interferes with the employee's basic rights it is viewed as much more serious than other dismissals and the maximum compensation that a court may force the errant employer to pay is much higher than in cases of ordinary dismissals. For example, the maximum compensation for the unfair dismissal of an employee fired for theft is 12 months' remuneration while the maximum compensation for an automatically unfair dismissal is 24 months' remuneration. This chapter looks at some examples of automatically unfair dismissal and its consequences for the employers.

MANAGEMENT IS SICK OF ABSENTEEISM

It is cold and 'flu season and absenteeism is approaching epidemic proportions. The challenge for employers is to distinguish the genuine cases of illness from those where employees are just sick of working.

The Labour Relations Act (LRA) requires that employers may consider dismissing employees incapacitated by illness or injury only as a last resort. While every employer is expected to go the extra mile, the larger and stronger the employer is the more it will be expected to do to accommodate the employee. For example, in the case of *Standard Bank of SA v CCMA* (2008, 4 BLLR 356) the employee, after 15 years of loyal and exemplary service, was injured on duty. The damage to her back made it impossible for her to carry on with her normal duties. The employee was eventually dismissed for incapacity, but this was after a long period during which the employer made continued efforts to accommodate the employee, including the following:

- The bank got advice from a doctor on how to help the employee.
- It looked for and found a series of alternative positions for the employee.
- Even though the alternative posts were more junior than her original job the bank did not reduce the employee's pay
- When the employee was in pain her boss would send her home for the day
- The bank gave the employee three extra months' paid recuperation leave.

All of the above did not satisfy the Court because the employer had failed to:

- Act on the medical practitioner's recommendation to get advice from an occupational therapist on how to accommodate the employee
- Give the employee a telephone headset and a comfortable chair in order to assist her to work with less pain
- Allow the employee to do the job of entering computer data out of fear that her medication might interfere with her concentration
- Consider the employee's request to work half day
- Allow the employee to state a case before dismissing her
- Consult technical experts before taking the dismissal decision.

The Court concluded from the above that the employer had not really wanted to keep the employee in its employ. It was acknowledged that the employer had genuine problems in keeping the employee on in its employ because:

- The employee had been absent for 74 days in one year and 116 days in the following year
- The employee admitted that she struggled to cope with the alternative jobs
- The employee often needed to go home early due to pain.

Despite the above, the Court found that:

- The bank would have been able to accommodate the employee because the cost of doing so would have been affordable for the bank
- The employee's inability to cope with the new work was partly due to the employer's reluctance to give her headphones and a comfortable chair.

The Court therefore found that the dismissal was unfair and that the bank had discriminated unfairly against the employee. This outcome confirms that any employer in such a situation must:

- Try to change the physical work station of an injured employee if such injury interferes with the employee's ability to work
- Try to change the employee's tasks
- Consult with the employee on these matters before dismissing him/her
- Obtain and carry out the recommendations of medical experts unless it can prove that this is truly not viable
- Before deciding that nothing more can be done to save the employee's job, get advice from a reputable labour law expert.

EMPLOYEES WHO BLOW THE WHISTLE ARE PROTECTED

The Protected Disclosures Act no. 26 of 2000 (PDA) protects employees from reprisals as a result of having blown the whistle on the employer. This applies whether the disclosure in question is made to authorities within or outside of the company/organisation concerned.

Under the PDA both employees and employers are protected. That is, employees are protected from reprisals when making disclosures in good faith and employers are, to a limited extent, protected from employees who make unfounded and malicious disclosures. Therefore, while the PDA encourages genuine disclosures it requires the employee, when making an external disclosure, to at least hold a genuine belief that the employer has acted wrongly.

Whistle-blowing employees are also protected by sections 186(2)(d) and under section 187(1)(h) of the Labour Relations Act (LRA). The former section classifies as an "unfair labour practice" any employer conduct short of dismissal resulting in "an occupational detriment" to an employee who has made a protected disclosure as per the PDA. The maximum compensation awarded to an employee successful in such a claim would be 12 months' remuneration.

The latter section of the LRA makes it automatically unfair for an employer to dismiss an employee for having made a disclosure protected in terms of the PDA. While few such cases have been reported in labour law it appears that the courts are trying to look after the interests of both employers and employees.

In the case of *City of Tshwane Metropolitan Municipality v Engineering Council of SA & another* (2010, 3 BLLR 229) the municipality's management rejected the job applications of white applicants chosen by the municipality's selection panel. Management's rejection of the white applicants was on the grounds that the posts were to be given to black applicants despite the fact that those black people who applied all failed an approved test. The managing engineer objected to the management's decision to appoint the candidates who had failed the test and sent a letter to this effect to his superiors and then to the Department of Labour. He expressed his concern that the appointees who had failed were not qualified to do dangerous electrical work.

In response to this the management disciplined the managing engineer and found him guilty of distributing his objection letters without due permission. He applied to court for an interdict against any form of sanction being implemented by the municipality. The Supreme Court of Appeal later found that the employer was not entitled to discipline the employee who had blown the whistle and ordered the employer to pay the employee's legal costs.

In the case of *Jane Arbuthnot v SAMWU Provident Fund* (2011, case number JS575/09) the employee was found to have been dismissed by the fund for having disclosed to the trade union's National Benefits Officer the contents of a legal opinion document rendered by two advocates to the management of the fund. According to the case report the opinion advised the fund on the potential liability of its trustees flowing from the so called "Fidentia scandal". The fund had invested money in a trust that was controlled by Fidentia and had thus lost a great deal of money. The trust's beneficiaries were minors. According to the case report the employee interpreted the legal opinion to state that the trustees ought to have monitored the performance of the trust properly and that such failure amounts to breach of fiduciary duty of the trustees.

The fund alleged that the employee had made the disclosure in bad faith contrary to her fiduciary duty to the fund.

The Labour Court found that:

- A key reason for the dismissal was the applicant's disclosure to the union's benefits officer
- The employee had good reason to so disclose the document
- She did not do so for personal gain
- She believed the information to be substantially true
- The PDA cuts across the fiduciary duty of the employee making the disclosure
- The employee had the interests of the fund's beneficiaries at heart
- The employee's decision to disclose the opinion to the union was a reasonable one
- The disclosure was protected in terms of the PDA
- The dismissal was automatically unfair.

The Court therefore ordered the fund to pay the employee 12 months' remuneration amounting to over R 287 000.00 plus costs.

In view of the above employers are advised to tread very carefully before acting against any employee who makes allegations involving employer wrongdoing.

DISMISSING ALCOHOLICS/ ADDICTS CAN BE COSTLY

It is legally very dangerous for employers to discipline and fire employees who commit offences due to illness or disability. For example, an employee who uses alcohol or narcotics and becomes addicted is legally classified as being ill and is protected by law.

Section 6 of the Employment Equity Act prohibits unfair discrimination against employees on the grounds of disability or illness. This means that an employer may not discriminate against an employee merely due to the fact that the employee is disabled. In fact the same Act obliges employers to find ways of recruiting and seeking ways to accommodate people with disabilities.

Furthermore, section 187(1)(f) of the Labour Relations Act (LRA) says that, "A dismissal is automatically unfair if .... the reason for the dismissal is .... that the employer unfairly discriminated against an employee, directly or indirectly, on any arbitrary ground, including, but not limited to race, gender, sex, ethnic or social origin, colour, sexual orientation, age, disability, religion, conscience, belief, political opinion, culture, language, marital status or family responsibility."

The fact that disability is included in the above list means, for example, that if your receptionist loses an arm in an accident (whether work-related or not) you cannot terminate his/her employment because you believe that a disabled receptionist looks bad to customers who come to visit. You would have to prove that this receptionist is in fact unable to work before you could even consider terminating his/her employment.

In the case of *Black Mountain v CCMA and others* (2005 1 BLLR 0001) the employee was dismissed for causing damage while driving drunk. The CCMA arbitrator overturned the dismissal. The employer applied to the Labour Court for the arbitrator's decision to be reviewed. However, the Labour Court, after looking at the employer's policy in regard to alcohol-related infringements, decided that:

- The employee had been wrong in what he had done
- The employer should have allowed the employee to go for rehabilitation
- The dismissal was unfair
- The employer was required to reinstate the employee and to give him back pay for a period of 18 months
- The employer was to pay this money to the employee with interest.

In the case of *Mthethwa v Capitol Caterers* (2007, 5 BALR 469) the employee was dismissed after he was off ill from work for two weeks. The CCMA ordered the employer to reinstate him with full back pay because the employer had failed to follow the incapacity laws.

The above cases make it clear that, although employees can be dismissed for abusing sick leave, absence without permission and poor work performance:

- Sick employees are strongly protected from unfair treatment aimed at their disabilities
- Alcohol abuse can be seen as an illness in South African law
- Employers are legally required to adhere to their own policies
- Treatment must be considered before dismissal of a sick employee can be considered
- The incapacity procedure prescribed by law cannot be ignored.

Therefore all employers are advised to:

- Check with a labour law expert as to whether or not the circumstances merit dismissal
- Explore every alternative to dismissal before considering terminating the employment of a sick employee
- Genuinely and thoroughly involve the incapacitated employee in the process of consideration of alternatives, giving the employee ample opportunity to state his/her case
- Formally place on record every step taken in the above process
- Ensure that the entire process is planned and managed by an expert in labour law and industrial relations.

EMPLOYERS MUST CHANGE THEIR ATTITUDES TO GENDER REASSIGNMENT

Section 6(1) of the Employment Equity Act (EEA) prohibits employers from unfairly discriminating, directly or indirectly, against an employee on numerous grounds including gender and sex.

In my view gender discrimination occurs, for example, where the employer forces males to belong to a benefit scheme such as a medical aid but exempts females. A further example of gender discrimination would be where men are promoted into managerial positions at the expense of women who are suitable for the posts.

On the other hand "sex" discrimination may refer to the instance where, regardless of the employee's gender, the employer carries out an unacceptable sex-related act against him/her. For example, the employer may have harassed the employee sexually by grabbing his buttocks. If, for instance, the harasser and victim were both male there is clearly no gender discrimination but rather unfair behaviour relating to sex in the sense of sexual desire. Even if the employer and employee were of different genders the act is a sexual one and the gender of the parties becomes incidental. What is primary is that the employer infringed on the employee's right not to be touched in a sexual manner.

In the case of *Benjamin v University of Cape Town* (2003, 11 BLLR 1209) Mr Benjamin was turned down for a position of Senior Subject Librarian. However, the position was given to a woman. Benjamin alleged in the Labour Court that this amounted to unfair discrimination based on sex. However, in my view, this should have been a gender discrimination dispute because Benjamin did not allege that there was any sexually related behaviour. That is, his complaint revolved purely around the gender classification of the successful and unsuccessful job candidates.

Employers need to remember that sexual discrimination and sexual harassment are legally not confined to touching in a sexual way. Sexual harassment can be any sexually related act that is unwelcome in the eyes of the recipient such as the display of 'candid' posters, sexual internet visuals, dirty jokes, sex-related 'playfulness', crude language or even physically related compliments in the workplace.

Employers also need to remember that if they allow such incidents to occur, it is the employer (the company or organisation) and not the actual perpetrator who will land up in court. In the case of *Ntsabo v Real Security* that I mentioned in a previous article the Labour Court found that a sexually harassed employee had been unfairly discriminated against by her employer. This was not because the employer itself had sexually harassed the employee but because the employer did not take the necessary action to deal with the behaviour of the perpetrator. As the employer thereby infringed the provisions of section 60 of the Employment Equity Act the Court awarded substantial damages against the employer.

It is also possible that discrimination can take place that involves both sex and gender discrimination at the same time. For example, in a company where women are not promoted into management positions because of their gender the male MD may offer a female employee a promotion if she sleeps with him. Or he may refuse to consider her application because she has refused to sleep with him. This involves both a barrier against employees because they are women and sexually motivated behaviour prejudicial to the victim.

Another example of gender discrimination is highlighted in the case of *Atkins v Datacentrix (Pty) Ltd* (2010, 4 BLLR 351). Here the newly appointed employee was dismissed after informing the employer that he planned to undergo gender-reassignment surgery. The employer denied that the planned surgery was the reason for the dismissal and claimed that the employee's failure to disclose his plans prior to employment constituted misrepresentation meriting dismissal. The Court rejected this claim. It found that the employee had not been obliged to divulge his gender reassignment plans and that the principle reason for the dismissal was the employer's dislike of the planned gender reassignment. The dismissal was therefore automatically unfair and the Court ordered the employer to pay the employee R100 000 in compensation.

In the light of the above employers need to protect themselves by:

- Updating their attitudes and employment policies so as to focus on the employee's ability to do the job rather than on outdated concerns as to irrelevant characteristics of the employee. These policies also need to be designed to prevent sexual harassment
- Training management and employees in these revised policies.

CHAPTER CONCLUSION

It is clear from the above that the breaching by employers of the basic rights of employees is not tolerated in South Africa. The consequences of such employer breaches are often dire as regards the extremely high monetary cost thereof and as regards the employee relations fallout and reputational damage. Once the damage has been done it is immensely difficult to repair. As a result employers are advised to implement proactive measures so as to prevent such damage from occurring. These include clear, effective and legally compliant employment policies, thorough communication of these policies and, above all, intensive and ongoing training of management on the implementation policies designed to protect both the organisation and its employees.

CHAPTER 8

DISCIPLINE – HOW TO BALANCE LABOUR LAW COMPLIANCE WITH BEST PRACTICE

Every South African employer is forced to do a tough balancing act between trying to run a productive workplace on the one hand and having to comply with highly restrictive labour legislation on the other hand. Where we focus too much on worker productivity and good conduct we are in danger of losing sight of our labour law obligations. Where we are too intent on legal compliance productivity may suffer.

This chapter enables the reader to grasp key legal requirements as a means of avoiding over-interpretation of the law. It also identifies what employers can do in practice to achieve the right balance.

DON'T BYPASS YOUR OWN DISCIPLINARY POLICIES

Section 188 of the Labour Relations Act (LRA) gives the employer the onus of proving that it has been procedurally and substantively fair in dismissing employees. This forces employers to act with great care and expertise in gathering evidence and in designing and applying their disciplinary policies. The Labour Courts are most intolerant of employers who do not follow their own disciplinary policies and who cannot justify their dismissal decisions based on the facts of the case at hand.

No Labour Court decision illustrates these points better than the one delivered in *Riekert v CCMA and others* (2006, 4 BLLR 353). In that case Riekert was fired for having gained access to confidential information without authorisation and for undermining the good relations of company management. He took the employer to the CCMA but the arbitrator upheld his dismissal.

He therefore took the arbitrator on review to the Labour Court where the judge made the following findings:

- The CCMA arbitrator had recognised that the employer had a very extensive disciplinary code but had not adhered to it
- Since the employer's disciplinary code was incorporated in his employment contract the employee was entitled to insist that it be complied with
- Despite the above, the arbitrator found that the employer had complied with the basic requirements of natural justice and that disciplinary codes were mere guidelines
- While it is true that disciplinary codes are merely guidelines this does not entitle employers to deviate from procedures as they like
- It was unclear how the arbitrator arrived at the conclusion that the hearing was substantially fair since, contrary to the employer's own code, the chairperson of the hearing had neither kept any minutes of the proceedings nor provided any explanation for his decisions
- The employer had waited six months from the time it became aware of the misconduct before bringing the charges against the employee. This was despite the employer's own disciplinary code that required that charges be brought within a reasonable time
- The employee had been denied the opportunity to call witnesses
- The CCMA arbitrator had been wrong in accepting the employer's deviation from its own code in the absence of any compelling reason for such deviation
- No witnesses had been brought in respect of the charge of undermining good relations of company management and the arbitrator had heard nothing to provide any basis for that charge
- The arbitrator had not applied his mind to his decision that the employee was guilty of the charge of accessing confidential information without authority. The employer's witnesses were not even able to remember the date of the alleged incident
- The arbitrator's finding that the employee had not been frank in his testimony had been neither justified nor reasoned
- The arbitrator had failed to apply his mind to the evidence at all
- The arbitrator's award was set aside
- The dismissal was substantively and procedurally unfair
- The employer was ordered to pay the employee R100 000 in compensation plus interest
- The employer was to pay the employee's legal costs.

This case is of great importance as it provides employers with a number of extremely valuable lessons including that they should not:

- ignore their own disciplinary codes

- allow any unnecessary delays in notifying employees of disciplinary charges
- prevent an employee from bringing witnesses to his/her disciplinary hearing
- forget, before attending a disciplinary or arbitration hearing, to gather and prepare all evidence thoroughly.

POOR CONDUCT CAN MEAN POOR MANAGEMENT

Occasionally employees misbehave or misperform because they do not want to work and prefer to get fired. However, in my experience this is more the exception than the rule. More often, consistent poor conduct or poor performance reflects a management that is either underskilled or unwilling to manage employee conduct. As a result we may well find that employees:

- Spend hours chatting on the phone
- Fail to work according to quality standards
- Do private chores during working hours
- Refuse to carry out instructions
- Fail to check their work
- Abuse sick leave
- Have no pride in their work
- Misuse the internet
- Send private e-mails during working time
- Steal from the employer
- Get into fights
- Miss deadlines
- Waste production materials
- Arrive for work late, take long lunch hours and go home early.

It is not necessarily the manager's fault that employees want to misbehave or to slack off. Laziness, disinterest or lack of caring can be due to the employee's own character. However, where this is so, it is up to the manager to implement corrective measures that must either change the employee's behaviour or, where this has been properly tried and failed, result in possible dismissal. That is, every manager and supervisor must know how to:

- Quickly recognise rebellious or demotivated employees
- Engage with them in such a way that they are quickly aware that their behaviour will not be tolerated

- Guide wayward employees along the correct path
- Institute swift, timely, firm and appropriate disciplinary action that is not only effective but is also seen as fair by the CCMA or bargaining council.

Many managers are unable to deal with errant employees effectively and just as many are unable to discipline employees within the bounds of the law. This results in employees getting away with serious misconduct which is badly damaging to the employer. For example, in the case of *Faltyn v Buffalo Flats Community Development Trust* (2005, 2 BALR 183) Faltyn was dismissed for losing cash belonging to the employer. The employee alleged that the cash had been stolen from him. He had collected the cash the previous day and, instead of handing it in as he was supposed to have done, he had kept the cash with him. He had left work early without permission to do a personal errand and had been mugged the following morning on the way to work while he still had the cash in his possession.

The CCMA arbitrator accepted that:

- The employee could have handed in the money on the day it had been collected
- The employee should have spoken to his employer about his personal problem requiring him to leave work early
- The employee deserved to be dismissed.

Despite this the arbitrator ordered the employer to pay the employee financial compensation. This was because the same manager who had decided to charge the employee also presided over the disciplinary hearing. The fact that the manager had made the decision to charge Faltyn meant that the manager would have had knowledge of the incident prior to the hearing. For the same manager to then preside over the hearing rendered him a potentially biased chairperson because his prior knowledge of the incident could have influenced his judgement.

This is one of thousands of cases where such a technical error on the part of a manager has cost the employer money and has benefited an employee who was clearly guilty and deserving of dismissal. Often, this kind of error is the fault of the manager because the manager should have known better. However, more often than not it is the fault of the manager's employer for having failed to:

- Train the manager in the requirements of labour law
- Give the manager access to labour law experts who could advise the manager on how to deal with the case in question.

INVESTIGATING MISCONDUCT IS A MUST

Most managers are busy people and therefore claim nor to have time to investigate reports of misconduct or poor performance. It is often for this reason that managers may implement discipline hastily without first investigating the validity of the reports. This may occur due to feelings of anger or to ignorance of the labour law pertaining to disciplinary process. Investigation of misconduct allegations is a crucial step in legally acceptable disciplinary action and cannot be bypassed.

In the case of *Ngake v Incredible Connection (Pty) Ltd* (2011, 2 BALR 202) the employee was dismissed for dishonesty due to the loss of a great deal of stock. At the CCMA the arbitrator found that the employee had not been proven guilty of dishonesty and should not have been fired on such grounds. However, the arbitrator accepted that the employee's conduct had made continued employment intolerable because the substantial stock losses were due to her unacceptable failure to perform her work properly. Despite this, the arbitrator ordered the employer to pay the employee financial compensation because it had failed to investigate the cause of the stock losses despite the legal obligation to do so. Had the employer conducted a thorough investigation it would have been able to show either that the stock losses were due to the employee's poor work performance or that, contrary to the arbitrator's finding, the employee had in fact been dishonest.

The investigator should ideally be, but does not have to be, the same person who is going to present the case for the employer at the disciplinary hearing. (This person is normally known as the 'complainant' or 'initiator'.)

What is the purpose of investigation?

Investigation is an exercise designed to test allegations or suspicions, to find out what really happened and to establish whether there are grounds for disciplinary action. If the investigation shows that there probably was serious wrongdoing the evidence gathered will also be used to prepare and present the case against the employee at a disciplinary hearing.

How long should the investigation last?

There is no specified time period for completion of an investigation. However, the investigation must commence without delay and must only be halted when the investigator is fully satisfied that no stone has been left unturned. The length of the investigation depends on the nature of the case, the amount of evidence and the availability of witnesses and other evidence. Typically, a good investigator will find that the more evidence he/she uncovers, the more leads there are. It is only when this process of following all lines of inquiry has been exhausted that the investigation can be halted.

Must the employee know of the investigation?

It is not a standard legal requirement that employees be informed that there is an investigation on the go. This is more particularly so if:

- an issue, and not a person, is being investigated; or
- informing the suspect could genuinely enable him/her to interfere with and jeopardise the investigation.

Nevertheless, employers should be very careful about interfering with the employee's right to privacy. This is especially so where the investigation probes the employee's private life instead of workplace matters.

Suspension during investigations

The employer should only consider suspension if there is a real danger in keeping the employee on the premises. Any such suspension must be with pay, in writing and must make clear that it is only a temporary measure.

What makes a good investigator?

Concluding an investigation that optimises the chances of a successful disciplinary hearing requires a great deal of skill. Investigators need to know how to:

- Identify relevant witnesses, documents and other evidence
- Engage with witnesses so as to elicit the true and complete facts
- Recognise a new lead when it arises
- Keep within the laws limiting the rights of an investigator
- Put all the facts gathered into a clear and comprehensive report
- Question suspects without letting on that they are suspects.

DON'T DELAY IN DISCIPLINING EMPLOYEES

Sex-related acts are not always sexual harassment.

In the case of *Maepe v Commission for Conciliation, Mediation and Arbitration & another* (CLL Vol. 17 June 2008) a senior commissioner at the CCMA was brought to a disciplinary hearing on charges of sexual harassment and improper or disgraceful conduct. A CCMA receptionist had accused the senior commissioner of having professed his love for her, blown her kisses and told her that he clutched her photo to his chest.

The disciplinary hearing was chaired by another senior commissioner who dismissed the accused commissioner who then referred an unfair dismissal dispute to the CCMA. The arbitrator found that the employee's conduct did not constitute sexual harassment because the receptionist had not indicated that the employee's advances towards her were unwelcome and because the employee might not have realised that his actions were unwelcome. While the arbitrator found that the employee was guilty of making inappropriate sexual advances he replaced the dismissal with a final warning. This was despite having found the employee to have lied under oath at the hearing.

The CCMA, in its capacity as employer, applied to the Labour Court on review. The Court duly overturned the arbitrator's decision. On appeal the Labour Appeal Court (LAC) decided that the dismissal had been unfair but agreed with the employer that reinstatement was inappropriate because a commissioner who cannot respect the oath when he testifies cannot be allowed to continue in a job where he administers the oath to others.

The LAC found the dismissal to be unfair because there was no evidence that the employment relationship had either been materially damaged or had become intolerable. On the contrary, the employer had allowed the employee to continue working for five months after his conduct had been reported.

The LAC's decision is confusing. It agreed that the employee had been guilty of inappropriate behaviour towards the receptionist. It also agreed that, because of the fact that the employee had lied under oath, he should not be allowed to continue in his job. This being so, why was the dismissal unfair? Did the Court expect the employer to find a different post for the employee that did not involve administering the oath? Had the employer attempted to find such an alternative vacancy without success, would the dismissal then have been fair?

The outcome of this case is a lesson to all employers not to delay the implementation of the discipline of an employee for too long because this can result in the CCMA or a court deciding that the employment relationship has not been irrevocably destroyed and that the dismissal is therefore unfair. Item 3(4) of the Code of Good Practice: Dismissal in Schedule 8 of the LRA states that: "Generally, it is not appropriate to dismiss an employee for a first offence, except if the misconduct is serious and of such gravity that it makes a continued employment relationship intolerable." The item gives a few examples of serious misconduct including gross dishonesty, wilful endangering of the safety of others, wilful damage to the property of the employer, physical assault on the employer, fellow employee or client, and gross insubordination.

The CCMA arbitrator and later the LAC appear to have taken this item of the Code into account in deciding that the misconduct was not serious enough to destroy the employment relationship and to merit dismissal.

In the light of the above employers should:

- If they believe that the misconduct does merit dismissal, be able to prove that the employee has made the continued employment relationship intolerable by his/her actions
- Inform themselves as to how to prove that a particular act of misconduct does merit dismissal before deciding to dismiss the employee
- Not assume that every sexual act constitutes sexual harassment or that every perpetrator of such acts automatically deserves dismissal
- Understand that they not only have the legal duty, under the Employment Equity Act (EEA), to protect their employees from sexual harassment, but they also have, under the LRA, the duty to protect alleged perpetrators from unfair discipline.

This is a difficult and dangerous tightrope to walk. Employers should therefore get advice from a reputable labour law expert in order to decide how to deal with such matters. This will help avoid the employer falling off the tightrope hung between the EEA and the LRA.

If CCMA commissioners cannot agree amongst themselves as to what is and is not fair, then lay employers and managers cannot expect to be able to make such judgements on their own. One factor that could possibly have affected the judgment of the CCMA in the Maepe case is that the CCMA, as employer, may have been too close to the case to be able to come to a consistent decision. Employers should therefore realise that the use of an external expert is important in ensuring that a proper legal and objective decision is taken.

UNFAIR DISCIPLINE CAN CAUSE CONSTRUCTIVE DISMISSAL

Constructive dismissal means that the employee resigns and claims that the resignation occurred not because the employee wanted to leave but as a result of the employer's intolerable conduct.

Due to the fact that the employee alleges that the resignation was involuntary and was intentionally or unintentionally coerced by the employer, the resignation becomes a constructive dismissal. It is possible that this terminology originated from the idea that such a resignation submitted under duress can be seen to have been 'constructed' or 'created' by the employer.

In order to convince an arbitrator or judge that unfair constructive dismissal has in fact taken place the employee must show that:

1. The employment circumstances are so intolerable that the employee could truly not continue to stay on

2. The unbearable circumstances were the cause of the resignation of the employee

3. There was no reasonable alternative at the time but for the employee to resign in order to escape the circumstances

4. The unbearable situation must have been caused by the employer

5. The employer must have been in control of the unbearable circumstances.

The labour law on constructive dismissal was born out of case law and was later codified in the Labour Relations Act No. 66 of 1995 (LRA). Section 186(1)(e) includes in the definition of dismissal the situation where "...an employee terminated a contract of employment with or without notice because the employer made continued employment intolerable for the employee".

It must be stressed that questionable acts of the employer will not always constitute unfair constructive dismissal. This will depend on the extent to which the employer's conduct falls within the five tests for constructive dismissal outlined earlier in this chapter.

However, employers need to be careful in interpreting the meaning of these five tests. For example, test number 3, where the employee must show that he had no reasonable alternative but to resign must not be simplistically interpreted. For instance, it is often the case that the employee theoretically has the option of remaining in the employment relationship and referring an unfair labour practice to the CCMA or other tribunal. Where the employee fails to do so and resigns instead, this will not always mean that he has failed test number 3. Passing this test will depend a great deal on whether, under the circumstances at the time, the employee could reasonably have been expected to stay on in the employer's employ for purposes of referring the unfair labour practice dispute. Truly unendurable circumstances would make such a route unreasonable.

Employees must be equally careful not to misinterpret the law. Where, for example, an employer notifies an employee of a disciplinary hearing, this could genuinely be seen as unbearable to the employee. However, a resignation by the employee for purposes of avoiding the disciplinary hearing is unlikely to constitute unfair constructive dismissal. For example, in the case of *Mvamelo v AMG Engineeering* (2003, 11 BALR 1294) the employee was informed that he was to be called to a disciplinary hearing for theft and that criminal charges would also be laid. He resigned and claimed constructive dismissal but lost the case because it was found by the arbitrator that he had resigned to avoid the disciplinary steps of which he had been notified.

However, where disciplinary steps have been taken unfairly and this renders the employment circumstances intolerable this can constitute constructive dismissal. For example, in the case of *Solidarity obo Van Der Berg v first Office Equipment (Pty) Ltd* (2009, 4 BALR 406) the employee was found to have been performing his work poorly. As a result the employer decided to stop paying him his salary and replaced it with a commission structure. The employee resigned and went to the CCMA where it was found that the employee had been a victim of unfair constructive dismissal. This was because the employee could not be expected to continue employment under such intolerable circumstances.

Employers need to be extremely careful that they do not discipline employees unfairly. Otherwise the employer might have to pay tens of thousands of rands in compensation and legal costs.

THE VALIDITY OF PRIOR
WARNINGS IS A VEXED ISSUE

A disciplinary warning is an oral or written statement made by an employer informing the employee that his/her conduct or performance level is not acceptable and that any further failure to meet the required standards will result in stronger measures being taken. In this sense a warning is not a punishment. Instead it is a notification that punishment or other corrective measures could follow.

The giving of a warning is appropriate when it has been established that a less serious offence (one with relatively mild potential consequences) is committed. The level of warning (oral, written or final warning) to be used depends on the level of seriousness of the offence and on whether previous valid warnings have been given.

Where the offence is very mild a counselling session may be better than a warning. For example, if an employee is five minutes late for work for the first time a mild rebuke or counselling session will suffice and is less time consuming for the employer.

Where an offence is very serious or a final warning has already been given, then in some cases, a warning is unlikely to have the desired effect, and stronger discipline may be appropriate.

Is the employer entitled to combine a warning with other measures?

The LRA is silent on this question. It would be unfair to punish an employee twice for the very same offence (i.e. for the same incident). However, as a warning is not, in my view, a punishment it can be argued that a warning could fairly accompany another corrective measure. For example, where a driver is guilty of damaging the employer's vehicle it may be appropriate for the employer to give the driver a refresher driving course but also to warn him/her that, should he/she again damage employer property, stronger action will be taken.

Can an employee be dismissed for a repeat offence after having received a final warning for a similar offence?

The answer to this question is 'yes' provided that:

- there is no reasonable alternative corrective action to the dismissal; and
- the final warning is valid.

When is a final warning valid in terms of being usable in justifying a subsequent dismissal?

There is a point of view that a disputed final warning cannot be used as an aggravating circumstance to justify a subsequent dismissal. This view is linked to the notion that the employee, when disputing the dismissal can, at the same time, dispute the validity of the final warning that motivated the dismissal. However, I am of the alternative view that should the employee wish to dispute a final warning, he/she can only do so within 90 days of having received that warning. To be allowed to raise it later at the unfair dismissal arbitration stage is to me unfair unless condonation for the lateness of disputing the warning has been properly applied for and has been granted.

However, the employee would have the right to argue at any stage that the final warning was invalid if the warning had passed its expiry date by the time the subsequent incident of misconduct took place. In the case of *NUMSA and Others v Atlantis Forge (Pty) Ltd* (2005, 12 BLLR 1238) the employer dismissed a group of employees who had embarked on an unprotected strike. The dismissal was based largely on the fact that the employees had previously received a final warning for similar behaviour. However, the Labour Court reinstated the dismissed strikers because the final warnings in question had expired by the time the employees committed the second offence. In this case the employer's policy was for expired warnings not to be taken into account.

In *Numsa obo Ngwenya v KZN Motors* (2011, BALR) the commissioner found that, where the employer's policy does not require expired warnings to be removed from the employee's record or to be expunged, lapsed warnings may be taken into account when the offence is repeated.

This is a strange finding because it nullifies the purpose of the requirement for warnings to lapse which is to provide the employee with a clean slate. As a result I suspect that the decision could be overruled in future case decisions.

In *NUMSA obo Mabuslea v Premfit Engineering cc* (2011, 7 BALR 733) the commissioner stated that it is accepted that a previous warning can only be taken into account if it is for an offence similar to the one that the employee is currently being disciplined for. This view appears to be shared by most commissioners. But, as the LRA does not deal with this issue, it leaves scope for arbitrators to reach their own conclusions. Employers should ensure that previous warnings are similar enough in nature to validate them for use in the current case.

FAULTY SUSPENSIONS CAN HANG EMPLOYERS

It is very dangerous for employers to confuse suspension with dismissal. While a dismissal is a permanent termination of the person's employment, suspension is merely a temporary halt on the employee's right to provide services to the employer. Suspensions are carried out in a variety of forms and circumstances including:

1. One form of suspension is a temporary layoff of employees due to operational circumstances. For example, an employer may find itself with little or no work for its employees but may be unable to afford to pay its employees indefinitely without revenue coming in. The employer may, in such circumstances, give the employees a section 189 notification of possible retrenchment. Then, during the retrenchment consultations, either party may suggest temporary layoffs as an alternative to retrenchment. This might be implemented where the employees agree to the layoffs and there is some hope of more work and revenue being acquired in the future. In such circumstances the employees would not be paid but would still be employees of the employer.

2. Employers must be careful not to hire new employees in place of employees who have been laid off as this would indicate that there had been no good reason for the layoffs and the employer could well be forced to pay the employees for the layoff period. Where there is a large number of workers or where the layoff period is a long one this payment could come to an extremely high amount.

3. The employer's intention behind a suspension may be to make the employee's working circumstances so uncomfortable that he/she resigns. This motive is both illegitimate and dangerous. Employees sometimes resign on being suspended and charge the employer at the CCMA with constructive dismissal. However, the employee will not easily succeed with such a charge because such an employee is obliged to go through the disciplinary process rather than resign. Should the employee claim at arbitration that the suspension was a sham on the employer's part, the employer must be given the opportunity to show that it had good reason to suspend the employee and that there was some basis for the suspicion of misconduct.

4. The employer may need to investigate serious allegations made against the employee. Where the employee is in a position of official or unofficial power the suspension may be necessary in order to ensure that his/her presence at the workplace will not interfere with the investigation. This is a legitimate reason for suspension but the employee must be on full pay during the suspension period. The employer must be

sure not to breach a contractual right of the employee otherwise a civil suit could result. For example, where the employment contract or another contract provides that the employer must provide the employee with training and the suspension materially interferes with such training this could constitute a breach of contract.

5. The employer may have a need to avert the danger of the employee repeating the alleged offence. For example, if the employee is suspected of assaulting a colleague, a suspension may be merited to avert the possibility of a repeat assault. Again, the employee must be on full pay during the suspension period and the danger in question must be real.

6. Punishment of the employee by the employer. Here, the employee is normally suspended without pay. However, such suspensions are often illegitimate. This is because:

   - Cutting an employee's pay may breach the provisions of the Basic Conditions of Employment Act (BCEA)
   - The employer may have no fair reason for punishing the employee and withholding his/her pay. Such suspensions are too often implemented while the employer is in a fit of rage.

The dangers for the employer are that the employee could challenge the fairness of the suspension itself or could take the eviction as a dismissal and take the employer to the CCMA or bargaining council on this basis.

Suspension without pay may, in certain circumstances, be legitimate. This might be, for example, where the employee already has a final warning for the same type of offence but the employer does not necessarily wish to dismiss the employee. Should the employer approach this situation in the right way it may be able give the employee a choice of dismissal or an agreed suspension without pay for a limited period (preferably not more than two weeks).

In the case of *Mabitsela v SAPS* (2004, 8 BALR 969) a policeman was suspended without pay pending a charge of murder. The police regulations do allow for such suspensions to be without pay. The arbitrator found that it had been unfair to implement the suspension without pay.

This case shows that, even where regulations allow employers to suspend employees without pay this may still be found to be unfair under the circumstances. If a suspected murderer can win such a case it would be even easier for employees who have committed lesser offences to win their cases.

CHAPTER CONCLUSION

The law allows employers to discipline employees. It could even be argued that the law encourages such discipline. However, this should be seen in context from two points of view. Firstly, the law sees discipline not as synonymous with punishment or retribution but rather as a measure for correcting bad behaviour, as a means for teaching employees the right way. This is so that stronger corrective measures such as dismissal become unnecessary. Secondly, employers need to focus on the long-term goal of developing employees to be able and willing to take care of their own self-discipline. This will free the employer from much of the hassle of disciplinary action and will also promote the dignity of each employee who can avoid the humiliation of being disciplined.

*Correcting bad behaviour makes stronger corrective
measures such as dismissal unnecessary*

Dismissal procedure

CHAPTER 9

UNDERSTANDING WHAT FAIR DISMISSAL PROCEDURE IS

Even where an employer convinces an arbitrator that the employee fully deserved to be dismissed the employer can still lose the case and be forced to pay the employee compensation for unfair dismissal. This is simply because the law requires employers to follow a number of procedural requirements. Where the employer fails to meet these requirements it may be penalised. For example, where an employer fires an employee caught red-handed stealing money but fails to give the employee a chance to present a defence, an arbitrator can order the employer to compensate the guilty employee due to procedural unfairness.

This chapter highlights key procedural requirements and the consequences of ignoring them.

WHEN IS A FORMAL DISCIPLINARY HEARING NECESSARY?

The Labour Relations Act, via its Code of Good Practice: Dismissal, makes it clear that, while the disciplinary process can, under certain circumstances, be informal, the employee should nevertheless be told what case he has to meet and be given a proper opportunity to prepare and present his response.

While it is clear that the above-mentioned Code of Good Practice provides that the disciplinary hearing need not be formal section 188(1)(b) of the Labour Relations Act (LRA) requires that the employer has the onus of proving that a dismissal was procedurally fair. The key question is: How can the employer go about proving that the dismissal was procedurally fair without using formal processes to ensure fairness and to demonstrate that the procedure was indeed fair? For example, The Code of Good Practice does accord the employee the following procedural rights:

- The right to be informed as to what the charges are – proof would be a written charge sheet, receipt of which has been signed by the accused employee
- The right to a proper opportunity to prepare – proof would be a written notice of hearing, given to the employee well in advance of the hearing, receipt of which has been signed by the accused employee well in advance of the hearing date
- The employee's right to be heard and to present a defence – proof would be minutes of the hearing showing that the employee had a chance to state his case, use an interpreter and representative, bring witnesses and cross-examine evidence brought against him/her.

Consequently, once one introduces the use of records such as minutes, hearing notices and charge sheets, one is converting the disciplinary process into a formal one. In my view this conversion is reinforced by the need to separate the complainant role from the presiding officer role in order to eliminate bias.

However, it appears that my view is in conflict with that of one Labour Court Judge. In the case of *Avril Elizabeth Home for the Mentally Handicapped v CCMA and others* (2006, 9 BLLR 833) the finding of the Court suggests that avoiding of bias at a disciplinary hearing is not a requirement. Other findings that came out of this case are as follows:

- Video coverage does not have to be absolutely conclusive to be accepted; it need only satisfy the balance of probabilities requirement
- The procedure bringing about a dismissal does not have to be a formal enquiry unless the parties have agreed that it will be a formal hearing.

I am in agreement with the honourable Court as regards the principle of balance of probabilities and as to the fact that The Code of Good Practice does not require a formal hearing. I have, however, explained why, in practice, it is very difficult for an employer to comply with the requirements of The Code of Good Practice without using the mechanisms of a formal process. This is necessary, not because the Code says so (which it does not) but rather to make sure that the employer can satisfy its onus of proving that it has complied with the content and spirit of that Code.

As regards the apparent finding that an unbiased chairperson is not necessary at a disciplinary hearing I respectfully believe that, if the Court really meant to say this, its decision cannot be correct and will be overturned sooner rather than later. I would prefer to believe that the Court only meant that the test for bias of the chairperson should not be as stringent as that applied in criminal law.

My view is based on the fact that The Code of Good Practice requires that the employee is afforded the opportunity to present his/her case, and the central core of labour law requires fairness. I submit that no employee can present his/her case fairly before a biased chairperson. To allow biased chairpersons to chair internal disciplinary hearings and then dismiss employees would make a mockery of such hearings. The employee would lose his job and livelihood unfairly and could then lose his/her house, car and other assets while he/she is waiting for the labour law process at CCMA and Labour Court to take its course. Allowing such a situation would be akin to allowing a kangaroo court.

In summary, the employer's onus to prove that all the employee's rights have been complied with makes a formal and expertly controlled disciplinary hearing essential in my view. This holds true even if the only procedural rights an employee has are those few specifically provided for in The Code of Good Practice.

While the officials who carry out the corrective procedure do not need to be lawyers they do need to be well skilled in disciplinary procedure in order to make sure that each and every legal right of the employee is strictly adhered to.

Therefore, managers must either be thoroughly trained in disciplinary process or the employer must hire a reputable labour law expert to chair its hearings.

PRESIDING OFFICERS MUST BE UNBIASED

Hearing chairpersons should not count their chickens before they hatch.

Employers too often get rid of employees for reasons unacceptable in law. Some of these reasons include:

- The employer dislikes the employee for reasons unrelated to the workplace
- The owner wants a more attractive secretary
- The employee is unwilling to grant her superior sexual favours
- The employee has clashed with a key executive who has threatened to resign
- The employee has reported the employer to SARS, the Department of Labour or Department of Health for violating the law
- The manager is under pressure to perform and uses the dismissed employee as the scapegoat for performance problems
- The employer feels that it is time that it shows the workers who is boss and picks on the first employee who makes a mistake

- The shop steward stands up for the employee's rights and is labelled as a troublemaker.

Employers then conspire to get rid of such undesirables through the use of a number of tricks including:

- Firing the employee orally and then pretending that the employee absconded
- Framing the employee for poor performance or misconduct
- Provoking the employee into committing misconduct
- Setting up a disciplinary hearing where the presiding officer has been primed in advance to fire the employee.

This latter trick clearly renders the presiding officer biased. This constitutes a serious breach of the employee's right to fair procedure. Where the employer is caught out using such a biased presiding officer the CCMA has no mercy. The employee is likely to be reinstated with full back pay or to be granted heavy compensation to be paid by the employer.

Such bias on the part of a disciplinary hearing chairperson can be discovered in a number of ways including:

- The chairperson grants the complainant (person bringing the case for the employer) the opportunity to obtain more evidence, take adjournments or interrupt the employee, but does not grant the employee similar rights
- The presiding officer ignores evidence brought by the employee
- The chairperson is chosen to hear the matter despite having been the one who caught the employee breaking the rule. In the case of *FAWU obo Sotyatu v JH Group Retail Trust* (2001, 8 BALR 864) the arbitrator found that the manager who chaired the disciplinary hearing had been the one who had apprehended the employee. This was found to indicate bias and was unfair. The employee was reinstated with full back pay
- The chairperson says things early in the hearing that indicate that he/she has decided in advance that the employee is guilty.

For example, in the case of *Fourie & Partners Attorneys obo Mahlubandile v Robben Marine cc* (2006, 6 BALR 569) the employee was dismissed for attempting to remove several frozen chickens that he had hidden in a bucket. The arbitrator accepted that the employee was guilty of the offence but still found the dismissal to be unfair. This was primarily because the chairperson of the disciplinary hearing had revealed his bias by asking the employee at the beginning of the hearing, "Do you have an excuse for stealing the chickens?"

The fact that arbitrators do not hesitate to punish biased or inept presiding officers means that employers should:

- resist the temptation to 'fix' the outcome of disciplinary hearings in advance
- avoid misusing disciplinary processes to pursue private agendas
- ensure that only impartial and properly trained persons chair disciplinary hearings.

LAWYERS MAY BE ALLOWED AT DISCIPLINARY HEARINGS

Employers have normally disallowed external legal representatives to represent accused employees at disciplinary hearings. This is mainly due to the provisions of Schedule 8 of the Labour Relations Act (LRA) which states that, when an enquiry is held into an employee's alleged misconduct "The employee should be allowed ...... the assistance of a trade union representative or fellow employee."

However, case law seems to have shifted these goalposts. In the case of *MEC: Department of Finance, Economic Affairs and Tourism: Northern Province v Schoon Godwilly Mahumani* (Case number 478/03 SCA. Report by Dr Elize Strydom distributed 30 January 2005) the employee was refused the right to an external legal representative.

The employee went to the High Court to dispute this ruling. The court found that the ruling of the presiding officer of the disciplinary enquiry was wrong and ordered that the employee be allowed to have legal representation at the disciplinary hearing.

The employer appealed against this judgment to the Supreme Court of appeal which decided that the accused employee at a disciplinary enquiry, could, under certain circumstances, be entitled to be represented by a legal representative at a disciplinary hearing. This court found that clause 2.8 of the employer's disciplinary code labelled the code as a guideline that may be departed from under appropriate circumstances. This gave presiding officers the right to use their discretion in deciding whether to depart from the prohibition on legal representation.

In the case of *Molope v Mbha* (2005, 3 BLLR 267) an area manager was dismissed for unauthorised use of funds and was brought to a disciplinary hearing. The accused employee chose a colleague to represent her but, shortly before the disciplinary hearing, this colleague decided not to represent Mbha. The employee therefore applied for a postponement in order to obtain another representative but the employer refused. The hearing continued and the employee was dismissed. The CCMA found the dismissal to be fair in all respects. However, while the Labour Court agreed that the dismissal was substantively fair, it found the dismissal to be procedurally unfair. This was because the employer had refused to postpone the hearing. The Court also said that "it is now established that one of the requirements of a procedurally fair hearing embraces the entitlement of an employee to be represented thereat by a co-employee or a trade union official or a lawyer". This last finding appears, at first glance, to mean that employees at disciplinary hearings are automatically entitled to representation by outside parties such as union officials and lawyers. However, on closer scrutiny, this might not be what the Court was saying. The Court said that such representation was a right that employees must be given at "hearings". The Court did not say 'disciplinary hearings'. Thus it is therefore possible that the Court was referring to hearings in general and included hearings at the workplace, at CCMA and at court. Should this have been the Labour Court's intention then legal representation at internal disciplinary hearings need not be seen as an automatic right.

However, it is not clear what the Court in the Molope case meant and the Mahumani decision still exists. Employers are therefore advised, when receiving applications for external representation, to consider whether:

- The complexity level of the case is high
- The consequences of an adverse finding could be serious
- There would be no significant prejudice to the employer if legal representation would be allowed
- The employee's ability to deal with the case is low in comparison to that of the employer.

The above case findings have major consequences for employers engaging in disciplinary hearings. In particular:

- An employee's request for legal representation can no longer be dismissed out of hand. While such requests must not always be granted, they must be given very careful consideration
- This in turn means that employers will need to ensure that their presiding officers are highly skilled in chairing disciplinary hearings. This is so as to be able to make the right judgement as to whether to allow legal representation or not and also to be able to deal with the legal challenges posed by attorneys and advocates at disciplinary hearings
- Managers must be thoroughly trained in disciplinary process and the employer must use genuine labour law experts to chair and/or prosecute hearings.

DOUBLE JEOPARDY MEANS DOUBLE WHAMMY FOR EMPLOYERS

Double jeopardy occurs where an employee is disciplined twice for the very same offence. Under exceptional circumstances a second disciplinary process for the very same incident of misconduct might be justified if the employer is able to present evidence that:

- is new and has therefore not been presented at the first disciplinary hearing; and
- is relevant to the charges; and
- is significant enough to merit a new hearing; and
- the first sanction imposed was grossly unfair under the circumstances.

However, even these factors are not properly interpreted and applied by employers who continue to:

- Give employees warnings and dismissals at the same time
- Reopen cases that should be left alone
- Set up new disciplinary hearings without good reason after the employee has already been disciplined for the offence
- Open new hearings with newly formulated charges that are merely a different way of wording the same charge in respect of which the employee managed to avoid dismissal.

Some case law may serve as a timely warning to employers to proceed with extreme care in these matters.

In the case of *Constant Pretorius v the SA Bureau of Standards (SABS)* (*The Star*, 29 October 2003) it was reported that the SABS dismissed Pretorius for the illegal sale of crash-test bodies. But it appears from the report that he had already been given a 12-month final written warning for this very offence in August 2002.

It should be understood that the dismissal may well have been legally acceptable had Pretorius received a final warning for the illegal sale and thereafter committed another similar offence within the 12-month period during which the warning was valid. Then, had he been found guilty at a new disciplinary hearing, a dismissal for the second offence could have been within the bounds of the law.

In the case of *Rakgolela v Trade Centre* (2005, 3 BALR 353) the employee was dismissed for misappropriation and misuse of a company cell phone. He lodged an internal appeal in terms of the employers appeal policy. On appeal the dismissal was overturned and replaced with a final warning. The employer then charged the employee again for the same incident of taking the cell phone and added a new charge of telling lies during the original hearing.

After the employee's original dismissal had been overturned on appeal the police reported that the employee had lied about not having taken the cell phone home. The employer used this report as ammunition to recharge the employee and fire him a second time. However, the fact that the employee had lied had already been established by the appeal chairperson. The CCMA therefore found that there had been no new evidence justifying the second hearing and dismissal.

The CCMA found that the employee had been the victim of double jeopardy as he had been disciplined twice for the same misconduct. The employer was ordered to pay the employee 12 months' remuneration in compensation for the unfair dismissal.

In *Marebati and another v South African Police Service* [2014] 11 BALR 1075 (SSSBC) two police constables received final warnings for assaulting a journalist. Later they were dismissed, allegedly for a different offence. The arbitrator found that the dismissal was essentially for the same offence and ordered that the constables be reinstated retrospectively. This means that the employer had to bear the unpleasantness of taking the employees back and bear the cost of the back pay of the employees.

Where double jeopardy occurs it is often because the employer needs to get the employees out by hook or by crook. This could be due to a personality clash, to the fact that the employees are considered to be a troublemakers or simply because the employer has genuinely lost trust in the employees.

Whatever the reason the employer is neither free to act on it before ensuring that the dismissal would be fair; nor can the employer dismiss employees for reasons that the employer feels are fair. What is fair or not is determined by:

- the legal provisions of the Labour Relations Act (LRA);
- complex principles of fairness emanating from case law;
- the factual circumstances of each individual case; and
- how the CCMA or bargaining council is likely to react to the case.

The lay employer will not easily be able to assess his/her case against these four factors. This is because:

- The employer is often too emotionally embroiled in the case
- He/she might not have the legal knowledge and analytical ability necessary to assess the merits of the case accurately and objectively.

CHAPTER CONCLUSION

Of the two types of fair dismissal that an employer is required by law to prove procedural fairness is by far the easiest to prove. This is because, once the employer has codified its disciplinary procedures in line with legal requirements, it is merely a matter of ensuring that management follows the laid-down procedural rules to the letter.

There is no doubt that such slavish adherence to procedural rules can be onerous but this will never be as onerous as having to clean up the mess when unprocedural management behaviour is punished at the CCMA, bargaining council or Labour Court.

Unprocedural management behaviour

What is a fair reason for dismissal?

CHAPTER 10

WHAT IS A FAIR REASON FOR DISMISSAL UNDER THE LAW?

The previous chapter explained that employers must afford employees their procedural rights so that the process leading towards dismissal properly enables the accused to have a fair hearing. This chapter highlights where employers go wrong in arriving at the decision to dismiss their employees. That is, the law of substantive fairness requires that, in order for a dismissal to be fair the employer must have a reason that is appropriate under the circumstances of the case.

WHEN IS DISMISSAL FAIR?

Case law reveals countless reasons given by CCMA arbitrators for an employer's dismissal decision to be deemed unfair.

For example, in the case of *Moloi v Quithing Construction and Developers CK* (2007, 8 BALR 720) the accused was given a final warning after he had been repeatedly late for work. When he refused to sign for receipt of the warning the employer dismissed him for his negative attitude. The CCMA found that the dismissal was unfair because the employer had failed to give the employee a hearing to answer to the charge of refusing to sign for receipt of the warning and also found that refusal to sign such a document does not merit a dismissible offence. Employers should learn the following from this case:

It is very risky to dismiss an employee for something as nebulous as 'negative attitude'. Rather, the charge should relate directly to something specific that the employee did that he/she was not supposed to do. For example, it is better to charge the employee for late coming than for negative attitude if the employer believes that the negative attitude is causing the late coming.

Where an employee refuses to sign a written warning or other document served on him/her by the employer it is not safe to discipline the employee for such refusal. It is only necessary to get a third party to sign as witness that the employee has been given/ offered the document in question and the employee refused to take it.

In *Fourie v Sabre Footwear (Pty) Ltd* (2007, 8 BALR 700) the employee was dismissed for having sexually harassed a colleague. Although the degree and nature of this incident of sexual harassment was very serious the CCMA found that the dismissal was too harsh because it was an isolated incident and was unlikely to be repeated. In the light of the seriousness of this offence and in view of the heavy laws protecting employees from sexual harassment this finding appears somewhat surprising. However, it should be kept in mind that the policy of the employer in this case provided for counselling for a first offence of sexual harassment. Nevertheless, no employer should be expected to adhere to such a policy in a case of serious sexual harassment.

In *NUFAWSA obo Munjanja v Peter Osborn Furniture cc* (2007, 3 BALR 231) the employee was dismissed after taking his colleague's cell phone used for business purposes. The arbitrator found that dismissal was too harsh a sanction in this case because the charge had been "unauthorised possession" of the cell phone and had not alleged that the employee had been dishonest. Also, the employer had failed to bring any evidence to show that the relationship of trust had been destroyed.

In *FAWU obo Mbatha & Others v Sasko Milling and Baking* (2007, 3 BALR 256) a number of employees were dismissed for failing to follow emergency procedures. The employees were instructed to evacuate the mill and to meet at the emergency assembly point after a strong smell of gas was detected. However, some of the employees delayed leaving the building while others left the premises altogether instead of going to the assembly point. Individual hearings were held. While some of the errant employees received final warnings others were dismissed for gross insubordination. However, the arbitrator found that the dismissals were too harsh because the dismissed employees had shown "genuine" remorse. The dismissed employees were therefore all reinstated.

The remarkable point relating to this finding is that the dismissals were found to be too harsh, not because other employees had only received final warnings for the very same offence, but because the employees had shown "genuine remorse". This suggests that any employee can get away with gross misconduct merely by showing remorse as long as the arbitrator is convinced that the remorse is genuine. What is more astonishing, in the light of the CCMA's strictness as regards consistency, is the arbitrator's acceptance of the fact that some employees were dismissed for the same offence for which others received final warnings. The fact that separate hearings were held does not justify this decision as the employer could still have ensured consistent outcomes by commuting the penalties of those who were dismissed.

The general lesson to be learned by employers from the above cases is that arriving at a sanction that is going to satisfy the CCMA or bargaining council is extremely difficult. The surprising arbitration findings outlined above are but a few amongst many astonishing findings recorded in case law.

The question that employers will ask themselves on being made aware of this problem is: 'How do I decide on a penalty that is effective and fair to the employer, but at the same time avoids the ire of the CCMA or bargaining council?'

'SHOOT FROM THE HIP' EMPLOYERS ARE BREACHING PROBATIONARY LAW

Employers frequently misuse probation agreements to get rid of employees instantly because:

- the employee has committed misconduct
- the employer wants to make space for a friend or cousin of the owner
- the employee 'does not fit in'
- a manager 'does not like the employee's face'.

As probation is not a licence to fire, 'James Bond' employers who think they have '007' licences to fire at will are likely to fall foul of 'Dr No' arbitrators at the CCMA. In labour law, 'probation' simply means 'testing the employee's work performance'.

A probationary employee is one who has a conditional employment contract (written or unwritten). That is, the continuation of the contract is conditional on whether the employee's work performance during the probationary period shows that he/she is or is not able to carry out the work properly. While this describes the purpose of the probationary period it does not mean that the employer has a free licence to fire the probationer if the employer believes his/her performance to be unsatisfactory.

The employer is allowed to extend the employee's probation period in order to further assess the employee's performance. This might occur, for example, where the employee shows promise but has made some errors or the opportunity for evaluation has been reduced during the initial probation period.

However, before extending the probation period the employer is required to give the employee the opportunity to make representations as regards the proposed extension.

The biggest mistake that employers frequently make is believing that the conditional nature of the probationary employment significantly reduces the probationer's labour law rights. On the contrary, the employer that places an employee on probation has a number of legal obligations including:

- Making it clear that the employee is on probation
- Clarifying the length of the probation period
- Setting reasonable performance standards including:
  - specifying for and explaining to the employee the performance standards required
  - evaluating and monitoring the employee's performance against the set performance standards
  - informing the employee of performance shortcomings
  - issuing warnings to the employee where he/she is failing to meet the required standards
  - assisting, guiding, counselling, training the employee where necessary
  - before dismissing the probationer, giving him/her an opportunity to state his/her case.

For example, in the case of *Fraser v Caxton Publishers* (2005, 3 BALR 323) the employee was fired for falsifying her CV and for incompatibility. She took the matter to the CCMA where the arbitrator agreed that she was indeed guilty of this misconduct and that it was serious enough to merit dismissal. Despite this the arbitrator found the dismissal to be unfair because the employer had not given the employee a chance to defend herself against the charges.

In the case of *Tharratt v Volume Injection Products (Pty) Ltd* (2005, 6 BALR 652) the employee was dismissed during his probation period for poor performance. As the employer had failed to investigate the cause of the poor performance the CCMA found the dismissal to be unfair. The employer was therefore ordered to pay the employee compensation equal to three months' remuneration.

These cases highlight the fact that probationary employees are strongly protected by labour law. At the same time, probationary employees often do not work out as well as was hoped. While the law allows the dismissal of such failed employees the employer must follow strict procedures first.

Probation can be a very useful tool for the employer but must only be used after the employer has ensured that the following was correctly implemented:

- Designing a probationary policy and procedure
- Setting realistic performance standards
- Designing measures for monitoring and evaluating work performance
- Training management in probation law and in the implementation of the probation policy and procedure.

TWELVE REASONS FOR
EMPLOYERS TO BE CAUTIOUS

Labour law, born from South Africa's Constitution, is there primarily to protect employees. Central to this purpose is the principle that the jobs of employees must be protected. Labour law very reluctantly allows employers to terminate the employment of workers but only after the employer has proven that the employee deserved to be dismissed and that the employee had a fair hearing prior to dismissal.

The Labour Relations Act (LRA) has twelve sections devoted, in effect, to protecting employees' jobs and to the imposition of extremely stringent obligations on employers contemplating the dismissal of employees. These 12 sections are heavily reinforced by the Code of Good Practice: Dismissal attached to the LRA in the form of Schedule 8. This Schedule is itself divided into eleven items or sections all devoted to the protection of the jobs of employees. This Code stresses that dismissal must be the last resort taken by employers and details numerous factors and steps that employers must consider and carry out before contemplating dismissal. The code focuses on protecting employees from dismissal in circumstances of alleged misconduct, poor work performance, illness, injury and strikes. Further reinforcement comes from the Code of Good Practice on Dismissal Based on Operational Requirements that contains twelve items setting out the employer's obligations when contemplating retrenchment. Here the main focus is the employer's obligation to find ways of avoiding termination of the worker's employment.

But perhaps the most powerful reinforcement of these provisions are the countless employee-friendly decisions at CCMA, bargaining councils, Labour Court and Labour Appeal Court. The arbitrators and judges presiding over these cases are obliged by the LRA to assume the employer to be guilty until it proves itself innocent of unfair dismissal. This principle is implemented despite that fact that it directly contravenes section 35(3)(h) of the Constitution of South Africa which provides that all accused persons (including juristic persons such as employers) are entitled to be assumed innocent until proven guilty.

This means that the requirement to protect the jobs of South African employees is considered by the authors of the LRA to be more important than the innocence presumption provision of the Constitution; a provision that has been upheld and respected in the constitutions of civilised and democratic states around the world for well over a century.

In practice, the above means that there are no short cuts for employers. Employers either follow the law or lose the case. For example, in the case of *Mthethwa v Capitol Caterers* (2007, 5 BALR 469) the employee, a catering manager was apparently told that he had 'dismissed himself' after he had failed to attend work for two weeks. In a default decision the CCMA arbitrator found that:

- Absence from work due to illness or injury will only merit possible dismissal if its duration is unreasonable
- There is a difference in law between absenteeism and abscondment
- Absenteeism rarely warrants dismissal for a first offence
- Disciplinable absenteeism normally contains the elements that the employee is not at work, no permission is given for the absence and the employee failed to inform the employer of the reason for his absence
- An employee on authorised absence cannot be guilty of absenteeism unless the sick leave is being abused
- There is no principle of law to support the view that the employer appeared to have had that employees "dismiss themselves" after a certain period of unauthorised absence
- The dismissal was both procedurally and substantively unfair
- The employer was required to reinstate the employee with full back pay.

In *Ngubane v Shell Ridley Park Motors* (2011, 4 BALR 353) Ngubane's dismissal was found to be unfair because he had not been given an opportunity to state his case.

These cases are typical of thousands of cases where employers apply outdated principles and fail to understand the fact that, over the past 11 years, the labour law pendulum has swung very far to the side of employees and job preservation. All of this makes it clear that, in South African law, the jobs of employees are sacrosanct. Thus, employers must exercise extreme care before treading on the rights of employees.

While many employers have successfully dismissed errant employees it will come as no surprise that such success is normally based on the fact that the employer has carefully avoided all the legal protections of employees. This the employers have done via appreciating the legally disadvantaged situation they are in and taking strong steps towards the levelling of the playing fields.

YEARS OF SERVICE A MITIGATING FACTOR

Many employers, when considering dismissal, do not mind taking into account the fact that the guilty employee has long service. However, having weighed this against the seriousness of the offence and aggravating factors, the employer should be allowed, within reason, to make a decision on the penalty. Should a penalty of dismissal then be made in a case where the employee has been grossly derelict in his duties, the employer normally intends for the employee to stay fired. This is because:

- No enterprise can run effectively and harmoniously with employees who break the rules, destroy trust or fail to do their duty
- The employer needs to replace the errant employee and will therefore not have a post available for a dismissed employee who is reinstated
- The employer wants all employees to know that if they cross the line they will be out of a job
- The return of a dismissed employee therefore undermines the harmony and effectiveness of the workplace and the authority of management.

The employer therefore has a very strong need to know that its dismissal decision will not be interfered with. However, the Labour Relations Act (LRA) dilutes the employer's right to dismiss by:

- Laying down numerous and stringent criteria for deciding whether a dismissal decision should stand or not
- Giving arbitrators and judges the right to overturn dismissal decisions.

It is the above provisions that have plagued many employers over the past eleven years and have resulted in many thousands of employees being reinstated. However, recently a brief glimmer of light appeared in the employers' gloom. Some years ago, Rustenburg Platinum Mines dismissed a Mr Sidumo for failing in his duty as a mine security officer. Mr Sidumo failed to follow the required loss-prevention procedures to be utilised for searching employees employed in a high security area. Mr Sidumo disputed the dismissal at the CCMA. The arbitrator accepted that Mr Sidumo had been guilty as charged but decided that the dismissal decision was too harsh.

The employer attempted to get this award overturned at Labour Court on the grounds that, where an employee is indeed guilty of a serious offence, the CCMA should not have the right to interfere with the sanction imposed by the employer. Both the Labour Court and Labour Appeal Court dismissed this argument of the employer.

Rustenburg Platinum then went on appeal to the Supreme Court of Appeal where it was decided that arbitrators should approach the sanction of the employer with some deference and should only overturn it if it is way out of kilter with what would be fair. In other words, the Court said that, even if the arbitrator believed that a sanction other than dismissal would be more fair, if the employer's decision was still within the bounds of fairness, the arbitrator should not interfere with the employer's decision. This was because it was the employer's function to impose a sanction and because the employer has the prerogative to decide, within reason, how strong its sanctions should be. This decision was hailed by employers because it supported the need for employers to be able to protect their interests from the threat of errant employees and it represented an important swing in the pendulum towards a balance between the rights of employees to fair labour practice and the right of employers to run their businesses effectively.

However, the trade union movement saw the decision as a threat to the tight hold they had achieved over the past eleven years over labour legislation. As a result the matter was taken to the Constitutional Court. In the case of *Sidumo v Rustenburg Platinum Mines Ltd and others* (October 2007, *Skills Portal* newsletter) the Constitutional Court overturned the decision of the Supreme Court of Appeal. The Court said that arbitrators are not required to defer to employers' decisions and must instead take all relevant circumstances into account in deciding if the employer's sanction decision was fair.

This decision marks the unsuccessful end of a seven-year battle waged by employers to regain their right to decide how strong their sanctions for serious offences should be and thence to preserve the employer's prerogative to run their own businesses. The Constitutional Court has decided that the law protecting the jobs of employees must remain paramount.

In their disappointment employers should not lose heart and be deterred from dismissing employees who deserve it.

APPLY YOUR WORKPLACE DISCIPLINE CONSISTENTLY

The Code of Good Practice: Dismissal (the Code) in Schedule 8 of the Labour Relations Act (LRA) has been, in effect, provided for in section 188(2) in Chapter 8 of the LRA. This chapter provides for this Code as part of its purpose of ensuring that employers accede to the rights of employees not to be unfairly dismissed as required by section 185(a) of the LRA.

Item 3.(1) of the Code requires all employers to adopt disciplinary rules that "create certainty and consistency in the application of discipline". This means that the employer's rules should apply equally to all employees unless deviation from such consistency can be fully justified objectively due to genuine operational or other existing circumstances. Thus, for example, the rule that only managers will be entitled to use the employer's vehicles for private purposes could be a fair one if it is based on the objective fact that such perks for managers are necessary to attract and retain employees at this key organisational level. However, disciplining junior employees for damaging the employer's vehicles while letting off scot free managers who cause similar damage would not be likely to be accepted by the CCMA.

Item 3.(6) of the Code states that "The employer should apply the penalty of dismissal consistently with the way in which it has been applied to the same and other employees in the past, and consistently as between two or more employees who participate in the misconduct under consideration." However, the Code also provides, via item 3.(5) that, "When deciding whether or not to impose the penalty of dismissal, the employer should in addition to the gravity of the misconduct consider factors such as the employee's circumstances ....., the nature of the job and the circumstances of the infringement itself." Read together, items 3.(5) and 3.(6) of the Code require the employer to apply disciplinary measures (especially the measure of dismissal) consistently where the circumstances prevailing are similar and not simply where the charges against employees are similar.

The importance for consistency of the similarity of circumstances is well illustrated in the case of *CSA obo Nduli v CCMA* (2011, 2 BALR 137). In this case a CCMA commissioner was dismissed for submitting fraudulent travel cost claims to the value of approximately R42 000. Part of the employee's defence was that other CCMA commissioners who had submitted false cost claims had not been dismissed. The arbitrator (a CCMA commissioner) found that:

- The employer party (i.e. the CCMA) had proven that the dismissed employee had been guilty of submitting a number of falsified cost claims
- Employers are required to apply discipline consistently
- However, the employer is entitled to take circumstances into account when deciding on penalties for those who have committed similar offences
- The employee's offence, although of the same nature as that of her colleagues, was more serious than theirs because of the size and range of her fraudulent conduct
- The dismissal of the CCMA employee was therefore fair.

However, in the case of *SACCAWU obo Lentsha v Boxer Superstores (Pty) Ltd* (2010, 12 BALR 1294) the dismissal of a cashier was found to be unfair. The cashier had given

R1 000 to a customer despite the fact that the electronic banking system located at the cashier's till had rejected the customer's debit card cash withdrawal request. The employee's dismissal was found to be inconsistent and therefore unfair because another employee who had made a similar mistake had not been dismissed and because of the dismissed employee's long service and expression of genuine remorse. The arbitrator ordered the employer to reinstate the employee.

In the case of *Westonaria Local Municipality v SALGBC and others* (2010, 3 BLLR 342) the employee was dismissed for having falsely claimed, at her pre-employment interview, that she had achieved matriculation. However, it was established that another employee had been forgiven for having submitted a false matriculation certificate as part of her job application. The bargaining council arbitrator found that:

- this constituted inconsistency on the employer's part
- the failure to dismiss the other employee indicated that such dishonesty does not necessarily destroy the trust relationship; and
- the dismissal was therefore unfair.

The employer was ordered to reinstate the employee. The employer then took the matter on review to the Labour Court which upheld the arbitrator's finding.

The above should be seen as a warning to employers that, in order to avoid flouting the complex principles of consistency, they should apply the principle of consistency and indicate when to sacrifice it in favour of the legal requirement to differentiate between sanctions due to dissimilarity between the circumstances of different cases.

FIRING THE LOT COULD PUT YOU IN A SPOT

Employers frequently suspect that serious misconduct has occurred but are unable to prove which employee or employees are responsible.

Some case law has given the impression that, in such circumstances, group dismissals may be justified. This impression has been given by two important cases: those involving Score Supermarkets and Snip Trading.

In the case of *NUSFRAW obo Gomez & others v Score Supermarkets* (2003, 8 BALR 925) a group of managers were dismissed as a result of stock losses amounting to six million rand. While there was no proof that these managers had stolen the missing stock they were held responsible for the losses and disputed their dismissals at the CCMA. The arbitrator found that the markedly poor management of the business by the dismissed employees (and others) had led to the losses and that this justified the dismissal.

Again in the case of *FEDCRAW v Snip Trading (Pty) Ltd* the arbitrator ruled in favour of group dismissals. Here, the employer had a policy which held every employee responsible for stock losses. When stock disappeared several employees were fired despite the fact that the employer had not specifically proven that any one of these employees was guilty of the stock losses. The arbitrator found that the concept of group responsibility was fair under the circumstances as the employer's interests had to be taken into account.

In the case of *Foschini Group v Maidi & others* (2010, 7 BLLR 689) the store's entire staff were dismissed due to the loss of 28% of the store's stock valued at R207 000. The Labour Appeal Court found that:

- The stock losses at the store had, according to the employees, never previously exceeded 3%
- A thorough investigation had been carried out establishing that there had been serious stock losses
- The employees were unable to prove their claim that there had been a break-in at the store on the night before they were challenged with the stock loss
- The employees had been unable to prove that the losses were for reasons beyond their control
- This meant that the employees were responsible for the losses
- Each employee was culpable for the failure of the group to avoid the shrinkage
- As it is extremely difficult for an employer to prove that shrinkage is due to the acts of particular employees, the employer is entitled to include, as terms in employment contracts, the employee's duty to avoid shrinkage beyond reasonable limits
- The dismissals were fair.

The outcomes of these three cases have misled a number of employers into believing that group dismissals are fair. However, this will not always be the case. It will depend on the extent to which the employees specifically have responsibility for prevention of losses and have the means of preventing losses. It will also depend on the viewpoint of each individual arbitrator.

For example, in the case of *FEDCRAW obo Mthimunye v Rewmoor Investments 543 (Pty) Ltd* (2008, 2 BALR 142) the entire staff working the retail store were dismissed after the employer suffered serious stock losses. The CCMA found that:

- The notion of collective guilt was repugnant
- Despite the existence of a clause in each employee's contract to the effect that prevention of stock losses formed part of their conditions of employment the employer had failed to prove that the dismissed employees were responsible for the stock losses.

As a result all the employees were reinstated with full back pay.

The correct actions of the employer will differ from case to case depending on a number of legal subtleties and interpretations. An important difference between the Rewmoor case and the Foschini case appears to be that the employer in the Foschini case was able to convince the court that there were no other likely reasons for the stock losses other than the negligence and/or dishonesty of the employees. The provision of such proof requires, amongst other things, tight security measures and meticulous records and evidentiary techniques that show how tight security is. The purpose of this approach is to show the court that:

- There was no way that a large volume of stock could go missing over the relevant period of time other than due to the misconduct of staff; and
- The dismissed employees must either have been involved in the theft, or knew about it or were negligent in not knowing about it.

This, combined with showing that the employees had a duty to protect the employer from such losses will go a long way towards making a group dismissal stick.

BEWARE DISCIPLINING EMPLOYEES FOR OFF-SITE MISCONDUCT

What rights do employers have to discipline employees for misconduct perpetrated outside the workplace? While employers have very few rights under the Labour Relations Act (LRA) they do have the right to discipline and even to dismiss employees for work-related misconduct. However, a dismissal will only be upheld by the CCMA, bargaining council or Labour Court where:

- The employer has properly followed a stringent, complex and time consuming disciplinary procedure laid down by labour law; and
- The employer can prove, on balance of probability, that it had the right to dismiss the employee in the light of the facts of the case.

Whether the employer had the right to dismiss the employee will depend on the employer proving a number of things, including that:

- The employee knew the rule that he/she allegedly broke
- It was a fair rule and was consistently applied
- The employee was guilty of breaking the rule
- The breach of the rule was so serious as to merit dismissal
- Dismissal was justified despite mitigating circumstances.

In addition to the above factors the employer will not be entitled to dismiss an employee for conduct that has nothing to do with the employer. For example, the employer may not normally dismiss an employee who neglects his/her children or assaults a fellow nightclub visitor. But what if the employee was wearing his/her workplace uniform at the time of the assault? The employer may then be able to make out a case of bringing the name of the employer into disrepute.

Thus, despite the fact that the alleged misconduct occurred outside the workplace it can still occur within the context of the work relationship. And, if it does, then the employer may, in certain circumstances, still have the right to discipline the employee.

For example, in the case of *Saal v De Beers Consolidated Ltd* (2000, 2 BALR 171) it was alleged that the employee who worked for the mine had assaulted and raped a woman at a mine village and the employee was therefore dismissed. Although the rape was not proven at the CCMA the commissioner agreed that the employee was guilty of assault. The employee claimed that his dismissal was unfair because:

- a criminal case had been laid against him
- the alleged assault had taken place outside the workplace; and
- the incident had occurred outside normal working hours.

However, the CCMA decided that the criminal case had no bearing on the labour law matter and that, despite the time and place it happened, the employee's misconduct still fell under the employer's jurisdiction because:

- the employment relationship and the business of the employer had been affected by the assault; and
- the employer had a direct interest in the wellbeing of the residents of the mine village; and
- the employee knew that even assaulting a non-employee in the town infringed the employer's rules.

The CCMA therefore upheld the dismissal.

In the case of *CEPPWAWU obo Faku v Eco Tanks* (2007, 11 BALR 997) the employee was dismissed for being intoxicated, for insubordination and for verbally abusing the employer in the presence of other employees. This incident occurred outside the workplace. The arbitrator found that the employer had no right to dismiss the employee for intoxication and insubordination because these incidents occurred off the employer's premises. However, the act of abusing the employer in front of other employees did affect the work relationship and fell within the employer's jurisdiction.

In this case, had the employee been dismissed for insubordination only (outside the premises) the arbitrator would have found the dismissal to be unfair because the arbitrator had found that the insubordination was not relevant to the employment relationship. Every case taken to CCMA or bargaining council will potentially have a different outcome because circumstances differ as do the viewpoints of different arbitrators.

BRING PROOF THAT TRUST
HAS BEEN DESTROYED

An integral element of an employment relationship is the need for and the right of the employer and employee to trust each other. This is a two-way street and either party could forgo his/her right to continue the employment by destroying the trust relationship.

Thus, where an employer has mistreated an employee so badly that he/she is forced to resign this could contribute to a constructive dismissal finding. That is, an important element of a successful constructive dismissal claim is the employee's proof that he/she could no longer trust the employer to treat him/her fairly.

This challenge is also faced by employers when trying to justify the dismissal of employees. When taken to CCMA, bargaining council or Labour Courts, employers have a very challenging job to do in trying to win their cases. This is because the law requires the employer to be able to prove that:

- The procedures followed in dismissing the employee were fair in all respects
- The rule that the employee allegedly broke existed at the time and that it was a fair rule
- The alleged transgressor knew the rule

- The rule had been consistently applied
- The employee was in fact guilty of the alleged offence
- The offence was serious enough to merit dismissal as opposed to a lesser penalty such as a warning
- The employee's conduct irretrievably destroyed the trust relationship rendering continued employment intolerable.

It must be remembered that the employer cannot merely allege that the trust has been destroyed. It must convince the arbitrator at the CCMA or bargaining council that this is a fact. As feelings of trust and mistrust are by definition subjective, providing factual evidence and proof of the destruction of trust is very tricky. Due to the fact that the extent of an employer's ability to tolerate untrustworthy behaviour is not universal, different employers will have different points at which they draw the trust line. The way that many judges and arbitrators deal with this thorny problem is to ask themselves whether, in light of the facts presented to them, a reasonable employer would or would not be able to tolerate continued employment. However, this approach does not resolve the subjectivity dilemma. Instead, it merely shifts part of the focus of the problem from the question: "what is tolerable" to the questions: "what is a reasonable employer?" and "what would a reasonable employer be able to tolerate?" The answer to the latter two questions is still subject to the individual opinions, experience, beliefs, background and tolerance levels of the presiding judge or arbitrator.

Added to this danger is the fact that South Africa's Constitution, the Labour Relations Act (LRA), codes of good practice and case law decisions are permeated by the principle that it is the employee who is entitled to fair labour practice and to protection from unfair dismissal. In effect, section 188 of the LRA dictates that an employer, accused of unfair dismissal, is guilty of the alleged unfairness if the accused employer is unable to prove itself innocent. Thus, even the Constitutional protection that an accused is assumed innocent until proven guilty is not available to the employer. Therefore, where the employer is unable to convince the judge or arbitrator that the dismissal was fair, the dismissal will most likely, by default, be ruled to be unfair.

The uneven weight of onus placed on the employer by labour law means, in practice, that the employer has to arrive at the court/CCMA/bargaining council with solid evidence of everything it is required to prove as summarised in the seven points listed earlier in this article. Even where the employer is able to present convincing proof of the first six criteria it will still lose if it cannot convince the arbiter that the employee's conduct irretrievably destroyed the trust relationship, rendering continued employment intolerable.

In the case of *Edcon Ltd v Pilemer NO* (*Contemporary Labour Law* Vol 21, No. 1, August 2011) the Supreme Court of Appeal found that it is insufficient for an employer merely to state that the employee had destroyed the employment relationship. Evidence will have to be led to show why the employer believes this to be the case. This means that the employer must bring evidence relating to the nature of the employee's job, the nature of the offence, the degree of seriousness of the offence, the employers disciplinary code, the employee's past record, the nature of the employer's business and other relevant factors showing why the employer cannot trust the employee.

EXTERNAL PRESSURE DOES NOT JUSTIFY DISMISSAL

The CCMA has frequently upheld the dismissal of employees fired for misconduct. We have been directly involved in a great many cases where employees have been fired and, after appealing to the CCMA, have remained fired.

It is not the firing of employees that the law has a problem with. It is not dismissals that raise the ire of CCMA arbitrators. Instead, it is unfair dismissals that result in the employer being forced to reinstate the employee and/or being forced to pay the employee exorbitant amounts of money in compensation.

In order to be free to fire employees who deserve dismissal employers need to understand and accept the difference between fair and unfair dismissal. This is because, if the employer has an employee who is causing mayhem or is costing the employer money or is threatening the security of the business or is otherwise undesirable, the employer cannot afford for the employee to be reinstated. The reason for this is that it is exceptionally difficult later to dismiss or discipline an employee who has been reinstated by the CCMA or other tribunal.

So, while the law does allow dismissals, it also requires the employer to be able to prove that the dismissal was both procedurally and substantively fair.

"Procedurally fair" relates to whether the employee was given a fair hearing.

Whether a dismissal is "substantively fair" relates to the fairness of the dismissal decision itself rather than to the disciplinary procedures. Specifically, for the dismissal to be adjudged to be substantively fair, the employer would have to show that:

- the employee really did break the rule
- the rule was a fair one
- the penalty of dismissal was a fitting one in the light of the severity of the offence; and
- the employee knew or should have known the rule.

Properly trained CCMA arbitrators consider all the above factors together with the circumstances of each individual case in deciding if a dismissal was fair and whether the employee should stay dismissed or should be reinstated.

In the case of *White v Pinnacle Point Investments (Pty) Ltd* (2008, 1 BALR 91) White took up a post with the employer as CEO. Thereafter the employer discovered that White was in dispute with his previous employer which also happened to be the bank used by the new employer. The new employer then dismissed the employee claiming that the reason for the dismissal was the employee's refusal to divulge the true reason for the dispute with the old employer. It also claimed that it had failed to hold a disciplinary hearing because of exceptional circumstances. The arbitrator decided that:

- There were no exceptional circumstances justifying the failure to hold a hearing. Believing the outcome to be a fait accompli does not exempt the employer from giving the employee an opportunity to be heard
- The reason for the dismissal was not that the employee had failed to divulge the true reason for his dispute with the bank. Instead, the true reason was pressure from the bank on the employer to fire the employee
- The employer had not held its own investigation into the bank's allegation that the bank's money had found its way into the employee's bank account
- The dismissal was procedurally and substantively unfair
- The employer was to compensate the employee for the unfair dismissal.

The outcome of this case shows that employers will lose if they merely take the word of a third party as to the guilt of an employee or if they succumb to pressure from the third party to dismiss the employee.

INTOLERABLE EMPLOYMENT RELATIONSHIP PIVOTAL TO JUSTIFY DISMISSAL

Labour law accepts the firing of guilty employees only if dismissal is the last resort. The Code of Good Practice: Dismissal provides that, where employers are considering dismissing an employee they should be able to justify this drastic sanction by proving that the employee's misconduct is so serious that it makes continued employment intolerable. One factor that could constitute such intolerability is the employee's breach of the trust relationship.

For example, the employer is entitled to claim that, where an employee is found guilty of dishonesty, the trust element of the employment relationship has been damaged. However, this does not necessarily mean that the damage to the trust relationship is always so bad that it is irreparable.

It is a well accepted principle that:

- Employees are expected, as part of their employment contract, to behave honestly and in the interests of their employers and that
- trust is an important element to consider in deciding whether the employment relationship of a dishonest employee should continue.

However, the employer's right to dismiss the dishonest employee for breach of trust depends on the answers to a number of questions including:

- Was the trust really destroyed?
- Was the position that the employee occupied one where trust was a key factor?
- Was there an alternative corrective measure available short of dismissal?
- Has the employer acted consistently? For example, have other employees, committing similar offences, been dismissed due to the destruction of the employment relationship?
- Did the employee try to cover up the dishonest act with further dishonesty or did he/she immediately own up and show genuine remorse?

The intolerability of the continuation of the employment relationship can be caused by misconduct other than dishonesty or breach of trust, for instance, an employer could argue that an employee who sexually harassed a colleague severely damaged working relationships between employees and/or damaged the employer's reputation. However, the employer must still prove that this damage was serious enough to make continued employment intolerable.

Persuading an arbitrator that the employment relationship has truly been destroyed is very difficult. This is because:

- The modern arbitrator is more and more likely to look for reasons to preserve the employee's job.
- The concept of intolerability has at least as many subjective elements as it has objective elements. What the angry employer feels to be intolerable might not be seen in that light by an arbitrator who is more emotionally removed from the situation.

In the light of the above employers should:

- If they believe that the misconduct does merit dismissal, be able to set aside their anger and prove objectively that the employee has made the continued employment relationship intolerable by his/her actions.
- Ensure that their charging officers and hearing chairpersons are given thorough and updated training. This training should include input on what types and quality of evidence might qualify to justify a claim of intolerable employment relationship.
- Consider outsourcing the chairing of the disciplinary hearing to a labour law expert in cases where the case is too hot to handle for internal management.

TRAPPING AND ENTRAPMENT NOT THE SAME

Employers are at a very serious disadvantage at the CCMA because:

- The employer is the accused at arbitration in the same sense as the defendant in a criminal case
- The employer is normally required to present its case first
- The employer is assumed, from the outset, to be guilty of committing unfair dismissal until it proves itself innocent.

These three factors make it extremely difficult for the employer to convince the arbitrator that the dismissal should be upheld. The employer will not even get to first base until it has persuaded the arbitrator that the employee was guilty of the misconduct or poor performance that resulted in his/her dismissal.

There are some number of employers who do fully appreciate the uphill battle they have in proving the employee guilty, and who appreciate why such proof of guilt is crucial to winning at arbitration. However, even these enlightened employers are still stuck with the problem of how to prove the employee's guilt. Employers use a variety of methods to prove guilt, some of which are neither recommended nor legal. Methods that are legitimate and potentially effective include:

- Carrying out a thorough investigation so as to gather relevant facts
- Using documents as proof
- Backing up the documentary proof with video footage, audio evidence and polygraph test results
- Calling witnesses to give truthful and relevant testimonies
- Trapping the suspected employee.

Methods that are illegitimate and dangerous include:

- Falsifying documents and taped evidence
- Getting witnesses to lie
- Coercing the accused employee into confessing
- Entrapping the suspected employee illegally.

Often employers get confused between the method of trapping the employee (which is legal) and illegal entrapment. Entrapment occurs where the employer lures the employee into carrying out misconduct that the employee would not have carried out but for the ensnaring methods of the employer. For example, the employee is suspected of using illegal drugs at the workplace. The employer hires a detective to pose as an employee and the detective offers to sell the suspect some Mandrax. The employee refuses the drug but the detective then persuades the employee to accept the drugs by taking one himself giving one to the suspected employee for free. The employee is caught taking the Mandrax and is dismissed. In this case, the employer has engineered a situation where the employee was pressured into taking the Mandrax (because the detective used strong persuasive methods to get the employee to take the Mandrax).

On the other hand a legitimate trap would be, for example, where the employer suspects that the employee uses a particular vacant office to shoot up with heroin at tea time. The employer would be entitled to wait until the employee goes into that office, give him/her time to begin the injecting process and then go in and catch the employee red-handed. This is not entrapment because the employer did not unfairly induce the employee to take drugs.

While the examples I have given above of legal trapping and illegal entrapment represent two very different methods of catching an employee out, there are many cases where the line between trapping and entrapment is blurred. For example, in the case of *Mbuli v Spartan Wiremakers cc* (2004, 5 BALR 598) the employer set the suspected employee up by getting a colleague to ask the suspect to supply him with wire for private purposes. The suspect then sold to the colleague, at half the normal price, some wire taken from the employer's stock. The employee was caught, disciplined and dismissed. He complained to the bargaining council that he had been entrapped illegally because the employer had set him up. The arbitrator found that the trap was a fair and legal one because:

- The employer had suffered a serious shrinkage problem
- The trap was set due to reasonable suspicion against the employee
- The employer did not go beyond giving the employee the opportunity to commit the offence. That is, the trapper did not pressure the suspect into supplying the wire, did not use persuasive measures such as comradeship or sympathy and did not exploit any weakness of the suspect employee.

This case reveals the subtle factors that can distinguish between legal trapping and illegal entrapment.

BEWARE CANCELLING CONCLUDED EMPLOYMENT CONTRACTS

The courts have found that the employee is protected by labour law from the moment the employment contract is concluded even if the employee has not yet started work; and even if the contract has only been orally agreed.

According to section 213 of the LRA an employee is:
"(a) any person, excluding an independent contractor, who works for another person or for the state and who receives, or is entitled to receive, any remuneration; and
(b) any other person who in any manner assists in carrying out or conducting the business of an employer..."

This definition seems to strongly imply that the employer's legal obligations begin on the day that the employee physically begins work. However, this is not necessarily so. For example, in the case of *Wyeth SA (Pty) Ltd v Manqele* (*People Dynamics*, September 2003, page 39). Manqele was offered a position by the employer as a sales rep. The parties concluded a written contract of employment in terms of which he was to commence work on 1 April. Prior to Manqele beginning work, he was advised that the employer was no longer prepared to employ him. In terms of the contract of employment, Manqele had been entitled to a company vehicle. The employer believed that Manqele had made a misrepresentation as to the status of the car he had chosen, and on this basis took the view that there was no contract, as the parties had not reached agreement as to the condition of the motor vehicle stipulated in the letter of appointment.

Manqele took the matter to the CCMA where the arbitrator ruled that Manqele had become an employee the moment he accepted Wyeth's offer of employment. Wyeth took the arbitrator on review at the Labour Court on the grounds that the arbitrator had arrived at an "unjustifiable conclusion in ruling on the definition of an employee".

That is, Wyeth argued in the Labour Court that Manqele did not become an employee merely because of the employment contract. This argument is supported by an earlier Labour Court finding in the case of *Whitehead v Woolworths (Pty) Ltd* (1999, 20 ILJ 2133). In that case the Court found, according to the report, that a person who is party to a contract of employment but who has not yet commenced employment is not an employee for the purposes of the LRA.

However, despite the Woolworths case finding, the Court, in the Manqele case, found that, as a party to a valid and binding contract of employment, Manqele was an employee for the purposes of the LRA.

The employer then took the matter further to the Labour Appeal Court (In *Wyeth SA (Pty) Ltd v Manqele & others* 2005, 6 BLLR 523) but lost yet again. The Court upheld the earlier decisions by the CCMA and Labour Court that Manqele had achieved legal employee status the moment his employment contract was signed.

In the case of *Gumbe v Electro Inductive Industries* [2012] 1 BALR 1 the arbitrator found that the employee had been telephoned and offered a position, and that he had accepted. His contention that he had been dismissed was correct; a contract of employment had been concluded when the applicant accepted the offer, and the termination of that contract constituted a dismissal, even though the employee had not yet commenced service.

These decisions pose a number of concerns for employers:

- Firstly, the fact that two different benches of Labour Appeal Court judges (Woolworths on the one hand and Wyeth on the other) made two such diametrically opposed decisions on a matter as fundamental as this one creates major uncertainty as regards the law
- Secondly, where the parties have agreed in principle that the employee will get the job it is now not clear whether a disagreement on the terms of the employment does or does not delay the legal validity of the contract of employment.

In the light of these dangers employers should:

- Avoid entering into employment agreements until all the terms and conditions have been dealt with thoroughly
- Ensure that, before offering anybody a job, there are no obstacles to allowing the candidate to take up the position
- Make it clear that the discussion of the terms and conditions of a contract in no way constitutes an offer of employment.

CHAPTER CONCLUSION

The above makes it clear that employers have to be able to prove that their rules are fair, that their employees know the rules, that these are consistently applied, that the dismissed employee was guilty of the offence and that dismissal was the most appropriate remedy under the circumstances.

This is a huge task for employers especially since, what the employer truly believes is a fair sanction, can and often is overruled by the arbitrator or judge.

The legal standard for these five legs of substantive fairness is high. As a result employers have no choice but to place their own standards of fairness at this high level. This can only be achieved through ensuring that the implementers of discipline and dismissal have a thorough understanding of what the law sees as fair. Therefore, nobody should be placed in a position of leadership before being fully trained in the management of discipline.

Workplace misconduct and its consequences

CHAPTER 11

WORKPLACE MISCONDUCT
AND ITS CONSEQUENCES

While it is true that our law strongly protects the rights of employees it also allows employers to discipline and, where appropriate, to dismiss them. This chapter highlights examples of misconduct that can lead to the dismissal of employees.

INSUBORDINATION NOT ALWAYS DISMISSIBLE

Item 3(4) The Code of Good Practice: Dismissal (the Code) lists some examples of offences that might merit dismissal even in the absence of prior warnings. Included in this list is the offence of "gross insubordination". The concept of insubordination means "refusal to obey a lawful and reasonable instruction".

Despite the potential seriousness of "insubordination" employers would be wrong to assume that the refusal to obey a lawful and reasonable instruction will always justify dismissal. In fact, refusal to obey an instruction may, in some cases, not even constitute misconduct!

In the case of *MITUSA obo Clarke v National Ports Authority* (2006, 9 BALR 861) the employee, a Tug Master, was dismissed for refusing to obey a lawful and reasonable instruction from the tug boat's Pilot. The Pilot had instructed the Tug Master to tie the tug's rope to the bow (front) of the ship to be boarded. However, the employee refused to do so on the grounds that it would be dangerous to follow the instruction. As the employee had already received a final warning for insubordination she was fired.

The arbitrator found, amongst other things, that:

- In terms of the employer's policy and international practice Pilots carry out boarding operations at their own discretion
- Decisions of Pilots as regards boarding operations are final
- The instruction given by the Pilot had been both lawful and reasonable

- However, when manoeuvring their vessels to carry out the Pilot's instructions Tug Masters must avoid risks
- According to standing orders, should the safety of the tug be at risk, the Tug Master may disregard the Pilot's instruction
- Had an accident occurred after the rope had been secured to the front of the vessel the Tug Master would have been blamed
- While the Pilot's instruction was lawful and reasonable and may have been seen by others as being a safe one the Tug Master had the right to a different opinion and to act on that differing opinion because she was responsible for the tug's safety
- Contrary to the subsidiary charges the employee had neither been argumentative nor had behaved in an unprofessional manner
- Despite the validity of the Pilot's instruction the Tug Master had not committed insubordination; she had exercised her professional discretion as she had been entitled to do
- The dismissal was substantively unfair
- The employee was to be reinstated with full back pay which amounted to eight months' remuneration and benefits.

The remarkable aspect of this case is that the arbitrator found the dismissal to be unfair despite the fact that the employee had definitely disobeyed a lawful and reasonable instruction. The reason for this unusual finding was based on the unique circumstances of the case. These were:

- The employee did not believe the instruction to be reasonable on the grounds that it was unsafe
- Her opinion was based on her own view of what was dangerous practice
- Her opinion was within the bounds of rationality
- Her refusal to obey the Pilot's instruction was based, not on a desire to flout authority, but rather on her professional opinion relating to safety which, according to orders, was paramount
- There appeared to be a personal issue influencing the dismissal.

Employers must therefore avoid basing dismissal decisions on personal attitudes. Instead, expert advice should be sought to establish whether the employee truly committed an offence.

MANAGERS PROHIBITED
FROM BITING SUBORDINATES

When an employer contemplates disciplining an employee it is required by The Code of Good Practice: Dismissal (the Code) found in Schedule 8 of the Labour Relations Act to consider a number of circumstances before dismissing a guilty employee. For example, the Code requires the employer to consider the gravity of the misconduct, the employee's past record, length of service and personal circumstances. Case law has added to the factors that could or should be considered including factors such as the seniority of the employee, aggravating circumstances, provocation and other extenuating circumstances.

Collins Concise Dictionary defines 'extenuating circumstances' as circumstances that cause an offence or fault to appear less serious or to mitigate or weaken.

However, in the labour law context I tend to think of mitigating and extenuating circumstances as being slightly different from each other. I see mitigating circumstances as any circumstances that might reduce the seriousness of the offence whether such circumstances emanate directly from the actual incident or not, whereas I see extenuating circumstances more narrowly, as only those emanating directly from the relevant incident as opposed to general circumstances such as length of service that have no bearing on the merits of the misconduct.

An example of extenuating circumstances based on my definition is provocation. In both criminal and labour law, and especially where an assault or other abusive behaviour has taken place, provocation generally has an important role to play in considering the level of penalty of the offender.

Assault at the workplace is normally seen as serious misconduct because of:

- the harm or potential harm to the victim of the assault
- the potential disruption of workplace harmony
- the potential for the employer to be sued for vicarious liability by the assault victim
- the loss in working time due to the need for an assaulted employee to take sick leave
- the loss of business if the victim of the assault is a client.

Despite this, employers sometimes bungle disciplinary action against alleged culprits, and this is often because of the anger attached to incidents of assault or other unsavoury acts. This can be disastrous for the employer because section 188(1)(a) of the Labour Relations Act (LRA) makes it clear that the employer cannot fire an employee without good cause.

One area where employers struggle with misconduct penalties in general is where provocation is alleged. The employer got it right in the case of *Francis v The Clicks Organisation* (2010, 3 BALR 325). In this case Francis, a manager, told a subordinate to stop chewing gum. It is reported that, when he refused in an insubordinate manner, she assaulted him and bit him to the extent that she had blood on her mouth. When she was fired for this act she told the CCMA that she had been provoked by his refusal to stop chewing gum and by his attitude. The arbitrator found that the subordinate's behaviour did not amount to provocation at all. Instead his behaviour amounted to insubordination which should have been dealt with via proper disciplinary measures. This, together with the seriousness of the assault, and the manager's relative seniority to her subordinate rendered the dismissal substantively fair.

However, in *CEPPWAWU obo Mudau v Super Group Supply Chain Partners* (2009, 2 BALR 123) a shop steward was dismissed for, amongst other things, swearing at supervisors. The arbitrator found that he had been provoked into this behaviour because his supervisor had used an obscene term while addressing the shop steward. The dismissal was therefore unfair.

The above decisions tell us that it is important for employers:

- To deal with all alleged acts of misconduct coolly, calmly and without biting the offending employee
- To ensure that their managers are trained never to speak abusively to employees
- To give very careful and reasoned consideration to allegations of provocation by employees accused of misconduct. This is in order to establish whether the alleged act constituted provocation or not, whether the provocation was significant enough to be pertinent and whether the seriousness of the offence and/or aggravating circumstances outweigh the extenuating circumstances
- To keep themselves constantly updated with case law decisions that can affect the fairness of their disciplinary decisions.

CONFLICT OF INTERESTS

It is inherent in the nature of employment relationships that, as the employer is paying the employee for his services, he/she is obliged to be loyal to the employer and to devote his/her efforts to the interests of the employer. The employee should therefore carry out his/her work diligently and according to the employer's instructions, avoid bringing the employer's name into disrepute, and avoid activity that could clash with the employer's interests. For example:

- In order to avoid corruption employees involved in procurement services should not have private relationships with the employer's suppliers
- Employees who do not have permission should neither carry on businesses that compete with that of the employer nor carry on any other work that could impair the employee's ability to serve his/her employer.

However, there are limits to the employee's duty of loyalty. That is:

- The employee is not obliged to carry out any illegal instructions
- The employee would not be obliged to forego his own legal rights to work limited overtime hours.

Where a managerial employee joins a trade union this could well result in a conflict of interests. This is because management and trade unions often become adversaries. That is:

- They bargain against each other at wage negotiation time
- Unions organise strikes against management
- Management sometimes dismiss union members who go on strike
- Managers prosecute misconduct hearings against union members and union representatives attend these hearings to defend their members.

It is therefore natural for management to discuss confidentially the tactics they will use to protect the employer from union action. A manager who attends such meetings and then informs his trade union of management's plans has a conflict of interests and is behaving disloyally towards his/her employer.

In the case of *FAWU v The Cold Chain* (2007, 7 BLLR 638) the employee accepted a management position but refused to relinquish his posts of shop steward and union office bearer. He was then retrenched. The employer claimed that the employee could not properly carry out his managerial duties if he was involved in trade union activity. The Labour Court decided that:

- The employee had a right in terms of South Africa's Constitution and the Labour Relations Act (LRA) to be involved in union activity

- The potential conflict between the roles of unionist and manager could be dealt with via the disciplinary procedure if the employee was unable to carry out his managerial role effectively
- The dismissal was automatically unfair
- The employer was to pay the employee nine months' remuneration in compensation.

In this case the Court found that the employee's rights outweighed the employer's concerns of conflict of interest.

In *NUMSA obo Thobalo v Equipment Design & General Engineering (Pty) Ltd)* (2010, 11 BALR 1136) the employee was dismissed for offering to sell an electric motor to a client of the employer for his own gain. The employee claimed that he had intended that the client would be invoiced by the employer as usual and had no idea that it would appear that he had arranged this deal for his own gain. The commissioner found that, while the employee was guilty of misconduct, there was no proof that he had profited from the scheme and that the dismissal was unfair.

From the above cases it appears that, where the law protects employee rights, the employer's interest will often come second. However, while employers must hesitate to act against employees merely due to the employees' affiliations, they still retain the right, in certain circumstances, to discipline employees if their affiliations actually interfere in practice with the execution of their duties. For instance, the Court in the FAWU case discussed above, said that the employer would be able to discipline the manager if he failed to do his job. For example, should the manager purposely hold back on disciplining his/her subordinates because they are his co-union members, he/she should be subject to discipline himself/herself.

EMPLOYEES SHOULD NOT
FALSELY ACCUSE EMPLOYERS

Making unsupported allegations of unfairness against employers can be costly. This is partly because the CCMA, Labour Court, Labour Appeal Court and bargaining councils deal with approximately 190 000 cases per year and do not have time to waste on dealing with false claims. The majority of these cases are referred by employees and deal with issues relating to:

- dismissal for misconduct, poor performance, illness/injury or incompatibility
- discrimination

- retrenchments
- provision of benefits
- training
- promotion
- demotion
- suspension
- warnings
- pregnancy
- probation
- takeovers and mergers
- whistle blowing
- sexual harassment
- mutual interest dismissals
- victimisation due to the exercising of legal or organisational rights.

The majority of these cases contain employee allegations that are backed up, to one extent or another, by facts. On the other hand there are a significant number of dispute referrals that appear to be based on fabrication. I suspect this to be the case for a number of reasons:

- Firstly, employees lose approximately 40% of cases referred to CCMA arbitration. I accept that many of these cases have been lost due to poor provision of evidence by the employee rather than due to the fact that the allegations are false. However, at least some of these cases brought by employees will have been lost due to the complete lack of truth.
- Secondly, it is easy for employees to refer disputes to the CCMA and to most other dispute resolution bodies. The referral process is simple and free of cost. Employees are allowed to refer cases and to present their cases at conciliation, arbitration and at court on their own. They neither have to go to the expense of paying CCMA fees nor of hiring lawyers to assist them. This makes it tempting for dishonest employees to abuse the system in order to make some money.
- Thirdly, there are important motives for the bringing of false claims against employers. There may be employees (hopefully in the small minority) who bring cases against employers due to vindictiveness based on some unrelated matter or because they would rather extort money out of employers at the CCMA than earn their money honestly. I have been involved in assisting employers with cases where the employee simply refers a case to the CCMA or bargaining council as a means of evading discipline. This is a strategy where attack is the best defence.

Not only is such a practice dishonest but it is also a waste of the CCMA's and the employer's time and resources. It is therefore not surprising that the law provides for employees to be penalised for bringing frivolous or vexatious cases. Frivolous means trivial or insignificant. Vexatious means annoying and groundless. In such cases the employee can be ordered to pay part of the employer's legal costs.

For example, in *Simane v Coca-Cola Fortune* (2006, 10 BALR 1044) the CCMA agreed that the employee had been guilty of dishonesty. As he had lodged a case for unfair dismissal knowing that it was not genuine the CCMA awarded costs against him.

In *Ndwalane v The Magic Company (Pty) Ltd* (2006, 5 BALR 497) the employee was employed on the basis of a fixed-term contract. When it expired and he was told to go he lodged an unfair labour practice case against the employer. However, he brought no proof of unfairness and the arbitrator found his case to have been frivolous and vexatious. He was ordered to pay part of the costs of the employer.

While employees must beware of misusing the dispute resolution process, employers need to exercise caution as well. That is, employers should:

- Make sure that they do not give employees cause to take them to the CCMA or other dispute forum
- Avoid jumping to the conclusion that the employee's case will be found to be fabricated, frivolous or vexatious. That is, employers must not become complacent even when they feel sure that the employee's allegations are false. The employer still needs to prepare and present a solid case to prove the falsity of the employee's claims.

EMPLOYERS MUST PROVE DERELICTION OF DUTY CHARGES

Many employers like using Dereliction of Duty as a disciplinary charge when they want to inflict strong punishment on employees because:

- the phrase 'dereliction of duty' has a serious and damaging ring to it; and
- the penalty for a first offence of gross dereliction of duty could be dismissal.

However, employers need to be extremely careful before using this charge because it has a very specific meaning referring to an intentional or conscious failure of an employee to do his/her duty. Collins Concise Dictionary defines dereliction as "conscious or wilful neglect" (especially of duty). The Dictionary of English Synonyms lists, as synonyms for dereliction, "abandonment" and "desertion" which terms have a connotation of intentional failure to do one's duty. In practice, this type of misconduct occurs fairly frequently. Examples include situations where the employee:

- Abandons an asset of the employer in a place where it as at risk. For instance, a company driver might leave the company vehicle in order to visit a friend despite being well aware that the location is a crime-ridden neighbourhood
- Ignores the clients he/she is supposed to be serving in order to finish off the cashing up or administrative work early
- Knowingly fails to switch on the safety device of a machine operated by a subordinate or colleague
- Downloads data from a website that the employee knows is infested with viruses
- Fails to implement the spyware security procedures because he/she is in a hurry to leave
- Desserts his post as a security officer without an acceptable reason
- Gives the strongroom keys to an unauthorised person in order to be able to go on a long lunch.

Dereliction of duty cannot be used in every case where employees have performed their work poorly or failed to carry out instructions. Such problems can very often result, not from intentional or conscious decisions, but from lack of skill, faulty equipment, misunderstanding of the instruction, over-zealousness or other less sinister reasons. Regardless of how seriously the latter list of causes might be viewed they do not constitute dereliction of duty because they lack the element of intent or consciousness.

Furthermore, even where an employer truly believes that the employee's failure to perform is intentional, the employer still has the onus of proving this contention. The employer, enraged because he/she lost a client due to the employee's bungling, might fire him/her for dereliction of duty. The employer is basing the charge, not on evidence of intentional neglect, but on the infuriating and disastrous consequence of the botch-up.

Thus, where employers allow emotion to enter into the equation, they often come off second best at the CCMA or bargaining council. For example, in the case of *Joseph v Standard Bank of SA* (2001, 8 BALR 868) Joseph was dismissed for breaching the rule that there must be at least two officials present when money was being prepared for collection. The CCMA commissioner found that Joseph had in fact broken this rule and was guilty of dereliction of duty. However, as the manager concerned had charged the employee out of "spite" rather than out of concern for the security of the bank, the arbitrator found that the dismissal was unfair. The employer was therefore required to pay the employee 12 months' remuneration in compensation.

The main danger is that dereliction of duty is too often used as overkill when a charge of ordinary poor performance or negligence would do. However, the opposite mistake is also made. This is where the employee's poor performance is permeated with wilful failure to do his/her duty with serious consequences but the employer disciplines the employee for mere poor performance and gives him/her a warning. This gives the employee the wrong message that what he did was not serious. It also may set a precedent for other employees who might 'get away with murder' because the first case set too low standards on which performance is measured. The employer will then have to put up with a series of repeated cases of dereliction of duty and the damage it causes before being able to dismiss the employee.

In the light of the above dangers employers are advised to use experts in labour law to:

- Draw up their workplace rules and standards of performance
- Train management in implementing discipline and control
- Analyse suspected infringements in order to choose the legally appropriate wording for the charges against errant employees.

DISHONESTY WON'T ALWAYS MERIT DISMISSAL

Dishonesty has traditionally been seen as a serious offence and one that could render an employment relationship intolerable. This is because dishonesty damages the ability of the employer to trust the employee.

The Code of Good Practice: Dismissal (The Code) imposes a number of requirements on an employer who is contemplating dismissing an employee for misconduct. Three of these requirements are:

1. When contemplating dismissal, the employer should first consider factors such as the employee's length of service and previous disciplinary record.

2. The misconduct must be serious and of such gravity that it makes a continued employment relationship intolerable.

3. An employee should only be dismissed for an infringement if he/she has been found guilty of gross misconduct such as, for example:

    -   wilful damage to the property of the employer
    -   wilful endangering of the safety of others
    -   physical assault on the employer, a fellow employee or a client
    -   gross insubordination
    -   gross dishonesty.

In the past, where an employee has stolen from the employer, judges and arbitrators have accepted that such dishonesty, by its very nature, has rendered continued employment intolerable. However, more recently there has been a noticeable shift away from this view. It has been pointed out that the Code recommends dismissal for "gross" dishonesty rather than for all dishonesty and that therefore, not all acts of dishonesty make the employment relationship intolerable or merit dismissal.

Adding to the complexity of the debate is the fact that the concept of trust is a tricky one to define. However, I would like to suggest that, in a labour law context, the employee's duty of trustworthiness means that the employer has the right to expect the employee to behave honestly at all times without having to be monitored. The Courts have frequently supported this view and have therefore upheld employers' decisions to dismiss. In the case of *Shoprite Checkers (Pty) Ltd v the CCMA* (CLL Vol. 18 August 2008 case number JA 08/2004) the employee was dismissed for consuming the employer's food without paying. Both the CCMA and Labour Court found the dismissal to be unfair and the employer therefore went to the Labour Appeal Court (LAC) which found that:

-   The employee had a clean disciplinary record and had worked for the employer for nine years
-   However, the employee had acted in flagrant violation of the employer's rules
-   The trust relationship had broken down
-   The dismissal had been fair.

In the case of *Shoprite Checkers (Pty) Ltd v the CCMA* (CLL Vol. 18 August 2008 case number JA 46/05) the circumstances were amazingly similar to the one discussed above in that the same employer was involved and the employee was also dismissed for consuming the employer's food without paying. However, in this case the LAC found that the employee had 30 years of service and was a first offender. The LAC therefore agreed with the CCMA that the dismissal had been too harsh. It is very unclear whether it was the stronger mitigating circumstances of the second case that made the difference or whether the LAC judges sitting in the two cases interpreted the law differently.

Either way, the uncertainty makes it dangerous for employers to continue to rely on what used to be tried and trusted legal principles when dismissing employees. Instead, employers need now, more than ever before:

- To take note of mitigating circumstances but show clearly why they are outweighed by other factors
- To ensure that they are able to justify the dismissal by proving that the employee's conduct rendered a continued employment relationship intolerable
- To bring this proof to the CCMA and convince the arbitrator that the employee's conduct did not merely damage the working relationship but, in fact, destroyed it.

This is not an easy task because many employers do not have an in-depth understanding of what arbitrators see as 'intolerable' or as a 'destruction of trust'.

FALSIFICATION OF CREDENTIALS
NOT ALWAYS DISMISSIBLE

Employers too often fail to ensure that the qualifications submitted by job candidates are genuine. Common law entitles employers to know all facts about a prospective employee that are relevant to a job application. That is, the employee is obliged to:

- Divulge information relevant to the decision to appoint where it is clear that the employer requires such information
- Answer certain questions truthfully
- Desist from exaggerating job qualifications.

Divulging relevant information

For example, where an employee applies for the job of a driver he/she would be required to divulge that he/she does not have a driver's licence.

However, where the information withheld is not relevant to job suitability it would be dangerous for the employer to act against the employee. For example, in *Sylvester* v *Neil Muller Constructions* (2002, 1 BALR 113) the employee was fired for having failed to inform the employer that he had been given ill-health retirement by a previous employer. The CCMA found the dismissal to be unfair because the withholding of the information did not prejudice the employer.

On the other hand, In the case of *SACCAWU obo Waterson v JDG Trading (Pty) Ltd* (1999, 3 BALR 353) the arbitrator found that the employee was obliged to divulge to the prospective employer that he had a previous conviction for armed robbery and theft. However, he was only obliged to make this disclosure because the job he had applied for was that of bookkeeper. The job required the handling of money and the disclosure would have alerted the employer that he was not suited to the job.

However, employers need to view this finding with caution as it was made six years ago. Should such a case now be brought to the Constitutional Court it could be decided that the employee's past record was his own business, that he had paid for his past deeds and that his record should not be held against him.

Answering questions truthfully

Generally, job applicants are required to answer relevant questions truthfully during the screening process. However, what is relevant is a matter for debate. For example, a job applicant may well be able to claim that she was not obliged to answer truthfully a question as to whether she was pregnant because this has nothing to do with her ability to do the work. Her employer might then argue that the maternity leave would interrupt the continuity of the job.

However, the employer would then need to prove that the job required continuity and that no alternative interim measure could be implemented to solve the continuity problem.

It is not enough for the employer to prove the employee guilty of misrepresentation. The employer must prove that honesty is an essential requirement. *In NUMSA obo Engelbrecht v Delta Motor Corporation* (1998, 5 BALR 573) the employee had failed to disclose that he had been fired for theft by his previous employer. He had lied during his job interview by saying that he had resigned from the previous employer.

Delta Motor Corporation then fired the employee for misrepresentation. Despite the blatant lie told during the job application process the CCMA found that the dismissal was unfair and ordered the employer to reinstate the employee. This was because the employer had condoned a similar lie told by another employee.

Exaggerating job qualifications

In the case of *Hoch v Mustek Electronics (Pty) Ltd* (1999, 12 BLLR 1287) the employee was dismissed for having misrepresented her qualifications. The Labour Court ruled her dismissal to be fair because her dishonesty had destroyed the trust relationship.

Employers are warned however, that it is insufficient merely to allege that the employee has lied or exaggerated. The employee must be given an opportunity to respond to such allegations. In *Fraser v Caxton Publishers* (2005, 3 BALR 323) the employee was dismissed for embellishing her curriculum vitae. The arbitrator agreed that this misconduct merited dismissal. However, the employee had not been given a chance to respond to the employer's allegations. The arbitrator therefore ordered the employer to pay the employee compensation.

The above case law suggests that employers are allowed to take strong action against employees who were not entirely honest during the employment selection process. However, this principle only applies where the employer can prove that the employee had dishonestly hidden facts relevant to the inherent requirements of the job. Such proof must be brought to a disciplinary hearing chaired by an impartial chairperson who is fully competent to gather and process the evidence and arrive at a finding that will stand up in court.

POOR PERFORMANCE DOES NOT AUTOMATICALLY MERIT DISMISSAL

South African law does allow employers to decide what the proper standards of performance are, but only within reason. The employer will have, at the CCMA, a heavy onus to prove that:

- The employee knew what the required performance standard was
- The standard was realistically achievable
- The employee was given sufficient opportunity, guidance and wherewithal to achieve the standard
- It was the employee's fault that he/she failed to achieve the standard.

We look at each of these four requirements:

1. Did the employee know what the performance standard was?

It would be unfair to fire an employee for failure to attain a target if the employer had, for example, failed to inform the employee that he/she was required to make 10 sales per month, reach R2 million turnover per year, make 40 appointments per month, build 25 houses per year, pack 100 boxes per month or make 3 widgets per hour.

2. Was the standard achievable?

For example, if other employees have been able to type letters without making mistakes, the employee who keeps making errors despite having been counselled could be disciplined and possibly dismissed depending on the circumstances. However, the employer who is unable to prove the above would be in trouble at the CCMA.

In the case of *White v Medpro Pharmaceutica* (2000, 10 BALR 1182) the employee failed to meet her targets in nine out of ten months. The CCMA nevertheless found her dismissal to be unfair because the employer had set targets that were not achievable in the CCMA's view.

3. Has the employee been given sufficient opportunity to achieve the standard?

The CCMA will have a problem with the employer where, for example, the employee was appointed on a six-month probationary basis and is fired because his/her data capture work was not up to standard. The decision to impose a six-month probation period suggests that the new employee will need more than two weeks to get up to speed and will need to be given the guidance and resources necessary for success.

4. Was it the employee's fault that the performance standard was not met?

Dismissal will probably be adjudged to be unfair if the reason for the poor performance was that:

- the employer had failed to provide the employee with manufacturing materials
- equipment was faulty
- required training had not been given
- the employer's product was not in demand or
- some other reason beyond the employee's control.

In *UPSWU obo Mogodi v Ikageng Cleaning Services* (2007, 10 BALR 959) the employee was dismissed for poor work performance. However, the charges against the employee were very vague and brought in order to make a scapegoat of the employee. Therefore the employee was unable to prepare a proper defence and the employer failed to convince the arbitrator of her guilt. The employer was ordered to pay the employee 12 months' remuneration in compensation.

Instead of fabricating charges and blaming the wrong employee, employers need to:

- Investigate properly so as to identify where exactly the problem lies
- Set clearly achievable performance targets
- Adjust targets when changed circumstances dictate this
- Give employees a real chance to achieve the desired performance level
- Remove all obstructions to the achievement of the standards.

Employers should not dismiss under-performers without having attended to the above requirements and without having followed proper procedure.

DEAL CAUTIOUSLY WITH ABSENTEEISM

Ensure that the rights of absent employees are adhered to before dismissing.

The law considers absenteeism over short periods (a day or two) without leave or without good reason as minor misconduct. However, when even short periods of absence become the norm amongst a workforce this can constitute an extremely serious problem for the employer. This is obviously because employers rely heavily on the presence at work of their employees in order to get the work done. It is therefore a major source of frustration for employers when workers are absent. Where such absence is repeated or takes place over a protracted period, this frustration often turns into intense anger. This provokes the employer into wanting to get rid of the absent employee permanently so as to replace him/her with someone who can be relied upon to be at work.

However, such employers are often caught in the following vicious circle:

- The employer has an employee who is absent without leave
- The employer needs to hold a disciplinary hearing in order to get rid of the employee in a legally compliant manner
- But the employee is absent and the employer has no way of knowing whether the employee will be coming back

- The law says that employees are entitled to participate in disciplinary hearings brought against them because of the employee's right to defend his/her case
- But the employer is unable to get the employee to the hearing because the employee is absent and cannot be located.

That is, the very offence of unauthorised absence is preventing the employer from disciplining the employee. In their resulting anger, frustration and confusion employers often act before checking what the law allows them to do. They either:

- Immediately take the employee off the books and record that he/she has dismissed himself/herself; or
- Hold a disciplinary hearing in the employee's absence and fire him/her.

Employers are not entitled to work on the assumption that the employee has dismissed himself/herself. The courts have repeatedly said that, unless the employee clearly resigns, he/she has not terminated his/her employment. This raises the question as to what constitutes resignation. In my view resignation can be indicated in three ways:

- Firstly, a letter or note from the employee stating that he/she is leaving the employer's employ.
- Secondly, an oral statement by the employee such as 'I hereby tender my resignation' and the employee also packs up his/her things, physically departs and does not return by the employee's next shift. Section 37 (4) of the Basic Conditions of Employment Act requires notice of termination to be in writing unless given by an illiterate employee. However, in my view, the employee's failure to put the resignation in writing would not necessarily invalidate it if his/her actions made it clear that he/she was leaving. However, employers should act with great caution in such circumstances.
- Thirdly, the employee leaves without saying anything and goes to work full time for another employer in a permanent post. In my view this could constitute tacit resignation. Again, employers should act with great caution in such circumstances.

Where employers fail to exercise caution in dealing with employees who 'disappear' they usually end up on the losing end at the CCMA. For example, in the case of *Siswana v Thomas Restorations* (2007, 1 BALR 12) the employee disappeared for a month after informing the employer telephonically that he was at home attending to family business. The employer held a disciplinary hearing in the employee's absence and fired him. The arbitrator accepted that the employee had previously received several warnings for absenteeism. The arbitrator also found that the employee had been informed, when he phoned in, that he would face dismissal if he did not return to work the following day. The arbitrator found further that, after the first phone call, the employee had not attempted to contact the employer again. Despite making these findings the arbitrator still found the dismissal to be unfair because the employer had failed to attempt to contact the employee at his home and had failed to grant the employee a hearing when he returned after a month.

It is also crucial, where repeated absenteeism from work or from the workstations has become a common problem in an organisation, for the employer to carry out special investigations into the reasons for this. This includes industrial relations audits, hygiene investigations, employee control surveys and management competence assessments. Once the causes have been identified a strategy can be devised to resolve the problem.

CHAPTER CONCLUSION

While employees are very well protected from unfair dismissals and other unfair workplace practices they are not protected from the consequences of committing misconduct at the workplace. Employers are entitled to discipline and dismiss employees who break their rules where appropriate.

Case law is littered with examples where arbitrators and judges have upheld dismissals, demotions and other strong disciplinary measures. The challenge for employers is to be able to prove that the discipline was fair. The challenge for employees is simply to avoid breaking the employers' rules.

Deal cautiously with absenteeism

CHAPTER 12

HOW TO MANAGE FAIR DISCIPLINARY HEARINGS

Due to the numerous and often unclear laws protecting employees from unfair discipline and dismissal employers need to acquire substantial expertise to enable them to discipline employees effectively while complying with the law. One of these areas of essential expertise is the management of disciplinary hearings. This chapter deals with key practical aspects of effective disciplinary hearings.

DISCIPLINARY HEARINGS – BE PREPARED

Some time ago I was asked by an employer to assist with preparing for a Labour Court review case. The employer had dismissed the employee for theft but the CCMA had forced the employer to reinstate him. I was puzzled by the CCMA's decision because, on discussing the case with the employer, I unearthed strong evidence that the employee deserved to be dismissed. However, on further investigation, I discovered that most of the evidence against the employee had not been presented at the hearing. The reason for this was that the charging officer had neither conducted a proper pre-hearing investigation and nor had she properly prepared her witnesses and documents for the disciplinary hearing.

The result was that the evidence presented at the disciplinary hearing and at arbitration was insufficient to justify the guilty finding of the chairperson of the disciplinary hearing. Thus, the employer lost the case at the CCMA not because the CCMA arbitrator was biased, incompetent or mistaken, but because the case presented was very weak. This was tragic for the employer because existing strong evidence that would have won the case for the employer was not presented.

This same problem of weak case presentation occurs very often. There are two important reasons for this. The person presenting the case for the employer may be insufficiently trained and therefore unskilled in case presentation. Alternatively, the employer may have failed to prepare the evidence properly. The reasons for this failure include:

- The employer does not want to spend the time necessary to carry out proper preparations for the hearing
- The employer does not know how to prepare properly for a disciplinary hearing.

However, where the manager responsible for bringing the case on behalf of the employer fails to do so properly, the likelihood is that the CCMA arbitrator's decision will go against the employer. This is because the employer has the full onus of proving that the employee was guilty and that the misconduct merited dismissal as opposed to a less drastic and more corrective disciplinary step.

For this reason it is vital that all managers and other staff responsible for discipline acquire a full understanding of how to prepare for and how to present a case at a disciplinary or arbitration hearing. The steps for preparing a case include:

- Assessing the allegations to establish whether they have been brought in good faith or whether the accuser has a hidden agenda
- Investigating the circumstances of the alleged incident(s)
- Assessing the circumstances leading up to and surrounding the alleged incidents of misconduct
- Evaluating the evidence gathered in the investigation to establish whether it constitutes proof or not
- Formulating the charges to be brought against the accused at the disciplinary hearing
- Establishing who will present the evidence at the disciplinary or arbitration hearing
- Deciding which witnesses and other evidence will be used
- Preparing questions for the employer's witnesses
- Preparing questions to be used in order to cross-examine the evidence brought by the accused
- Preparing a draft closing statement.

In the case of *NUM and others v RSA Geological Services, a division of De Beers Consolidated Mines Limited* (2004, 1 BALR 1) the employer dismissed all the employees of its laboratory because a large quantity of kimberlite sample was found hidden on the premises. It was believed that the employees did this in order to falsely enhance their sorting rate and thus qualify for a performance bonus.

While the employer was able to prove that three of the employees had been involved in the scam there was insufficient evidence presented to merit the dismissal of several others. The employees were therefore reinstated.

Had the employer prepared properly for the hearing and had it brought sufficient evidence that all employees had been involved in the deception it would have been unlikely to have had to reinstate the dismissed employees.

This indicates the crucial need for expert skills in preparation for and presentation of evidence at a disciplinary hearing. Employers and managers are not born with these skills. They either need to hire in such skills or to arrange for managers to be trained in how to prepare evidence for disciplinary hearings and how to present such evidence successfully.

HEARSAY EVIDENCE CAN RENDER DISMISSALS UNFAIR

At a disciplinary hearing the chairperson should reject evidence that is legally inadmissible. One type of evidence that may be ruled inadmissible is hearsay evidence. This occurs, for example, where the person placing the evidence before the presiding officer is not the person who witnessed the incident. For instance, the complainant may call the bookkeeper as a witness who might testify that the accused employee had been seen by the accountant making false entries in the books of account. The bookkeeper's evidence is hearsay because he/she did not see the false entries being made. His/her evidence that the accountant saw the alleged incident is hearsay, indirect or second hand.

Another example of hearsay at a disciplinary hearing is where the complainant hands the presiding officer a written statement (with or without the writer's signature affixed) but the writer is not brought as a witness.

The reasons that hearsay evidence is considered as suspect at best and impermissible at worst include that:

- It increases the possibility that the evidence has been intentionally fabricated because the originator is not there to confirm it
- It increases the likelihood that there may be errors in the hearsay evidence placed before the hearing and that the person presenting it might have misunderstood the originator. In this sense hearsay evidence is akin to a rumour as, the more people to whom the story is relayed, the more it can be inadvertently altered. This renders the evidence unreliable
- The opposition party who may wish to dispute the evidence is not given the opportunity to cross-examine the originator of the evidence.

There are certain exceptional circumstances where hearsay evidence might be accepted to a limited extent. However, where a presiding officer of a disciplinary hearing illegally admits hearsay evidence in dismissing an employee this is most likely to result in the CCMA or bargaining council arbitrator ruling the dismissal unfair.

In *NUMSA obo Mnisi v First National Battery* (2007, 10 BALR 907) several employees were dismissed for stealing. The presiding officer admitted into evidence a tape recording of a statement by an employee. The arbitrator found the admission of this evidence to be hearsay because the maker of the alleged statement did not testify. The arbitrator therefore ordered the employer to reinstate all the dismissed employees with retrospective effect.

In the case of *Mhlanga v SA Mint Company* (2011, 1 BALR 7) the employee was dismissed for submitting a false school leaving certificate. At arbitration the employer submitted a report from a verification agency which showed that the employee's alleged school had no record of him having passed his final exams. The arbitrator found that this report constituted hearsay as it was neither issued by the school itself nor was it accompanied by any evidence that could authenticate it. Although the arbitrator also did not accept the applicant's evidence that he had fully completed his schooling he found the dismissal to be unfair and ordered the employer to reinstate the employee with full retrospective effect.

When a presiding officer of a disciplinary hearing is faced with hearsay evidence he/she must consider:

- Whether it should be admitted at all
- The reason that hearsay evidence is being brought instead of first-hand evidence. It may be that it is impossible for the originator of the evidence to testify because he/she has subsequently died
- Whether it should be admitted but be given less weight than it might otherwise be given
- Admitting the hearsay evidence will result in legal prejudice to the opposing party. That is, will the admission of this evidence substantially disadvantage the case of the opposing party?
- The inherent value of the evidence outweighs the potential disadvantages of admitting hearsay evidence.

Having to make these crucial yet highly complex decisions requires a solid understanding of the laws of evidence. It also requires substantial skill in weighing up the pros and cons and making a decision that is fair and pragmatic for the employer but does not infringe the labour laws protecting the employee.

WITNESSES ARE KEY AT HEARINGS

Should an employer fail to bring any witnesses to a CCMA arbitration the employer's representative will find it extremely difficult to win the case because witness testimony normally forms the crucial core of the procedure at any hearing.

The procedural guidelines laid down require the arbitrator to start off by explaining the arbitration process and rules. This entails explaining that:

- opening statements are made outlining what the parties intend to prove
- the employer is normally required to present its case first
- each time the employer's representative is finished questioning one of his/her witnesses the employee has a right to cross-examine that witness
- the arbitrator has the right to ask the witness questions for clarity and the employer is allowed to re-examine the witness, but only regarding the issues raised during cross-examination
- once all the employer's witnesses have been heard the employee presents his/her case according to the above listed steps.

After the arbitrator has explained and followed this process he/she must hear closing statements, assess the evidence and make the award. The evidence that the arbitrator assesses for purposes of deciding in favour of the employer or employee falls into three broad categories, viz:

- Documents
- Sundry items such as video tapes, stolen goods, photos and other items relevant to the case at hand
- Witness testimony.

While all three types of evidence are very important the testimony of witnesses is the most crucial of all. This is because it is difficult (and often impossible) to bring documentary or other evidence without using witnesses as a channel. For example, should the employer's representative need to bring a letter or a video tape as evidence against the employee, the representative will need to validate the letter or video by bringing, as a witness, the author of the letter or the person who filmed the video. Thus, witnesses are normally the conduit for all other evidence.

In the case of *Ntoyakhe v Open Arms Home for Children* (2007, 10 BALR 946) the employee was dismissed for, amongst others, assault and drunken driving. The CCMA arbitrator found that the employee had been fired at a hearing where the guilty verdict had been based on the evidence of people who had not been called as witnesses and on the contents of a police docket and a court record. The arbitrator rejected this and found the dismissal to be unfair despite the fact that the employee admitted that he had been guilty of assault. The employer was ordered to pay compensation to the employee.

Not only are witnesses the most crucial source of evidence, they are also the most difficult source of evidence to utilise. There are many reasons for this:

- Unless properly managed witnesses can disappear or fail to turn up at the arbitration hearing
- Unless properly prepared witnesses forget important details
- Witnesses can be bribed or otherwise persuaded to lie
- Unless expertly handled witnesses may get nervous during the arbitration hearing. They may therefore get flustered and so make mistakes.

Due to the fact that witnesses are the most crucial means of winning a case at arbitration and, at the same time, the most difficult evidentiary element to control, any party at arbitration should use the services of a labour law expert to:

- Identify well in advance all the witnesses that will be needed
- Prepare these witnesses to ensure that they will truthfully give the evidence relevant to the case of the party who calls them
- Work out which witnesses will be used to validate which documents and other evidence.

ALLOW EMPLOYEES TO ATTEND
THEIR DISCIPLINARY HEARINGS

Item 4(1) of the Code of Good Practice: Dismissal (the Code) attached to the Labour Relations Act (LRA) states, in effect, that the employer should conduct an investigation and allow the employee to state a case in response to disciplinary allegations as part of the requirements for rendering dismissals procedurally fair. Countless case law decisions have upheld this requirement.

Item 4(4) of the Code further states that, in exceptional cases, where the employer cannot be expected to comply with these requirements, it may dispense with the pre-dismissal procedures. There are very few circumstances where an employer can justify failure to allow the employee a hearing but such a situation could possibly occur where:

- Employees are on an unprocedural strike, there is chaos at the workplace and as a consequence, the employer is unable to communicate with the employees or to get them to attend a hearing
- The employee appears to have absconded and the employer, try as it might, is unable to contact the employee over a protracted period
- The employee refuses to attend the disciplinary hearing, waiving his right to be heard
- The employee fails to attend the hearing without an acceptable reason.

Employers are warned that, even if one of the four above scenarios occur, this will not automatically entitle the employer to dismiss the employee without a hearing. The employer will need to obtain advice from a labour law expert who will need to analyse and advise on each individual case with its unique set of circumstances.

This is crucially important because section 188(1)(b) places the onus firmly on the employer to prove that a dismissal was procedurally fair; and the holding of a hearing lies at the heart of procedural fairness. Thus, if the employer fails to prove that the employee was given the opportunity of a fair hearing the employer will most likely lose the case.

On the other hand, the law does not countenance the ploy used by employees where they absent themselves from hearings in order to avoid being disciplined or dismissed. If the employee claims to be unable to attend the hearing he/she is obliged to provide convincing proof of this. For example, in the case of *Old Mutual Life Assurance Co. (Pty) Ltd v Gumbi* (2007, 8 BLLR 699) the employer dismissed the employee for misconduct. He took the employer to the High Court on grounds that the disciplinary hearing had taken place in his absence. The Court found that the employee had wilfully excluded himself from the disciplinary hearing and dismissed the case.

The employee took the matter to a higher court, the Transkei Regional Court, which reversed the High Court's decision on the grounds that the employee had a valid reason for his absence from the hearing. That is, he was ill and produced a medical certificate.

The employer then took the matter to the Supreme Court of Appeal which found that:

- When the disciplinary hearing had first been convened the employee had proffered a medical certificate. The employer then withdrew the charges and, after the employee had returned to work, issued him with a new hearing notice. However, the employee's representative raised some spurious reasons for trying to halt the hearing. After a brief adjournment the employee's representative submitted another doctor's certificate and made it clear that he and his client would not be attending the hearing.

- The second medical certificate had been offered under questionable circumstances and had little value. The employee had thus used unacceptable means of trying to abort the disciplinary hearing. Had he truly been ill he should have applied in advance for a postponement.
- The employer therefore had the right to proceed with the hearing in the employee's absence and the dismissal was not unfair.

Employers should not misinterpret this decision. The dismissal was found to be procedurally fair because the proof of the employee's reason for his failure to attend the disciplinary hearing and the evidence therefor were found to be invalid. This does not mean that employers can now reject illness as a reason for an accused employee's absence from a disciplinary hearing. It also does not mean that all medical certificates can now be branded as invalid. What the Supreme Court of Appeal's finding does mean is that:

- Employers are allowed to question the validity of an accused employee's reason for absence from a hearing
- Careful judgement must be used in deciding whether the employee's excuse for absence is acceptable or not
- All the circumstances surrounding the employee's absence must be considered within the bounds of the law that gives employees the right to answer to the allegations brought against them.

CRACK DOWN ON DISRUPTIONS OF DISCIPLINARY HEARINGS

The presiding officer (PO) of a disciplinary hearing must hear the evidence from both sides properly in order to be able to consider it once the hearing is adjourned for purposes of a verdict. The PO then assesses the evidence collected at the hearing in order to decide whether the employee is guilty or not guilty of the charges.

Later in the process, if the verdict is guilty, the PO must decide on the corrective action most appropriate to the circumstances. However, this key task is more difficult to achieve if the PO's collection of the evidence is hampered unduly. Such obstacles could, for example, include the absence of key participants, unjustified objections raised, unnecessary adjournments and disruptive behaviour by the parties at the disciplinary hearing.

Absence of key participants

Participants in a disciplinary hearing would typically include the presiding officer, the accused, the accused's representative, the complainant (person bringing the charges on behalf of the employer), an interpreter (where required), witnesses and a scribe. Sometimes a HR advisor also attends for procedural reasons.

Where the accused fails to attend, continuation of the hearing in his/her absence should only be considered as a possibility if it is established that the employee has chosen not to attend without good reason.

The employer must, at the outset, ensure that the accused's representative and witnesses are released from duty in order to be at the hearing. The employer must also offer to arrange for an appropriate interpreter if the hearing is not being conducted in the accused's home language.

Objections

Where parties raise procedural objections the PO must give these serious consideration, assess their validity and deal with those problems that merit correction.

Adjournments

Such interruptions may be necessary where parties need time to consider responses to issues raised during the hearing. POs need to be expertly trained to know how to evaluate each such request and to decide whether it would be proper to grant them or not. Also, POs might themselves need adjournments, in order, for example, to consider objections or proposals raised by the parties.

Disruptive behaviour

Complainants seldom, if ever, behave intentionally disruptively during disciplinary hearings because an orderly hearing is in the best interests of their goal to prove the employee guilty. Therefore, while the complainants might use underhand tricks, disruption of the process is unlikely to be amongst them.

However, where the accused and his/her representative know that he/she is guilty and that they have no legitimate way of defending the charges, it may happen that they use disruptive tactics such as walk-outs, shouting, threats, hammering the table or toyi toyiing. Such parties trade on the fact that the accused has a basic right to be present at his/her hearing and for his/her representative to be present as well. They may behave badly in the hope of either having the hearing scrapped altogether or with the aim of getting evicted from the proceedings. Such eviction could then be used at the CCMA as grounds for procedurally unfair dismissal.

Only properly skilled POs will be able to deal with such disruptive tactics. On the other hand, untrained POs may mishandle such behaviour in the following ways:

- Try to ignore the disruptions regardless of the harm they cause. A danger of this approach is that the complainant could be distracted from presenting a full and fair case. Also, witnesses could feel intimidated and the PO could lose concentration.
- Lose his/her temper and become abusive, thereby adding to the disruption. This is unprofessional and plays into the hands of the perpetrators.
- Immediately evict the accused or representative. This would be too hasty a remedy and could result in the employee succeeding at the CCMA with an unfair dismissal case.

While lack of space does not allow elaboration, POs need to be given intensive training on hearing control strategy. Such strategy includes a graduated, cautious yet firm and effective approach towards ensuring an orderly and evidence-friendly disciplinary hearing.

CROSS-EXAMINATION IS A RIGHT

At a hearing arranged to discipline an employee both parties are entitled to bring witnesses. These witnesses may come from inside or outside the workplace. The accused employee has the right to cross-examine the witnesses brought by the employer.

The employer is not compelled, in every case, to bring witnesses that it chooses to leave out of the hearing. However, where the hearing chairperson, in making his/her decision, relies on statements made by a person, the employer is required to call that person as a witness so that he/she may be cross-examined by the accused employee. For example, in *NUFAWSA obo Fortuin v Cori Craft (Pty) Ltd* (2007, 5 BALR 423) the employee was dismissed for stabbing a colleague in the arm. He was dismissed at a hearing where the stab victim's statement was introduced. However, the stab victim was himself not called as a witness. As this meant that the accused employee was unable to cross-examine the victim, the arbitrator found the dismissal to be procedurally unfair and ordered the employer to pay the employee five months' remuneration in compensation.

On the other hand, should the accused employee bring witnesses as part of his/her defence it is most important for the complainant to cross-examine those witnesses. The purpose of this is:

- To deny those things said by the witnesses that the complainant believes to be untrue
- To expose the weaknesses in the testimony of the witnesses
- To highlight the lack of credibility of the witness
- To ask the employee's witnesses any questions that could shed light on the employee's guilt.

It is essential that, once the complainant's witnesses have testified, the accused employee is given the opportunity to cross-examine them. That is, the employee must be allowed to question the evidence brought against him/her in order to be able to show the presiding officer the employee's side of the story.

It often happens that the employee, while cross-examining a witness, asks questions that appear to be irrelevant to the case. The chairperson is entitled, for purposes of clarity, to ask the employee how the line of questioning is relevant to the charges. However, the presiding officer is not entitled to interfere unduly with the employee's cross-examination of the complainant's witnesses. There is therefore a very fine line between what the chairperson is and is not allowed to do. This is a key reason why the presiding officer needs to be properly skilled in labour law and disciplinary hearings.

The Labour Relations Act (LRA) neither deals with the employee's right to cross-examination nor prescribes the extent to which the employee can digress from the point of the hearing. However, CCMA arbitrators and Labour Court judges insist that employees are given the right to cross-examine the complainant's witnesses. This is because such cross-examination is the democratic right of anyone accused in any formal process. Interfering with this right without sound reasons is likely to land the employer in serious trouble.

For example, in the case of *Aranes v Budget Rent a Car* (1999, 6 BALR 657) the arbitrator found that the disciplinary hearing chairperson had been wrong in intervening in the proceedings before the accused employee had been given a chance to cross-examine the complainant's witnesses. This was unfair because it would have been likely to have intimidated the accused employee and to have given him the impression that the chairperson had already made up her mind that he was guilty.

In the case of *Labuschagne v Anncron Clinic* (2005, 1 BALR 40 CCMA) the employee had been the administrative manager at the clinic. She had been dismissed for putting laxative in a cup of yoghurt that had been eaten by the hospital manager before he had embarked on an air trip. The employee admitted putting the laxative in the yoghurt but claimed that it had not been intended for the hospital manager. The arbitrator found that the chairperson of the disciplinary hearing had continually interrupted the accused employee while she was trying to question the complainant's witnesses at her disciplinary hearing. The arbitrator found this to be unfair and ordered the employer to pay the employee six months' remuneration in compensation.

Although the disciplinary hearing's presiding officer is the one in control of the hearing this does not give him/her the power to do anything he/she likes. The law restricts the rights and powers of the presiding officer and the CCMA is there to act as policeman should the presiding officer exceed his/her powers.

Whether the presiding officer steps out of line knowingly or unintentionally makes no difference. If such an error on the presiding officer's part potentially interferes with the rights of the accused employee the employer is likely to lose its case at the CCMA. This is the reason that employers are now, more than ever, tending to have their managers properly trained in labour law and in the management of discipline.

DISCIPLINARY HEARINGS MUST BE HONEST

Illegal entrapment occurs when the employer unduly induces an employee to break a rule as opposed merely to providing an opportunity for the employee to break that rule.

I mentioned that illegal entrapment is not the only unfair method used by parties to ensure that an employee is found guilty or not guilty. Numerous other unfair methods may be used at disciplinary hearings, appeal hearings and arbitration hearings. These unsavoury tactics include the falsification of documents, the influencing of witnesses, coercing employees to make admissions or confessions and tampering with audio and video tapes. It can also happen that the employer instructs the chairperson of a disciplinary hearing to dismiss the accused employee regardless of the evidence brought. It is even possible for a party to attempt to bribe or otherwise influence an arbitrator or presiding officer to make a decision contrary to the evidence.

Such methods might be used because there is a lot at stake. But this is obviously not a justification for dishonest practices. Let us look at these unfair tactics in more detail:

Falsification or Fabrication of Documents

This could take the form of:

- An employee getting a medical certificate forged by the doctor's assistant or from a business specialising in selling certificates
- The accused employee falsifying a letter from a supplier stating that the missing cash refund had not been given to the employee
- An employer fabricating a letter from a client complaining that the employee was rude to the client.

Parties must be wary of these and other means of bringing false documentary evidence. At a hearing a party is entitled to question the validity of a document. If a competent witness is not present to validate the document and to be examined as to its genuineness the opposing party has a right to oppose the admissibility of the document. However, the presiding officer has the discretion to allow such documents in certain exceptional cases. Even where a witness to the document is produced the other party has the right to challenge that witness's statements. For example, where the employee brings a doctor to the hearing to validate a doctor's certificate the employer is entitled to question whether the witness is a qualified doctor or to point out that the medical certificate does not bear an official PR number (practice number).

Influencing of Witnesses: For example, a manager acting as a charging officer could use his authority to intimidate one of his/her employees into giving false testimony against the accused. Alternatively, the employee could offer a witness money in exchange for lying at the hearing. Such tactics are unacceptable.

Coercing Admissions and Confessions: The employer could threaten to hold back the employee's pay unless he confesses to the misconduct. This is not only unfair, it is also dangerous because, if it comes out that the employer forced the confession, this taints the employer's case.

Tampering with Taped Evidence: Either party could make deletions or additions to audio or video tapes relevant to the case. However, technical experts are able to pick up such tampering quite easily. For this reason parties are strongly advised not to try such tricks because they are likely to backfire badly.

Instructing a Chairperson to make a False Finding: For example, a senior manager might tell his subordinate who is chairing a hearing to 'fire the accused come what may'. This is not only dishonest but will be detected and punished at the CCMA because the failure of the chairperson to link the dismissal decision logically to the evidence will be a dead giveaway.

Bribery of a Presiding Officer or Arbitrator: Such practices are highly illegal and, where detected, will nullify the presiding officer's decision. While bribery itself is not always easy to prove, it is not difficult to prove that the presiding officer who allegedly took the bribe was biased. This is because his/her decision, having been influenced by the bribe, will not fit with the evidence brought at the hearing.

In the case of *SACTWU obo Baaitjies and others v PEP Stores* (2004, 3 BALR 377) several shop assistants were dismissed when high levels of stock losses were discovered. The employees had all previously received warnings for the same offence of negligence leading to stock loss. The commissioner accepted that the employees were responsible for the stock losses and that the dismissal decision was justified. However, the Commissioner also found that the presiding officer was biased as he had discussed the case with the charging officer before the hearing. This rendered the dismissals unfair and the employer was ordered to pay each of the employees compensation.

The above makes it clear that there are no shortcuts to proving an employee guilty. The only way to succeed with this is for the employer to use available expertise to gather, prepare and present valid, truthful and relevant evidence and to convert that evidence into solid, unbreakable proof.

CHAPTER CONCLUSION

If the disciplinary hearing is not fair it is unlikely that its outcome will be found to be unfair. It is therefore crucial that employers prepare extremely well to ensure that there will be no unfairness attached to the hearing. A crucial aspect of this is ensuring that a fully competent and impartial person is appointed to preside over the hearing.

Such a presiding officer will not only be able to ensure fair procedure during the hearing but will also be able to deal effectively with falsified documents, recordings that have been tampered with, tactical disruptions of the hearing and witness tampering.

CHAPTER 13

EMPLOYERS MUST KNOW
THEIR RIGHTS AND OBLIGATIONS

There are a number of factors that make labour law a minefield for employers. These include the fact that South African labour legislation has been drastically amended to focus on protection of employees, so substantially increasing the legal obligations of employers. In addition, much of this legislation is unclear and open to interpretation. Furthermore, our eight labour acts are supported by numerous regulations and codes all adding to the obligations of employers. Moreover, a great many case law decisions are made every week and many of these add to the body of our labour law. Each of these decisions add to the shifting of the labour law goal posts which reduces the certainty that employers may have as to what the law expects of them.

Lastly, and of great importance, is the fact that labour law is based on the principle of fairness. Due to the facts that fairness is a subjective concept and that it is not defined in any labour act, each arbitrator and judge is able to use his/her personal judgement in deciding what is fair.

This chapter promotes the implementation of employer systems for ensuring that our complex and ever-changing laws are understood and adhered to.

WHO WILL GUIDE YOU THROUGH
THE LABOUR LAW MINEFIELD?

It is crystal clear that, for an employer, South African labour law is a minefield riddled with endless new and hidden dangers. That is, there are numerous labour acts, regulations, codes and determinations that are mainly focused on protecting employees. Some of these provisions are so incomplete or vague that they are often interpreted very differently by the arbitrators and judges appointed to implement them. And the laws keep changing.

All of this means that, as with income tax laws and actuarial science, the untrained layperson cannot be expected to understand and implement labour legislation or to travel through the jungle of labour case law without a guide. The only guide qualified to lead employers through this perilous and harsh terrain is a labour law expert with a track record of experience in labour law.

The question is, how do you distinguish a true labour law expert from one who will give you the wrong advice, half-baked training and failed litigation? We are frequently called in to fix up such messes but sometimes too much damage has been done to save the employer from serious losses.

The solution is therefore not in the cure but in prevention. That is, every employer needs to have available, at short notice, a labour law advisor who can help to ensure that the employer does not fall prey to the jungle's pitfalls all the time. However, it is extremely difficult to find and choose a labour expert who suits your needs and who knows what he/she is doing because:

- The lay businessperson may not know enough about the law to be able to assess whether the so-called specialist truly is a labour law expert
- There are a great many so-called labour experts around
- The brochures and other promotional materials you receive may look impressive but could be exaggerated
- The fee may be so low that it could tempt you to use the consultant.

With all these pitfalls it is extremely difficult to choose a labour representative who will keep you out of trouble rather than land you in it! There are a number of reputable and highly competent labour law experts in South Africa. The question is, how does the businessperson fight his/her way through the jungle of misinformation to find the right expert? A number of guidelines in this regard can be useful. Try to ensure that the labour expert you choose:

- Has a tertiary qualification in the labour relations field
- Has substantial experience as a labour law consultant or labour lawyer
- Has a solid, hands-on background in corporate industrial relations
- Is closely affiliated to a business labour forum through which he/she can keep in touch with the latest developments in industry, in trade union activity and in labour legislation
- Shows his/her updated knowledge of labour relations via publications, speaking at conferences and the presentation of seminars
- Has quick access to the latest labour statutes and to case law decisions
- Charges a fee that is affordable but not suspiciously low
- Is willing to share his/her knowledge via in-house training courses for your managers rather than trying to make you dependent on him/her

- Provides the full spectrum of labour law/industrial relations services – a comprehensive service rather than fragmented assistance. The services that should be offered include:

  ◦ Chairing of disciplinary hearings
  ◦ Representation of employers at CCMA and bargaining councils
  ◦ Labour relations consultation, labour litigation and legal advice
  ◦ Industrial relations and human resources policy development
  ◦ Review and drafting of employment contracts
  ◦ Retrenchment, restructuring and rightsizing
  ◦ Negotiating and drafting union recognition agreements
  ◦ Union wage negotiations and strike handling
  ◦ Writing of legal opinions on all Labour Law and IR/HR matters
  ◦ Conducting of IR audits
  ◦ Implementation of employment equity
  ◦ Mentoring of HR/IR executives, managers, officers and trainee HR/IR professionals.

Choosing the wrong expert is like using a blind guide. So, don't enter the minefield until you have an expert who can see and deal with the dangers.

EMPLOYEES HAVE A FIDUCIARY DUTY TOWARDS THE EMPLOYER

The more senior the employee the stronger the duty to be trustworthy.

South African labour legislation gives employees very strong rights including the right to join trade unions, go on strike, have a fair disciplinary hearing, protection from unfair demotions, be promoted under certain circumstances, minimum wages in many cases, sick leave, holiday leave, maternity leave, compassionate leave, overtime pay, consistent treatment, protection from unfair discrimination and representation at the CCMA by a trade union representative.

However, labour legislation imposes on employees few obligations. They are obliged to behave and work properly, to carry out the employer's lawful and reasonable instructions and to comply with their fiduciary duties towards the employer. Fiduciary duty refers to the employee's obligation to behave in a trustworthy manner. Specifically, this means that the employee may not:

- Place him/herself in a position where his/her interests conflict with those of the employer
- Make a secret profit at the expense of the employer
- Receive a bribe or commission from a third party
- Misuse the employer's trade secrets
- Give a third party the employer's confidential information
- Tell lies to the employer.

In the case of *Pillay v Rennies Distribution Services* (2007, 2 BALR 174) the employee was dismissed for signing a maintenance agreement without authority. The CCMA arbitrator found that the employee had lied about his signing of the maintenance agreement. The arbitrator said that, in telling this lie, the employee had breached his fiduciary duty towards the employer not to be dishonest. The seniority of the employee made his conduct even more serious. The dismissal of the employee was therefore upheld.

In *Botha v Grandyway (Pty) Ltd t/a Tops Gelvandale* [2016] 2 BALR 116 (CCMA) the applicant, a cashier supervisor, was dismissed for gross negligence after she had left her supervisor's till card unattended for several months. The card was used to approve fraudulent transactions while she was not at work, resulting in a loss to the employer of about R78 000. The Commissioner noted that the applicant had admitted that she had been negligent. The applicant was employed in a supervisory role, and her failure to keep the card in a safe place amounted to a breach of her fiduciary duty which justified her dismissal.

While this principle applies generally to employees it applies more strongly to senior employees. In deciding on the extent of fiduciary duty that an employee has the courts consider a number of factors including:

- The degree of freedom that the employee has to exercise discretion in making and executing business decisions
- The opportunity for the employee to exercise this discretion in his/her own interests
- The extent to which the specific circumstances open the employer to abuse of the employee's discretion
- The extent to which the employer relies on the employee for expertise and judgement in conducting the business
- The extent to which the employee is in a position of trust.

Clearly, the more junior the employee the less these fiduciary factors are likely to prevail. That is, junior employees normally do not have the right or duty to make crucial business decisions or the opportunity to misuse decision-making power.

The line between who is a senior employee and who is not and the line between who is in a position of trust and who is not are blurred. Whether, for example, a junior salesperson is in a position of trust or not depends on the specific circumstances of each case. Therefore, in order to protect itself from employees acting against the employer's interests every employer should:

- Build in checks and balances that prevent the abuse of power
- Inform all employees of their fiduciary duties in relation to their positions of trust
- Make sure employees at all levels know the seriousness of breach of their fiduciary duties
- Take swift, fair and consistent action against employees who breach their fiduciary duties.

LABOUR LAW TRAINING PUTS MANAGEMENT ON TRACK

The new legislation implemented in 2014 and 2015 necessitates that line management obtains labour law expertise in order to meet the stiff challenges posed by these drastic legislative changes. In the case of *NUFAWSA obo Matiti v Svencraft cc* (2007, 3 BALR 220) the employee, a shop steward, was dismissed for dishonest use of sick leave. The arbitrator found that the shop steward's dishonesty merited dismissal. However, despite this finding, the arbitrator found the dismissal to be unfair because the chairperson of the disciplinary hearing had been involved in the pre-hearing investigation. Had the chairperson been properly trained in labour law and disciplinary procedure this serious error is most unlikely to have occurred.

While this shows that labour law training for managers is an operational necessity employers find it difficult to decide what training to invest in and where to get the training. The answer to this problem lies in the principle that the training should be provided by someone who is both a labour law expert and a training expert. This will ensure both that the content of training is right and that the necessary learning is fully passed on to those that need it. In this way the employer gets maximum value for money.

For example, if an employer is about to invest in labour law/industrial relations training for management it shouldn't automatically assign its HR Officer to do the training even if this will be the 'cheapest' option, unless the HR officer is in fact the best expert in labour law and in training that the employer can find.

While HR/IR officers are often well versed in labour law they do not always have the technical training expertise to put this across to line management in such a way that it sticks.

It should be kept in mind that, firstly, should the in-house HR/IR practitioner conduct the training badly he/she will get the blame for it. Secondly, where an expert external trainer is used then the internal HR/IR practitioner will still get the credit for high-quality training provided that he/she ensures that the initial training is properly followed up. Train the trainer courses are also available.

Another problem lies with the fact that senior and line managers at whom the training is targeted often have the attitude of, "let HR handle daily disciplinary problems, I'll just mess it up". It is therefore important that the training is offered in such a way that the line managers see it as a tool towards success, and that it is presented in a fresh and stimulating way geared towards facilitating the manager's effectiveness and status. Employees who observe that their bosses know what they are doing when it comes to discipline and performance correction respect their bosses and seldom step out of line.

Management is under "too much pressure to waste time on training". The typical South African line manager and supervisor is much more a doer than a manager. But to say that a manager has no time to undergo training means that the manager is not delegating tasks sufficiently. Too many managers get caught in the vicious circle of being too busy "doing" and therefore having no time to manage and to develop management skills; and this itself is a problem which may have to be addressed via management training.

When line managers do attend IR or labour law training they sometimes forget what they learned after a week. The training programme therefore needs to be designed professionally in order to ensure long-term retention and effective carry-over onto the job.

Some line managers believe that unless their employees receive the same training as they do the exercise will be a waste of time. These managers are perfectly correct because, where employees are not trained on the LRA (for example) or get their input from union meetings they will look at labour relations from a very different perspective to that of the manager.

Insufficient funds are budgeted for such training. It is a never-ending source of wonderment to us that employers are not prepared to spend a few hundred rand on training a manager but do not mind taking the risk of having to spend tens of thousands of rand on going to the CCMA. We have represented countless employers taken to the

CCMA and bargaining councils because a manager mishandled a shop floor grievance or disciplinary matter and the employee was unfairly dismissed.

In some cases, because the line manager mishandled the matter, the line manager gets fired for incurring unnecessary legal costs! The company then faces another unfair dismissal case! Employers often lose potentially good managers this way at great cost, whereas proper training could have avoided the whole mess.

It is crucially important to get the training right first time. A badly trained manager is worse than one who has no training at all. Therefore, the cost of not using the right trainer far outweighs the need to save pennies by taking second best.

EMPLOYERS MUST PROTECT THEMSELVES

Labour law provides scant protection for employers.

In 1995 the old Labour Relations Act promulgated in 1956 was scrapped by the new ANC government. The old act was considered by the new government and the trade unions as failing to provide sufficient protection for employees. By 1995 South Africa's new constitution had entrenched labour law rights very strongly. Also, the ANC and COSATU (the largest trade union grouping) had formed an alliance. As a result of these developments the trade unions were easily able to force provisions into the new Labour Relations Act of 1995 (LRA) that suited the labour movement's agenda.

As time has passed the trade unions have been able to add further and stronger protections into the LRA. In addition, CCMA awards and Labour Court judgments have, over time, become more and more employee friendly. Examples of these burgeoning legal protections for employees include:

- Employees are entitled to join and participate in legitimate trade union activity without fear of being fired for this
- Employees are entitled to refuse to do the work of colleagues who are on strike
- Employees are entitled to a disciplinary hearing even where they are accused of being on an unprotected (illegal) strike
- Employees appear to have the right to motivate for permission to bring an external representative (e.g. a lawyer or trade union representative) to disciplinary hearings
- Employers may not terminate the employment of employees for reasons related to a takeover of a business as a going concern. This is irrespective of whether the termination takes place before or after the takeover

- Employers are obliged to renew fixed-term employment contracts if the employees concerned have a reasonable expectation of such renewal
- Where the employer considers an employee to have absconded (left the employment without resigning) it cannot replace the employee without following a set of onerous procedures
- Where an employee accuses an employer in court or at the CCMA of having dismissed him unfairly and the existence of the dismissal is established the employer is assumed guilty of unfair dismissal until it proves itself innocent
- The CCMA is entitled to overturn the sanction of dismissal imposed by an employer even if the dismissal sanction could be seen by reasonable people to be fair
- Where an employer contemplates terminating the employment of an employee it is required to follow complex and stringent procedures before it can do so. Many employers find these procedural requirements so onerous that they either try to bypass them or are afraid to ever dismiss employees
- The use of labour brokers and temporary employees was strongly curtailed on 1 January 2015 when the new LRA amendments became effective.

In the case of *Ntoyake v Open Arms Home for Children* (2007, 10 BALR 946) the accused, the resident manager of the children's home, was dismissed for appearing in front of the children in an intoxicated state. The CCMA agreed that Ntoyake was in fact guilty of this charge and that dismissal was an appropriate sanction. However, the arbitrator still found the dismissal to be unfair because the employee had not, at the disciplinary hearing, been given the chance to cross-examine those who had raised the complaint. That is, the employer's failure to facilitate the cross-examination phase of the disciplinary procedure caused it to lose the case.

As a result of these statutory provisions and case law decisions South African employees are amongst the best protected in the world today. It is clear that the intention of these laws is primarily to keep employees employed even if this results in difficulties for the employer. It seems that, based on recent patterns, as the new dispensation gets older the legal protection of employees is likely to continue to strengthen, and the ability of employers to run their organisations effectively could be increasingly hampered.

Despite this gloomy outlook employers are strongly encouraged not to crack under the strain. Instead they are encouraged to develop the following simple strategy which can be very effective in protecting the damage to their businesses that can be done by employees who take unfair advantage of labour legislation. That is, employers should:

- Develop in their management teams the ability to manage effectively situations involving errant, incapacitated or redundant employees

- Join an Employers Organisation (a union for employers equivalent to an employees' trade union) to represent the employer in dealings with unions and at the CCMA and bargaining councils.

LACK OF DISCIPLINARY
EXPERTISE CAN PROVE COSTLY

Making dismissal stick requires legal knowhow.

Many an employer has lost a case at the CCMA as a result of orders given by business owners and managers to: "Get rid of him now; we'll worry about the law later!" Little do they realise that 'the costs' they are shouting about could be immense. This is especially so if the persons charged with the job of getting rid of the offender do not have the necessary labour law knowledge and skills. Expertise is required in a number of areas including:

- Assessing whether what the employee is accused of actually constitutes an offence
- Ensuring that the employee gets a fair opportunity to answer to the charges
- Arriving at a fair verdict based on the facts presented
- Ensuring that the penalty is a fair one
- Preparing a watertight case to take to the CCMA or bargaining council to persuade the arbitrator that the employee deserved to be dismissed
- Presenting a persuasive case at arbitration.

None of the above tasks is easy and failure with them can prove extremely costly. For example, in the case of *Fidelity Cash Management Service v CCMA and others* (2008, 3 BLLR 197) the employee was dismissed for gross negligence, dereliction of duty for failing to arrange back-up vehicles, refusing to take a polygraph test and for twice appearing late for his disciplinary hearing. It was alleged that the employee's failure to arrange the back-up vehicles indirectly resulted in the robbery of one million rand.

The CCMA arbitrator found that the employee was not guilty of the charges brought against him and ordered the employer to reinstate the employee with retrospective effect. The employer took this decision on review but the Labour Court upheld the arbitrator's award. The employer then went on appeal to the Labour Appeal Court. The employer said that the employee had been in the wrong as he was absent from the control room for a period on the day of the robbery. However, the Court disqualified this allegation as it had not been included in the charges laid against the employee at his disciplinary hearing.

The Court further found that:

- The employee had been told that he did not have to undergo the polygraph test and that it was therefore not fair to dismiss him for refusing to take it
- The employee had the right to arrive late for his disciplinary hearing because it was his choice to waive his right to defend his case
- It had not been part of the employee's duties to arrange back-up vehicles; so he could not be punished for failing to do so
- The CCMA arbitrator's decision to reinstate the employee was reasonable and that the Labour Court had been correct in deciding not to overturn it
- The employer's appeal was therefore dismissed.

In this case the persons acting for the employer failed to convince the Court that:

- The employee's absence from the control room was part and parcel of the charge of dereliction of duty
- The employee's refusal to take the polygraph test was not so much a charge as an indicator that he had something to hide and therefore added to his guilt in respect of other charges
- The employee's late arrival on two occasions at his disciplinary hearing caused a delay of the hearing and therefore constituted misconduct
- Despite it not being in the employee's job description it had become the employee's normal duty to arrange back-up vehicles
- The CCMA's award was unreasonable.

It cannot be said unequivocally that the blame for the employer's loss of the appeal should be placed partly or completely at the door of those who presented the employer's case at the CCMA and in court. Case presenters can only work with what they are given and cannot change the facts of the case. It appears that the root of the problem could have stemmed at least partly from the preparation for the disciplinary hearing. The cost to the employer in this case included the expense of the hearings at CCMA, Labour Court and Labour Appeal Court as well as the cost of the back pay required by the reinstatement order.

CHAPTER CONCLUSION

Due to the fact that the law gives employers much fewer rights than obligations managing discipline and other workplace issues is a major challenge for management. Information is the primary tool that employers need to use to enable managers to manage both effectively and in accordance with the law. That is, employers must, in order to avoid falling foul of labour law, develop proper employment policies and procedures and train their managers on effective and legally compliant employee management. Employers must also include in the key result areas of all their managers and supervisors the requirement to know the labour law and how to manage workplace discipline and performance properly.

Lack of disciplinary expertise can prove costly

INDEX

A

abscondment, 146
absence, 42, 53, 58–59, 112, 116, 146, 165,
       180, 189–91
  authorised, 146
  employee's, 42, 181, 190, 206
  employer's, 58–59
  unauthorised, 146, 181
  of key participants, 190–91
absenteeism, 1, 107, 146, 180–81
  repeated, 182
abuse, 57, 104, 117, 171, 200–201
  racial, 97
addicts, 111
adjournments, 134, 189–91
Administrative Justice Act, 103
affirmative action (AA), 1, 5, 14, 16, 35, 63–67,
       73–74
  candidates, 16
  criteria, 28
  targets, 14–16, 64
Africa's labour legislation, 1
alcohol abuse, 112
alcohol-related infringements, 111
allegations, 62, 72, 101, 111, 127, 168, 171,
       178, 184, 190, 205
amendments, 5, 15
  new, 14
  new BCEA, 14
  new labour law, 12, 44
analytical ability, 139
anger, 61, 99–100, 102, 106, 119, 159, 167,
       181
  employer's, 99
anti-discrimination, 63
apartheid era, 63, 93
apartheid history, 93
apartheid regime, 65
appeal, 8, 14, 20, 24, 27, 29, 37, 46, 52–53,
       103, 110, 135, 138, 148, 205–6
  employer's, 8, 37, 206
  internal, 138
arbitration, 20–25, 27, 37, 59–61, 103, 127,
       159, 171, 183, 186, 188, 205
  awards, 13, 24, 28, 58

dismissal disputes, 23
  duties, 58
  findings, 143
Arbitration Foundation of Southern Africa
       (AFSA), 19
arbitration hearing, 21, 24, 28, 53, 56, 58–59,
       117, 184, 188, 194
arbitration proceedings, 58
arbitration process, 187
arbitration tribunal, 20
arbitrator, 3–4, 20–28, 37–39, 56–61, 72–74,
       115–16, 118–19, 147–51, 154–55, 157–
       59, 161–63, 174–78, 180–82, 186–88,
       192–94
arbitrator's discretion, 60
arbitrator's decision, 20, 26, 58, 111, 121
arbitrator's finding, 72, 116, 119, 150
arbitrator's rationale, 99
arbitrator's requirement, 25
ArcelorMittal South Africa (AMSA), 19
assault, 128, 153, 167–68, 187
  alleged, 153
  guilty of, 153, 188
  physical, 122, 175
assessment, 24
  objective, 68
automatic termination clause, 45–46
award compensation, 30

B

balance labour law compliance, 115
BALR (Butterworths Arbitration Law Reports),
       4, 6–8, 37–38, 124, 126, 141–42, 144,
       146, 149–51, 153–54, 172–73, 176–81,
       186–87, 192–94, 200–201
bargaining councils (BC), 3, 5–6, 10, 13–14,
       17, 19–22, 29, 41, 150, 60, 96, 138–39,
       143, 145, 152, 154–55, 171, 173, 205
Basic Conditions of Employment Act, 9, 29,
       36, 39, 47–48, 103, 128, 181
BEE legislation, 65
behaviour, 102, 105–6, 113, 117, 121, 126,
       168, 192
  abusive, 167

disruptive, 104–5, 190–91
employee's, 99, 102, 117
malicious, 61
motivated, 114
racist, 73
subordinate's, 168
unfair, 113
unprocedural management, 139
untrustworthy, 155
bias, 27, 73, 132, 134
biased chairpersons, 118, 133
BLLR (Butterworths Labour Law Reports), 2,
    17, 27, 31–32, 40–42, 46–47, 59, 70–71,
    73–74, 81–82, 84–85, 88, 100, 113–15,
    150–51
breaching probationary law, 143
bribes, 20, 25, 194, 196, 200

C

case law, 23, 35, 57, 82, 103, 123, 135, 137–
    38, 141, 150, 167, 182
case law decisions, 42, 56, 155, 168, 188,
    197–98
case presenters, 206
cases, 13, 20–21, 56–57, 59–61, 70–72, 84–86,
    107–9, 128, 131–33, 143–46, 150–54,
    156–57, 159–61, 170–72, 187–89
CCMA (Commission for Conciliation,
    Mediation and Arbitration), 9–10, 19–21,
    23–25, 27–29, 50–51, 56–62, 82–83,
    93–94, 96, 121–22, 141–45, 149–56,
    170–73, 175–79, 202–6
CCMA and non-CCMA arbitrations, 23
CCMA arbitration, 171, 187
CCMA arbitration proceedings, 25
CCMA arbitrator, 25, 55, 59, 111, 116, 118,
    122, 141, 146, 156, 183, 187, 193, 200,
    205
CCMA arbitrator's decision, 184, 206
CCMA commissioners, 46, 52, 56, 73–74, 122,
    149, 173
CCMA for unfair dismissal, 37
CCMA for unfair promotional practice, 101
CCMA guidelines, 23–24
CCMA hearings, 26
CCMA policy, 23–24

CCMA process, 51
CCMA rules, 57
CCMA/bargaining council, 58
CCMA's jurisdiction, 51, 80
CCMA's policy guideline for misconduct
    dismissal arbitrations, 27
CCMA surprises, unpleasant 56
chairing disciplinary hearings, 136
chairperson, 116, 132, 134, 183, 185, 193–96,
    201
    impartial, 178
    unbiased, 132
chairperson grants, 134
charge sheets, 61, 132
charges, 116, 118, 121, 127–28, 132, 137,
    141–42, 144, 149, 172–74, 180, 184,
    189–91, 193, 204–6
    criminal, 124
    disciplinary, 117, 172
    fabricating, 180
Chinese employees, 65
Circumstances that merit dismissal, 112
claim, 10, 28, 32, 37, 54, 58, 66, 109, 114, 119,
    123, 151, 158–59, 177
    applicant's, 61
    broker's, 6
    employee's, 53, 172
    false, 170–71
    unsubstantiated, 54
claim dismissal, 13
CLL (*Contemporary Labour Law*) Vols 25, 39,
    50, 54, 57, 76–77, 80, 82, 84–85, 121,
    175
Code of Good Practice, 122, 132–33, 145,
    148, 157, 165, 167, 174, 188
commissioners, 22, 24, 27–28, 45, 57, 59, 61,
    121, 126, 153, 170, 196, 200
    presiding, 56
    senior, 121
compensation, 2, 4, 9, 18, 29–30, 90, 114,
    116, 124, 131, 156, 188
    financial, 30, 118–19
    granted heavy, 134
    maximum, 9, 107, 109
    remuneration in, 4, 6, 43, 48, 71, 79, 138,
    170, 174, 180, 192, 194
complainant, 71, 119, 134, 185, 191–93

con-arb (conciliation and arbitration), 21–23, 97
conciliated settlement, 22
conciliation, 20–22, 171
conciliation meetings, 20, 22, 57
conditional employment contract, 143
conditions of employment, 5, 22, 37, 39–41, 67–68, 152
conflict resolution, 94
Constitutional and labour law protections of employees, 50
Constitutional Court, 20, 24, 88, 90, 148, 177
Constitutional protection, 155
Constitutional provisions, 19, 24, 97
constructive dismissal, 22, 98, 123–24, 127
    unfair, 123–24
    claim, 124, 98, 154
    finding, 154
contract, 6–7, 9–10, 13–14, 17–18, 32, 36–39, 43–46, 51, 89–90, 103, 128, 143, 161–63
    binding, 162
    written, 161
corrective action, 190
    reasonable alternative, 125
corrective disciplinary step, 184
corrective measures, 117, 125, 129
    alternative, 158
corrective procedure, 133
counselling, 106, 142, 144
Courts, 2–4, 16–17, 27–32, 44–48, 51, 53, 59–60, 70–82, 90, 97–98, 107–11, 113–14, 135–36, 161–62, 204–6
    civil, 36, 39
    highest, 24
    honourable, 132
Criminal Law Amendment Act (CLAA), 48–50
criteria
    fair, 44, 81
    job evaluation, 67
    objective, 83
  retrenchment selection, 83–84
cross-examination, 187, 192–93, 204

D

damaged management-employee relationships, 95
damaged working relationships, 158
defence, 131–32, 193
    employee's, 149
Director General of Labour (DGL), 64, 66
directors, 45–46, 64, 66
    deputy, 103
dirty hands, 60–61
dirty hands principle, 62
disadvantage employees/applicants, 98
disciplinable absenteeism, 146
disciplinary action, 104, 118–19, 129
    bungle, 167
disciplinary allegations, 188
disciplinary codes, 73–74, 103, 116
    employer's, 41, 73–74, 116, 135
disciplinary enquiry, 42, 135
disciplinary hearing, 31–32, 105–6, 117–21, 124, 131–32, 134–37, 157, 159, 178, 180–81, 183–86, 188–94, 196, 199, 203–6
disciplinary hearing chairperson, 134, 193
disciplinary inquiry, 53
disciplinary measures, 149
    proper, 168
    strong, 182
disciplinary policies, 115
disciplinary procedures, 24, 139, 152, 156, 170, 201, 204
    correct, 105
disciplinary proceedings, 31–32
disciplinary record, previous, 174
discipline, 57, 60, 110–11, 119, 122, 125, 129, 149, 152–53, 163, 165, 182, 184, 192, 194
    managing, 206
    strong, 74
    unfair, 122–23, 183
    unprocedural, 105
    employees, 121
    junior employees, 149
Disclosures Act, 98
discrimination, 69–70, 73, 113, 170
    racial, 73
    sexual, 71, 97, 113

dismissal, 20–24, 30–32, 39–43, 45–48, 72–74, 96–99, 107–12, 114–18, 121–23, 125–29, 136–38, 141–42, 144–59, 165–68, 174–79
  fair, 139
  fair misconduct, 24
  merited, 178, 184, 201
  mutual interest, 171
dismissal decision, 108, 115, 147, 156, 166, 196
  employer's, 141
  overturn, 147
dismissal dispute, 21
  unfair, 7, 10, 51, 74, 121
dismissing alcoholics, 111
dispensation, 93
  legal, 1
dispute, 19–22, 27, 29, 36–37, 39, 42, 51, 53–54, 61, 82–83, 97, 101, 126, 135, 157
dispute forum, 172
dispute referrals, 171
dispute resolution arms, 20
dispute resolution forums, 19, 23
  statutory, 19
dispute resolution process, 33, 172
  speedier, 21
dispute types, 29
documents, 23–24, 29, 50–51, 64, 110, 120, 141–42, 160, 183, 187–88, 194–95
  falsified, 196
  gazetted, 23
  legal opinion, 110
  tender, 89
DOL (Department of Labour), 63–65, 67, 110, 133
DOL inspectors, 64
drugs, 160
  illegal, 160

E
EE, *See* Employment Equity
EEA (Employment Equity Act), 14–15, 29, 36, 63–69, 71, 74, 97, 111–13, 122
employee compensation, 2–3, 8, 29, 41, 99–100, 144, 178, 196
employee rights, 11, 133–34, 170
employees during pregnancy, 47

employee's past record, 156, 167, 177
employee's trade union, 86
employer actions, 33, 96
employer and employee, 20, 22, 40, 45, 113, 154
employer's disciplinary code, 156
employer's failure, 10, 22, 66, 76, 204
employment, 5–6, 8–12, 37, 39–41, 45–46, 48–52, 67–69, 89, 91, 111–12, 123–24, 154–55, 158, 161–63, 203–4
  changes in terms and conditions of, 40
  probationary, 144
  sexual offender's, 50
Employment Act, 36, 47, 128
employment agreements, 37, 163
employment contracts, 6, 9–10, 17, 19, 29, 32, 35, 37–39, 45–47, 51, 116, 123, 128, 158, 161–62
Employment Equity (EE), 15, 29, 63–65, 67, 69, 71, 73–74, 111–13, 122, 199
employment law, 14
employment of sex offenders, 48
employment policies, 54, 114
employment relationship, 37, 42–43, 51, 60, 94, 100, 121–22, 124, 153–54, 156, 158–59, 168, 174–76
enforcing arbitration awards, 29
enquiry, 32, 135
  formal, 132
Equal Pay Code, 67
  work of equal value, 12, 67–68
errant employees, 118, 142, 147–48, 174
  dismissed, 146
evidence, 20, 22–25, 27–28, 86, 116–17, 119–21, 132, 134, 156, 171, 173, 183–88, 190, 193–94, 196
  anticipated, 23
  employee's, 21, 58
  factual, 155
  false documentary, 195
  insufficient, 184
evidentiary element, difficult, 188
evidentiary techniques, 152
expertise, 28, 57, 72, 115, 183, 196, 200, 205
  legal, 57
  technical training, 202
expired warnings, 126

F

fair disciplinary hearing, 183, 199
fair dismissal requirements, 46
fair hearing, 136, 141, 145, 156, 189
fair procedure, 50, 59, 79, 134, 196
fairness, 24, 43, 68, 70, 74, 82, 128, 131, 133,
       138, 148, 156, 163, 168, 197
   procedural, 24, 77, 139, 189
   substantive, 141, 163
fighting CCMA, 1, 5
fighting disputes, 96
final warning, 105, 121, 125–26, 128, 137–38,
       141, 165
   disputed, 126
firing, 5, 57, 90, 102, 134, 150, 156–57
fixed-term contracts, 9–10, 13, 43–44, 172
foreigners, 50–51
   employed, 51
   illegal, 51
formal disciplinary hearing, 131, 132
forums, 1, 11, 19
   business labour, 198
   senior dispute resolution, 20

G

gender, 63, 73, 111–14
   employee's, 113
gender discrimination, 113–14
   dispute, 113
gender reassignment, 112
   surgery, 114
General Public Service Bargaining Council, 27
Good Practice, 47, 122, 131–33, 145, 148,
       157, 165, 167, 174, 188
grievance, 7, 57, 61, 101
   formal, 105
   lodged, 98
groups, 11, 73, 85, 94, 126, 150–51
   designated, 64–66, 73
   non-designated, 73
guilty, 116, 118, 121, 134, 144–47, 149, 151,
       153, 155, 159, 173, 175, 190–91, 193–94,
       204–5
   finding, 183

   of unfair dismissal, 21, 204
   verdict, 187

H

harmonious relationships, 100–101
healers, traditional, 52–53
hearing, 21–22, 36, 57, 59–60, 103, 116, 118,
       121, 131–34, 136, 138, 141–42, 181–85,
       187–96, 206
   chairpersons, 133, 159, 192
hearsay, 185–86
   evidence, 185–86
High Court, 24, 135
   decision, 189
HR/IR professionals, 57
   trainee, 199
human resources policy development, 199

I

illegal workers, 50
illness, 29, 47–48, 54, 58, 107, 111–12, 145–46
   alleged, 54
   diagnose, 53
illness/injury, 170
Immigration Act, 50–52
implementing discipline, 174
implementing performance measurement, 83
incapacity, 21, 42–43, 100–101, 108
   procedure, 112
industrial action, 31, 80, 94–95, 104
industrial relations, 16, 112, 199
   corporate, 198
industrial relations audits, 182
inequalities, 74
insubordination, 61, 66, 96, 122, 142, 154,
       165, 168, 175
interdicts, 29, 31–32, 110
interpreter, 132, 191
intoxication, 154, 204
investigation of misconduct allegations, 119

J

jailed employees, 41
job grading, 67

job grading systems, 12, 14, 68–69
job losses, 13, 95
   avoiding, 75
judgments, 22, 59, 74, 97, 122, 135
jurisdictional finding, 51
juristic personality, 4

L

Labour Appeal Court (LAC), 20, 29–30, 37,
      40, 42–44, 46, 82, 84–86, 88–89, 121–22,
      145, 147, 162, 175, 205–6
Labour Court, 2–3, 8–10, 17–21, 24–25, 27,
      29–33, 45–46, 58–60, 66, 72–74, 79–82,
      88–89, 100–103, 110–11, 205–6
labour law, 9, 11–12, 13, 15–17, 18, 40–41,
      43, 49, 56–57, 63, 68, 97, 99, 118–19,
      143–45, 148, 155, 193–94, 197–99,
      201–4, 207
LAC, *See* Labour Appeal Court
law, common 35, 176
      criminal, 132
lawful trade union activities, 98
legislation, apartheid, 74
losses, 5, 8, 30, 43, 61, 84, 87, 90, 93, 95,
      104–5, 150–52, 167, 198, 200
   employee's, 30
   employer's, 206
   financial, 43
loss-prevention procedures, 147
LRA (Labour Relations Act), 7, 9–10, 21–24,
      29–32, 36–40, 46–48, 50–52, 56–57,
      75–76, 78–83, 87, 97–99, 122–23, 145–
      48, 167–69, 203

M

management competence assessments, 182
management systems, ineffective, 43
management teams, 204
managers, 26, 56–57, 72, 80, 86, 104–6,
managing workplace conflict, 93
Manpower Training Act, 38
maternity, 7, 48, 177, 199
MDPs (mentally disabled persons), 49–50
members of minority trade unions, 13
mentally handicapped, 132

meriting dismissal, 72, 122, 144, 153, 155,
      159, 165, 174–75, 178
minority trade unions, 13
misconduct, 21, 23, 27–29, 100–101, 118–19,
      122, 126–27, 137–38, 149–50, 152, 158–
      60, 165, 167–68, 173–74, 184
   alleged, 99, 119, 135, 145, 153
   committed, 58, 143
   constituted, 206
   dismissal arbitrations, 23, 27
   dismissals for, 23, 27, 170
   employee's, 77, 153, 158
   gross, 142, 175
   hearings, 169
   penalties, 168

N

National Economic Development and Labour
      Council, 11
National Intelligence Agency, 38
National Minimum Wage Act, 14
NEDLAC (National Economic Development
      and Labour Council), 11, 93
negligence, 152, 174, 196
   gross, 200, 205

O

objections, 22, 26, 32, 191
   formal, 22
   procedural, 191
   unjustified, 190
offence, 49, 67, 122, 125–26, 128, 134, 137–
      38, 141–42, 146–49, 155–58, 161, 163,
      165–68, 172, 174
   alleged, 32, 99, 128, 155
   disciplinary, 40
   employee's, 149
   sexual, 49–50
offender, 49, 167, 175, 205
   sexual, 49
organisational rights, 14, 171
out-of-court settlement, 20

P

PAJA (Promotion of Administrative Justice
    Act), 25–26, 103
penalty, 142–43, 147, 149, 157, 167, 172, 205
  lesser, 155
  maximum, 63
  severe, 72
performance, 110, 143, 174, 178–79, 207
  employee's, 143–44
  individual's, 69
  misconduct/poor, 98
performance correction procedure, 84
performance levels, 84, 125, 180
policies, 6–7, 10, 17, 23, 66, 73–74, 112, 114,
    142, 151
  comprehensive sexual harassment, 72
  employer's, 32, 111, 126, 165
  employer's appeal, 138
  internal, 35
  labour relations, 93
  probationary, 145
political reconciliation, 93
poor performance, 8, 29, 77, 81, 83–85,
    99, 117, 119, 134, 144, 159, 170, 174,
    178–79
post-dismissal hearing, 42
potential retrenchees, 5
pre-dismissal procedures, 188
pregnancy, employees 47–48, 77, 171
  reasons relating to, 48
pre-hearing investigation, 201
presiding officer (PO), 133–36, 185–86,
    190–96
  biased, 134
  disciplinary hearings, 194
  role, 132
  decision, 196
pre-suspension procedures, 104
private e-mails, 117
probation period, 143–44, 179
  employee's, 143
probation policy, 145
procedural rules, 139
Promotion of Administrative Justice Act
    (PAJA), 25–26, 103
prosecutions, 64, 67
Protected Disclosures Act, 109

R

racism, 73–74
  false accusations of, 73–74
rape, 49, 153
rebellions, 95–96
redundancies, 85
registered trade union, 14
regulations, 128, 197
rehabilitation, 112
reinstatement, 8–9, 13, 27, 30, 39, 42, 81, 91,
    93, 97, 98, 102, 112, 121, 146, 150, 183,
    185–86, 205–6
relationships, 3, 95
  hostile, 93
  intolerable employment, 159
  poor, 101
religious discrimination, 69
remedial measures, 102
remedying wrongs, 29
remuneration, 2–5, 9, 14, 18, 30–31, 36, 41,
    60, 68–69, 87, 107, 109, 111, 161, 166
  deferred, 68
  equal, 14, 68
Remuneration Committees, 68
remuneration policies, 68
representation of employees, 21, 31, 77–78,
    103, 136, 143, 199
  external, 79, 136
  legal, 32, 135–36
representation of employers, 78, 79, 187, 199
resignation, 123–24, 181
  forced, 98
  tacit, 181
responsibilities, 11, 35, 62, 68, 151
  family, 5, 48, 73, 111
  primary legal, 12
retrenchees, 81
  potential, 77–78, 91
retrenchment code, 83
retrenchment consultations, 76–80, 82, 127
retrenchment law 78
retrenchment procedure, 85
retrenchment process, 40, 81–82
retrenchments, 3, 5, 8, 15, 31, 40–41, 43–44,

57, 75, 77–86, 89–91, 95, 127, 171, 199
  avoiding, 75, 81
  contemplated, 77, 81, 145
  employee's, 4
  large-scale, 81, 83
  poor performance, 84
  unfair, 75, 81
rules, 24, 27, 33, 60, 71, 84, 147, 149, 153–55,
    157, 163, 173, 182, 187, 194
  bureaucratic, 54
  disciplinary, 149
  employer's, 55, 101, 149, 153, 175
  fair, 153–54
  internal, 33
  religious, 71
ruling, 24, 29, 51, 58–59, 80, 135, 162
  arbitrator's, 59
  bargaining council arbitrator, 186

S

salaries, 1–2, 18, 55, 69, 76, 90, 96, 124
  employee's, 17
sanction, 110, 137, 142–43, 147–48, 150, 158,
    204
  fair, 163
  of dismissal, 96, 204
sangomas, 52
separation package, 98
sex offenders, 48–50
sex-related acts, 113,121
sex-related infringements, 49
sexual acts, 49, 122
sexual advances, 121
sexual harassment, 71–72, 113–14, 121–22,
    142, 171
  guilty of, 71–72
shop stewards, 13, 76, 134, 168–69, 201
signing of employment contracts, 35
Skills Development Act, 38
skills levies, 2
South African dispute resolution system, 17
South African Labour Law, 16
South Africa's Constitution, 15, 24, 145, 155,
    169
South Africa's Labour Dispensation, 1
stealing money, 27

red-handed, 131
strikers, 80, 94
  dismissed, 126
Supreme Court of Appeal, 20, 24, 52, 90, 103,
    110, 135, 148, 156, 189–90
suspension, 49, 98–100, 103–4, 120, 127–28,
    171
  unfair, 99
  unreasoned, 102
  unwarranted, 103
  decision, 104
  period, 127–28

T

terminating fixed-term contracts, 43
termination, 6, 10–11, 31, 45–46, 83, 162,
    181, 203
  automatic, 45
  avoiding, 145
  permanent, 127
  premature, 19
  letter, 17
testimony, 23, 116, 187, 193
  false, 195
  relevant, 160
theft, 27, 107, 124, 152, 177, 183
THPC (Traditional Health Practitioners
    Council), 52
trade unions, 5, 7–8, 31–32, 35, 44, 75–78,
    85–86, 95, 106, 110, 135–36, 169, 199,
    203, 205
  joining, 98
  recalcitrant 76
  representative 64
traditional healer certificates, 52–53
Traditional Health Practitioners Act, 52
Traditional Health Practitioners Council
    (THPC), 52
tribunals, 96, 124, 156
trust, 110, 142, 147, 154–56, 158, 174–75
  destruction of, 155, 176
  lost, 138
  position of, 200–201
trust relationship, 142, 150, 154–55, 158, 175,
    178

U

Understanding South Africa's Labour Dispute System, 19
unfair conduct, 98
unfair discrimination, 12, 35, 63, 66–67, 69–70, 73, 111, 113, 199
unfair discrimination and harassment, 98
unfair discrimination disputes, 29, 66
unfair dismissal, 3, 6, 9–10, 20–23, 29–30, 37, 39, 71, 97, 99, 101–2, 104, 107, 155–57, 159
  alleged, 19
  claimed, 38
unfair dismissal, arbitration stage, 126
  cases, 30, 192, 203
  finding, 75
unfair labour practice, 22, 55, 98–99, 103, 109, 124
  alleged, 99
unfairness, 4, 170, 172, 196
  alleged, 71, 155
  procedural, 131
union wage negotiations and strike handling, 199
unions, 6, 11–12, 21, 32, 44, 60, 75–77, 80, 83, 89–90, 110, 169, 205

V

valid warnings, previous, 125
vexatious cases, 60, 172
victim, 113–14, 124, 138, 167, 192
  alleged, 72
  stab, 192
victimisation, 97–98, 102, 171

W

wage negotiation time, 169
warning, 47, 51, 55, 73, 104, 106, 125–26, 137, 141, 144, 150, 155, 171, 174, 181
  previous, 126
  prior, 125, 165
  received, 196
wellbeing, 153
  emotional, 53
whistle blowing, 171

employees, 109
witnesses, 23, 27–28, 116–17, 120, 132, 142, 160, 183–85, 187–88, 191–96
  competent, 195
  complainant's, 193–94
  employee's, 193
  employer's, 28, 116, 184, 187
  managed, 188
  prepared, 188
work contracts, 38
work performance, 81, 83–84, 101
  collective poor, 84
  employee's, 143
  evaluating, 145
  poor, 3, 83–84, 95, 112, 119, 145, 180
work permit, 50
work relationship, 153–54
workplace discipline, 148, 207
workplace disruptions, 104
workplace forum, 78
workplace misconduct, 165
workplace victimisation, 97
written warning, 141
  final, 137

www.ingramcontent.com/pod-product-compliance
Lightning Source LLC
Chambersburg PA
CBHW081501200326
41518CB00015B/2337